PENTECOSTALS IN THE ACADEMY
TESTIMONIES OF CALL

PENTECOSTALS IN THE ACADEMY

TESTIMONIES OF CALL

EDITED BY

STEVEN M. FETTKE
ROBBY WADDELL

CPT Press
Cleveland, Tennessee

Pentecostals in the Academy
Testimonies of Call

Published by CPT Press
900 Walker ST NE
Cleveland, TN 37311
USA
email: cptpress@pentecostaltheology.org
websites: www.cptpress.com
          www.pentecostaltheology.org

Library of Congress Control Number: 9781935931263

ISBN-10: 1935931261
ISBN-13: 9781935931263

Dedication

This book is also dedicated to all those unheralded and sometimes even unknown Pentecostal scholars who, from the days of Azusa Street, tried to provide people who had experienced the life-changing Pentecostal experience some clarity from the Bible and Church history about what had happened to them. Their work has proven to be invaluable in the formation of the modern Pentecostal tradition, and it is especially meaningful to those scholars who have tried to fill their shoes in the past one hundred years. 'God is not unjust; he will not forget your work and the love you have shown him as you have helped his people and continue to help them' (Heb. 6.10 NIV).

A book like this one could have had many more testimonies from Pentecostal scholars, including numerous people of various racial heritages. Indeed, we urged several to contribute. Despite our urging, we could not get them to respond to our invitations. This is not to say their contributions to Pentecostal scholarship are less worthy than those who have been included in this book – far from it. Instead, we would like to dedicate this book to their efforts, too. We would like to thank Jon Geniesse for his assistance in preparing the indexes.

TABLE OF CONTENTS

FOREWORD

From its origins at the beginning of the twentieth century, the Pentecostal movement often has been viewed by outsiders as a fringe group, economically deprived, socially lower class, even psychologically disordered. At least through the Second World War, Pentecostal religiosity was a frequent subject of sociologists and psychologists of religion, whose fields of study advanced markedly over the same period. Researchers tirelessly linked deep personal need with religious extremism. Speaking in tongues was taken at times to be an indicator of mental deviation or a marker of economic distress. In more recent decades, anthropologists have had a field day with ethnographic explorations of global Pentecostal communities – with notably greater neutrality.

But a shift occurred early in the second half of the twentieth century. In 1960, Thomas F. Zimmerman, top leader of the Assemblies of God, became the elected head of the National Association of Evangelicals. In that same year, the charismatic movement began: there were clear antecedents, but that is the year Episcopal rector Dennis Bennett drew national attention when he announced his personal experience of the Pentecostal baptism in the Holy Spirit, including speaking in tongues.

Shortly, Vatican II would renovate the Roman Catholic Church – among other changes allowing containment, rather than suppression, of the Catholic Charismatic Movement. That group itself was an outcome of the early 1960s from modest beginnings on the Catholic university campuses at Duquesne and Notre Dame. (Classical Pentecostalism also traces its origins to schools in Topeka and Houston, though of far lower collegiate status.)

If the Pentecostals were evangelicalized, the mainstream churches were pentecostalized. At least large segments of them were, but without the doctrinal and behavioral distinctives that marked classical Pentecostalism. The Pentecostal movement gentrified, moved back across the tracks, spawned megachurches trimmed of the group's more emotional 'distinctives'. As the century progressed, Pentecostals came to leadership and teaching posts in seminaries, bible societies, inter-church organizations, colleges, and universities. Some emerged in roles as federal appointees; others became significant figures in ecumenical circles.

Falling denominational walls, increasing ecumenical friendliness, and the emergence of a mood of post-denominationalism over the past half-century were signaled by the unplanned contrast of the cover photos for the July 2005 issues of two leading periodicals. The evangelical gold standard, *Christianity Today,* featured Pentecostal statesman Jack Hayford; while the top charismatic slick magazine, *Charisma,* portrayed Billy Graham. A generation earlier, the photos would have been reversed.

Still, a firm undertow of anti-intellectualism strongly persists in the classical Pentecostal tradition, unlike the root value placed on learning in such Christian traditions as the Reformed, the Lutheran, or even the Roman Catholic. A Bible verse often repeated by respected Pentecostal elders still rings in the ears of many bright young folk in their churches: 'But the anointing which ye have received of him abideth in you, and ye need not that any man teach you …' (1 Jn 2.2 KJV).

But if in Pentecostalism's first century there were not many wise, not many noble, among them, at the dawn of Pentecostalism's second century there are not a few. Here, in the pages that follow in this book, are accounts from ten card-carrying Pentecostal academics.

These scholars bear the distinguishing marks of the tradition. They have spoken in tongues and prayed for the sick. They have been baptized in the Spirit and, as some would add, sanctified. They champion the 'Four-fold Gospel' (or else the 'Five-fold Gospel', reflecting an abiding internal dispute over whether sanctification is separable from the baptism in the Holy Spirit as an instantaneous, post-conversional experience). And they look for an anytime Second Coming of Christ. They have been pastors. They know well the genre of 'testimony', individual reports of Christian experience – a reflection of the oral character of early Pentecostalism.

What follows in fact authentically extends old-time Pentecostal testimonies, accounts of how the Lord has worked in their lives.

But these are those who have blended Pentecostal ministry with academic careers. They and their peers – ten more could be named for each included here – have completed doctorates at research universities on four or five continents, published scores of books and articles in refereed journals, established archives and research centers, founded and edited academic journals, made television appearances, molded hundreds of students, engaged in scholarly interchange in the guilds of the academy, been elected to prestigious academic societies, given keynote addresses at national conferences, presided over institutions within and without their native tradition. Apart from those enterprises lie their care for, and participation within, all the churches.

The genre of scholarly memoirs fascinates, informs, and inspires. Here is a sample from just over the past two generations: a trio of Anglican scholars, C.S. Lewis, *Surprised by Joy: The Shape of My Early Life* (London: Geoffrey Bles, 1955); William Barclay, *A Spiritual Autobiography* (Grand Rapids: Eerdmans, 1975); J.B. Phillips, *The Price of Success: An Autobiography* (London: Hodder and Stoughton, 1984). Some such autobiographies reflect the institutions where the authors served: Princeton, in Bruce Metzger's book, *Reminiscences of an Octogenarian* (Peabody, MA: Hendrickson, 1997); Moody Bible Institute, Fuller Seminary, and Trinity Evangelical Divinity School recalled by Wilbur M. Smith in *Before I Forget* (Chicago: Moody Press, 1971); or, F.F. Bruce's days at Leeds, Sheffield, and Manchester portrayed in his book titled *In Retrospect: Remembrance of Things Past* (Grand Rapids: Eerdmans, 1980).

But few book-length autobiographies of Pentecostal scholars have yet been published (although Vinson Synan has one in the works). Here, in this book, are the collected stories of the first wave of Pentecostalism's second-century university scholars.

Readers will observe the durability of their commitment. They will catch glimpses of the gestation of an academic culture arising from a revivalistic community. They may be surprised at the breadth and depth of intellectual capacity. They will take cheer from the stock of personal faith and denominational loyalty.

These scholars and the scores of others they represent, along with hundreds of successors now fingering laptops in classrooms, nevertheless face a serious challenge. George Marsden, Notre Dame historian of American religion, somewhere observed that

Pentecostals these days are where the Methodists were a couple hundred years ago. Unbridled liberalism regrettably breeds a sustained threat to a tradition where religious experience is valued above theological substance, where 'doctrine' stands to be uncritically imported from the conservative churchly environment rather than crafted from fresh and informed engagement with Scripture – however loudly the loyalties to the Bible may be proclaimed. In the hearts and hands and minds of scholars like those whose academic testimonies are marshaled in these pages sits the future of Pentecostal intellectual spirituality. May God give them uncommon wisdom … and the soundest of successors.

Russ Spittler
Professor of New Testament, Emeritus and Provost, Emeritus
Fuller Theological Seminary, Pasadena, California, June 2012

Introduction: Testimony and God's Call

Steven M. Fettke[*]

Older believers reared in Pentecostal fellowships can fondly recall exciting testimonies of God's deeply felt presence. With great relish during testimony time in worship, Pentecostals would re-tell their stories of God's powerful move upon their lives: in salvation, Spirit-baptism, and ongoing experiences of the inner work of the Spirit. Such stories from the laity were the stuff of great inspiration and deep admiration, making testimony time for me a very moving part of Pentecostal worship during the early years of my Pentecostal experience. As deeply moving as were the testimonies from the laity of God's awe-inspiring presence, however, the real public attention on a powerful personal move of the Spirit came from the testimonies of call from pastors, evangelists, and missionaries.

Testimonies of call were and still are a special category unto themselves, very high on an unwritten but well-known 'list' of what was a kind of hierarchy of Pentecostal experiences. The very best to which one might aspire in Pentecostal experience, or so the community seemed to be emphasizing, was to be called to one of the five-fold gifts listed in Eph. 4.11: apostle (missionary?), prophet, evangelist, pastor and teacher (without the comma between pastor and teacher!). Those called to these (professional) ministry gifts are held in very high esteem in Pentecostal churches. Indeed, the apostle reminds us that we should honor such called people, 'The elders who direct the affairs of the church well are worthy of double hon-

---

* Steven M. Fettke (DMin, Columbia Theological Seminary) is Professor of Religion at Southeastern University in Lakeland, FL, USA.

or, especially those whose work is preaching and teaching' (1 Tim. 5.17).[1] Yet what if believers sensed the Spirit calling them to something else? Where would they find the language to describe that? And would their Pentecostal community understand that and thus embrace and support their call? Is it possible that God could also call the laity to their 'secular' work?[2] Is it possible that God's powerful call experience could be 're-scripted' to embrace more than just the call to be a missionary, pastor, or evangelist?[3] Is a call to a life of loving God with one's mind and to Pentecostal scholarship within the realm of God's concern?

Loving God With All Our Minds[4]

There is a long history of anti-intellectualism in modern Pentecostal history.[5] For some generations now Pentecostals have been 'trained' to be suspicious of the intellect.[6] Pioneers of the modern Pentecostal movement 'complained that those who gleaned information with their *mere human mind* were filled with only "head knowledge" and so had automatically forfeited the influence of the Spirit's teaching'.[7]

Many older Pentecostals can remember this old canard: Who would want to go to seminary when everyone who is truly 'spiritual' knows it is really a 'cemetery' where preachers go to die? To para-

---

[1] Unless otherwise noted, all citations of Scripture are from the New International Version (2011), International Bible Society.

[2] Steven M. Fettke, 'Who Are "the Called": Mission, Commission, Accountability', in *God's Empowered People: A Pentecostal Theology of the Laity* (Eugene, OR: Wipf & Stock, 2010).

[3] Mark J. Cartledge, *Testimony in the Spirit: Rescripting Ordinary Pentecostal Theology* (Burlington, VT: Ashgate Publishing, 2010).

[4] Cf. Mk. 12.30. Note these fine volumes representative of many excellent works highlighting the life of the mind: Richard T. Hughes, *How Christian Faith Can Sustain the Life of the Mind* (Grand Rapids: Eerdmans, 2001); George Marsden, *The Outrageous Idea of Christian Scholarship* (London: Oxford University Press, 1997); J.P. Moreland, *Love God with All Your Mind: The Role of Reason in the Life of the Soul* (Downers Grove, IL: Navpress, 1997); Mark Noll, *The Scandal of the Evangelical Mind* (Grand Rapids: Eerdmans, 1994); James Sire, *Habits of the Mind: Intellectual Life as Christian Calling* (Downers Grove, IL: InterVarsity Press, 2000); Clifford Williams, *The Life of the Mind: A Christian Perspective* (Grand Rapids: Baker Academic, 2002).

[5] Rick M. Nañez, *Full Gospel, Fractured Minds?* (Grand Rapids: Zondervan, 2005).

[6] See Nañez, *Full Gospel, Fractured Minds?*, chs 5-6.

[7] Nañez, *Full Gospel, Fractured Minds?*, p. 68 (emphasis in original).

phrase Nathaniel, 'Can anything good come out of seminary?' (Jn 1.46). And, at least in the minds of so many Pentecostals, what is worse than a seminary is a secular university graduate school of religion, those awful bastions of liberalism! Also, why would anyone spend time writing books and articles and teaching college classes where there is a 'real' world to be reached for Christ? Through what is now my fourth decade teaching in a Pentecostal university, many a student has asked me, 'When are you going to return to "the ministry"?' For those called to a life of the mind, to a life of scholarship, there has not been space for expression and affirmation within the Pentecostal metanarrative about call.[8]

Our abilities to reflect, reason, contemplate, and think creatively are indeed gifts from our Maker. Thus, to count these aspects of our nature as second rate, to court a prejudice against matters of the mind, or to hold our intellectual commodities in suspicion is not only classical anti-intellectualism but is sin. Furthermore, to champion a so-called *Full* Gospel belief system, yet to pit experience against logic, faith against reason, and spirituality against rigorous mental exercise, is to fall far short of operating within God's *full* counsel as communicated in his written revelation.[9]

In an increasingly pluralistic culture found world-wide thanks to satellite television and the internet, people are exposed to all kinds of worldviews and cultural expressions. In such a global community, there is an increasing need for believers to be able to 'test everything (and) hold on to the good' (1 Thess. 5.21). In a way, Pentecostal scholars serve as 'pastors of the mind'; that is, they help believers understand both the strengths and weaknesses of the ideas and worldviews circulating. In this way, Pentecostal scholarship provides an *apologia* for the faith. Apologetics is the disciplined defense of a position through the systematic use of reason. 'But in your hearts revere Christ as Lord. Always be prepared to give an answer to everyone who asks you to give the reason for the hope that you have. But do this with gentleness and respect' (1 Pet. 3.15).

---

[8] 'The Christian metanarrative refers to the general Christian story about the meaning of the world, the God who created, and humanity's place in it' (Kenneth Archer, 'Pentecostal Story': The Hermeneutical Filter for the Making of Meaning' in *The Gospel Revisited: Towards a Pentecostal Theology of Worship and Witness* [Eugene, OR: Pickwick Publications, 2011], n. 32).

[9] Nañez, *Full Gospel, Fractured Minds?*, p. 15 (emphasis in the original).

Pentecostal scholars also provide important instruction in the faith, reminiscent of the wisdom teachers of the biblical wisdom literature. The sages provided instruction in the ways of God and nature in the ancient world. One writer has suggested this, '"Coping with life," not "mastery of life," seems a more accurate description of the goal of the sages who remained aware of life's mysteries'.[10] On the other hand, another writer has said, '... wisdom (for the Hebrew) (was) skill in living. Wisdom deals with mastery of life'.[11] It begs the question for modern interpreters: Is everything figured out, or are believers given skills to deal with whatever issue arises? Indeed, believers would do well to ponder the notion of so many grandiose claims expressed in our culture – both within the church in sermon series on seven steps to success or in the secular world with business or real estate or personal growth seminars – that promise all the answers to life's questions. In light of the competing notions of having just the right formula to be successful versus having the necessary skills to handle what life brings us, believers can learn from sages – Pentecostal scholars – responses to life's dilemmas that are true to the biblical text, the work of the Spirit, and the way things really are in the nitty-gritty world.

Perhaps best of all, Pentecostal scholars help believers discover new insights into the biblical text or open new vistas of hitherto unappreciated or undiscovered truths. Two fine examples immediately come to mind. Amos Yong opened whole new ways of thinking when he proposed a theology of disability as a way of understanding the life of faith in a challenging modern world.[12] As a parent of a disabled son on the severe side of the autism spectrum, I was deeply affected by his fine work. Another excellent work is by Frank Macchia.[13] He opens new vistas of understanding about the doctrine of justification, showing how vital is the work of the Holy Spirit to the whole idea of God's plan of redemption.

---

[10] Roland E. Murphy, *Wisdom Literature and Psalms* (Nashville: Abingdon, 1983), p. 29.

[11] Elmer A. Martens, *God's Design: A Focus on Old Testament Theology* (Grand Rapids: Baker, 1994), p. 166.

[12] Amos Yong, *Theology of Down Syndrome: Reimagining Disability in Late Modernity* (Waco: Baylor University Press, 2007).

[13] Frank Macchia, *Justified in the Spirit: Creation, Redemption, and the Triune God* (Grand Rapids: Eerdmans, 2010).

Those called to the life of the mind – loving God in ways true to the intellect – provide a much needed service to the local church and to the world. Those who are called to serve as 'sages', wise and well-trained teachers, are gifts of God to the Body of Christ and worthy of honor for their gift and their call. 'Anyone who receives instruction in the word must share all good things with his instructor' (Gal. 6.6).

Testimony as Meaning-Maker[14]

There have been many works published proving that humans learn in the form of stories.[15] In one such work, the writer makes the point that people understand life events only as they are able to attach those events to a story. He claims that it is the only way people make sense of their world.[16]

We are so accustomed to our personal and cultural stories that we are largely unaware that we understand life by these stories. We are unaware, that is, until our understanding of these stories intersects with another very powerful story. It is then that we see that our stories have meaning and purpose, either a divine purpose or one less than divine! Such an 'intersection' occurred for believers when we heard the gospel story. It was that story – *the* story – that challenged the way we understood our culture's and our personal stories. When we heard *the* story – the gospel – and submitted our life story to *the* story, we had to go through a fundamental change in the way we perceived, devised, and proclaimed our stories. There is now a new reference point for our stories – the gospel – and that story causes us to rewrite our personal story. In a similar way, the Pentecostal experience of the baptism of the Holy Spirit creates a whole new means by which meaning is perceived: in terms of the Spirit's transactions within believers' lives.[17] Pentecostal believers hear these powerful stories of Spirit-inspired transactions through testimonies.

---

[14] Archer, 'Pentecostal Story', pp. 18-42.

[15] Trevor Hart, *Faith Thinking: The Dynamics of Christian Theology* (London: Society for Promoting Christian Knowledge, 1995), p. 107.

[16] Frank Smith, *To Think* (New York: Columbia University Press, 1991), pp. 63-64.

[17] See Archer, *The Gospel Revisited,* p. 25.

In these stories, Spirit-inspired transactions can be understood with Spirit-inspired perception. God's powerful presence draws people into the story-world created by those powerful testimonies of the work of the Spirit. The story-world created invites listeners to imagine a world where the same sorts of spiritual transactions are possible. In this story-world the Spirit is both actor and agent. The story is presented in such a way that though times, places, traditions, and even events may change, the story-world made possible by the work of the Spirit is not finally bound by these changes. Enabled by the Spirit as actor and agent, the story contains mysterious and often inexplicable elements that make possible future transactions for people willing to enter this world and hear and see with the ears and eyes of faith. This makes it possible for people of faith to live obediently according to the possibilities made available by the language and experiences related in the testimony. It is as if believers are provided a new lexicon and grammar of Spirit-inspired possibilities made flesh through believers' testimonies.

The *touchstone* for such testimonies of Spirit-inspired transactions is the biblical story, especially the biblical story of the Day of Pentecost in Acts 2: the introduction of the 'Latter Rain' of the Holy Spirit in 'the last days'. If the Bible is the authoritative starting point for Pentecostal testimony, then the way the Pentecostal community understands and embraces the experiential understanding of that biblical story through testimony becomes a kind of canon within the canon. After the outpouring of the Spirit described in Acts 2.4, the 'God-fearing Jews' (Acts 2.5) asked, 'What does this mean?' (Acts 2.12). Peter then interpreted the events that day by citing passages from the Hebrew Bible (Joel 2; Psalms 2, 16). The biblical passages became the *touchstone* for the experience of the Holy Spirit. Peter's experience and sermon became a means by which he could 'make meaning' out of the question posed, and, in a way, 're-script' the understanding of the work of God as expressed by this outpouring of the Holy Spirit. Peter's 'reading' of the selected biblical passages and his 'reading' of his experience of the Holy Spirit resulted in a revised understanding of God's 'new' work.

The Pentecostal community reads Scripture from a Pentecostal perspective shaped by its particular story. As in all readings, there will be a transaction between the biblical text and the community, and this will result in the production of meaning.[18]

This 'meaning-making' is possible because Pentecostals begin to recognize in the biblical narrative an unfolding 'plot' by which they hope to understand the Spirit's work.[19] All this activity of discerning the Spirit's 'meaning' is supposed to happen within the faith community. 'The community must discern what the text means and how that meaning is to be lived out in the community'.[20]

The limitation of this approach has to do primarily with the limitation of 'acceptable' Pentecostal experiences to those as determined by the professional ministers and not the whole discerning Pentecostal community. If 'acceptable' Pentecostal experiences of call are limited to those called to professional ministry, the community is not discerning the whole work of the Spirit, only the work of the Spirit specifically directed to the work of the professional minister. It would seem that there is a problem with perspective in the Pentecostal community on what it means to be called by God and to what God might be calling people.

If finding the 'plot' functions in the dynamic relationship between the biblical narrative and the experience of the Spirit, then certainly believers will want to know just where they might find themselves in God's plot line. However, if the possible 'characters' in God's plot line are severely limited only to certain key roles, then it will be difficult for those not identified as key players; they will be marginalized, forgotten, or ignored. If 'the making of meaning and the validation of that meaning will take place primarily within the community', and if 'authoritative meaning rests in the pragmatic decision of the community', then it is vital that the lexicon and grammar of the community include more than just a limited expression of a story of call.[21]

The Hebrew Scriptures contain many call narratives, most of them describing a call to be a prophet. These call narratives can often be traced to the tradition of Moses and his call experience.[22] Although many are familiar with the call narratives of Isaiah and

---

[18] Archer, *The Gospel Revisited*, p. 26
[19] Archer, *The Gospel Revisited*, p. 26
[20] Archer, *The Gospel Revisited*, p. 27
[21] Archer, *The Gospel Revisited*, p. 27
[22] Steven Merle Fettke, 'Moses, the Prophetic Model' (ThM, Columbia Theological Seminary, 1985).

Ezekiel, none is more detailed than Jeremiah's call narrative, presented in the biblical text in the form of personal testimony.[23]

There are at least two things striking about Jeremiah's testimony of call: (1) God's powerful word holds sway over the historical process as well as the stubborn resistance of the prophet, and (2) somehow, through human agency (Jeremiah) and divine fiat, God will have the final say in a situation that seems hopeless.

As Jeremiah was said to describe the way God dealt with him, Jeremiah (or the narrator?) appealed to what was commonly understood about connections with Moses: like Moses he claimed an inability to speak (Jer. 1.6a; cf. Exod. 4.10), and, when God dealt with Jeremiah, Jeremiah 'explained' his experience with God with what was known about Moses' teaching about prophetic experiences (cf. Deut. 18.18). However, what was 'new' about this call experience for Jeremiah was that Jeremiah was caught up in the very plan of God and placed 'over' nations and kingdoms (Jer. 1.10)! How difficult it must have been for Jeremiah to comprehend and find the language to express this exalted place God had decided Jeremiah would occupy in fulfilling his call! Even though Jeremiah was given divine promises of divine protection and presence (Jer. 1.7-9), Jeremiah still needed help in dealing with his fears and uncertainties about such a new and strange calling (Jer. 1.17-19).

In placing Jeremiah in this position of prophet to nations, God was giving him by virtue of his call *history-shaping power*. Without explanation – and without embarrassment – the text asserts that the final say about national politics or personal decisions rests finally in the word of God spoken through a God-called prophet. 'Judah imagines it can have security while retaining control over its own destiny. The prophetic alternative insists that security only comes by submission, which entails yielding control.'[24]

It is this *history-shaping power* in Jeremiah's call experience that so fascinates me. What if that notion were applied to all call experiences; that is, what if all who felt called to particular tasks began to understand their call experiences in terms of helping shape the 'history' of those to whom they had been called? Is it possible that be-

---

[23] For alternative interpretive views of Jeremiah's call narrative see Walter Brueggemann, *A Commentary on Jeremiah: Exile and Homecoming* (Grand Rapids: Eerdmans, 1998), pp. 24-25.
[24] Brueggemann, *Commentary on Jeremiah: Exile and Homecoming*, p. 29.

cause of obedience to my call experience, my influence on others for the good has helped 'shape' their personal history?

God can work newness, create historical possibilities *ex nihilo* precisely in situations that seem hopeless and closed. God works in freedom without respect either to the enduring structures so evident or to the powerless despair when structures are gone. God alone has the capacity to bring endings and new beginnings in the historical process (cf. Deut. 32.39; Isa. 45.7; Ps. 113.7-9).[25]

The New Testament has very few stories of call by which readers might try to make sense of their own experience of God's call. There are stories of the call of individual disciples (e.g. Jn 1.35-51). There is the general call to witness found in the Great Commission (Mt. 28.19-20) and through the empowerment of the Holy Spirit (Acts 1.8). 'Pastor' Timothy is reminded that he should not neglect his gift (presumably his 'ordination' to pastoral ministry, 1 Tim. 4.14). Peter reminds believers, 'Each one should use whatever gift he has received to serve others, faithfully administering God's grace in its various forms' (1 Pet. 4.10).

The most famous New Testament experience of call is the Apostle Paul's in Acts 9.1-19. This dramatic 'Damascus Road' experience has become a kind of touchstone itself for subsequent call experiences. In Pentecostal circles it has become a paradigm for ministerial call experiences. Some might even call it an impossible standard! In defending his apostolic ministry against what he called 'false apostles' (2 Cor. 11.13), the apostle himself tries to define the call experience of an apostle as having these characteristics: (1) the call comes directly from God (1 Cor. 1.1), (2) one has a vision of the risen Christ (1 Cor. 9.1), and (3) one has the ability to work signs, wonders, and miracles (2 Cor. 12.12), all of which are very reminiscent of Paul's experience. Somehow, this feels far too prescriptive and self-serving. Perhaps his best 'evidence' for his apostolic ministry, his call, is found in 2 Cor. 3.2-3: the converted Corinthians are the 'evidence' of Paul's call from God; they are recommendation 'letters' of the Spirit, the result of Paul's ministry to them. In other words, the effects of his call can be seen in those to whom he has been sent.

---

[25] Brueggemann, *Commentary on Jeremiah: Exile and Homecoming*, p. 25.

Paul's prescriptive definition of the apostle's call served his purpose in defending his apostolic ministry against what he considered false apostles, but it also created a kind of impossible standard for future call experiences. Who could possibly measure up to the dramatic events described in Paul's call experiences? Are professional ministers the only ones truly called by God? How can believers 'make meaning' or find the lexicon and grammar of call if their callings do not fit within the very narrow boundaries of the call to professional ministry as defined by missionary, pastor, evangelist? And where is the language of call available in the Pentecostal community for the lay people called to be excellent teachers, lawyers, assembly line workers, etc.? Who could compete with the accepted dramatic testimonies/stories of call from preachers who feel compelled to equal or 'one up' Paul's experience of call? In fact, with the near absence of testimony time in Pentecostal churches, where would Pentecostal believers even hear of 'different' kinds of call testimonies?[26] With usually only the 'platform' people – pastor, worship team – allowed to say anything in worship, there appears to be no room for any testimony of any kind from any laity in any congregational setting.

The New Testament experiences previously mentioned are all highly suggestive of dramatic kinds of experiences of the Spirit and involve equally dramatic results in practical ministry experiences, usually expressed in terms of emotionally charged events occurring in church worship services. The point of this volume is to highlight the call and life of those called to the life of the mind: Pentecostal scholarship. The call to this kind of life is not often filled with dramatic moments of practical ministry and blinding lights. This life is often filled with months and years of toil in studying the best writings of the best minds of the centuries. Working on graduate and doctoral degrees is not for the faint of heart and it is certainly not filled with chill bumps and hallelujahs. And life after graduation often means even more long and agonizing months and years of carefully crafting papers and books so that others might be inspired and/or enlightened. It can mean years of trying to teach bored and listless college students great biblical and theological truths. In a

---

[26] See Scott Ellington 'The Costly Loss of Testimony', *Journal for Pentecostal Theology* 16 (2000), pp. 48–59.

results-oriented, experiential Pentecostal community, all this smacks of wasted time and quenched Spirit.

It is my great hope that this volume of testimonies/stories of call to Pentecostal scholarship will itself be a testimony of God's mighty work in people and ways unfamiliar to most Pentecostals, as well as opening up a new lexicon and grammar of possibilities for those who are toying with a sense of call to Pentecostal scholarship. Is it possible that older Pentecostal scholars' stories of call included a 'reading' of Scripture that found space for a call to scholarship despite the negative message about education from their local Pentecostal church? Could it be that this volume might provide the 'language' by which young and upcoming Pentecostals might understand this 'strange' thing happening in their lives and these amazing gifts of learning and writing they have? Would it be possible that the stories in this volume will help the younger ones 'make meaning' of what they sense the Spirit speaking in their hearts about Pentecostal scholarship? If the popular Pentecostal metanarrative about call still highlights only the call stories of professional ministers, then perhaps this volume will give younger believers a glimmer of new possibilities of call as the Spirit tugs at their hearts to pursue the life of the mind. Perhaps these stories will inspire younger Pentecostals to investigate new paths hitherto unknown to them.[27]

In addition, a volume like this one might help younger potential Pentecostal scholars find ways to wrestle with and perhaps even reconcile their newly discovered scholarly insights in graduate school and their experience of emotionalism and the uncritical acceptance of dispensationalism and fundamentalism found in so many Pentecostal churches. Young scholars should not be made to feel that they must deny or abandon their deep experience of the Holy Spirit for a more mundane and more cerebral life of scholarship. To paraphrase Qoheleth, it is possible to hold on to the one (the life of the mind) without letting go of the other (a deep and ongoing experience of the Spirit; cf. Eccl. 7.18a).

---

[27] Kami L. Rice, 'Want to Encourage Civic & Social Engagement? Then Tell a Story', *CCCU Advance* (Spring 2011), pp. 23-25.

Imagining a 'New' Way of Experiencing God's Call

Pentecostals have shown a capacity for understanding a 'new' sense of God's calling. Just a little over a generation ago few would have conceived of the array of professional ministries now commonly accepted as 'authentic' expressions of call: worship leader and worship 'team', business and finance pastor, visitation pastor, seniors pastor, counseling pastor, and arts and drama pastor. Two generations ago there were very few, if any, full-time, paid professional children's pastors or youth pastors. Children and youth were served by dedicated lay people rather than by specifically designated professional ministers whose call to such groups was recognized and embraced by the Pentecostal community.[28]

In addition to these 'newly' embraced understandings of call, there are calls to social service in the Assemblies of God which are now recognized as 'authentic' expressions of God's call: Healthcare Ministries (doctors, nurses, dentists serving the medically needy in the poorest parts of the world) and Convoy of Hope (providing food and life's physical necessities in places of great need or where natural disasters have occurred). All these 'new' expressions of ministry and opportunities for understanding of call are fine and needed, but is it possible to imagine an even greater expansion of understanding God's call and place of call?

'Imagining' is the capacity to host and embrace a world other than the one that is in front of us. It is the freedom to recognize that the 'given' world in front of us is not 'given', but is constructed by word, gesture, symbol, and icon. It is the courage to refuse the given world and to act toward a new world that arises out of a different tradition, a different vision, and a different practice.[29]

This volume can be the starting place for Pentecostals to begin imagining that God's call and place of call is greater than just the 'new' array of professional ministers and ministries within the local church and the 'acceptable' social services provided by ancillary organizations. Yes, a call to Pentecostal scholarship is one of those 'new' places of call.

---

[28] However, note that all these still fall within the ranks of the professional minister, basically extensions of the work of the professional pastor, evangelist, and missionary.

[29] Walter Brueggemann, 'On Out-Imagining', *Vantage* (Winter/Spring 2011), p. 16 (a publication of Columbia Theological Seminary, Decatur, Georgia).

However powerful and important professional ministers (even the expanded list of professional ministers) are to the continued work of Pentecostal experience, these ministries cannot continue to be the only means understood by Pentecostals as 'authentic'. It is interesting that in his excellent and inspiring story of a call to scholarship in this volume, one of the preeminent 21st century Pentecostal scholars still felt compelled to try to 'explain' his call and his work in terms of the ways Pentecostals understand the work of the pastor, evangelist, and missionary.[30]

I am 'imagining' a new day in which Pentecostals can testify of God's call upon their lives in ways unique to a particular calling that is not necessarily expressed in terms of pastor, evangelist, or missionary. Yes, it is important to endorse and support the work of the pastor, evangelist, and missionary, but it is equally important to endorse and support, without even a hint of defensiveness or embarrassment, God's call to other kinds of authentic Spirit-inspired work, including the call to Pentecostal scholarship.

I am also hoping this volume will help Pentecostals to learn better to listen to what the Spirit might be saying and doing. The art and practice of listening has great potential for 'meaning making' and imagining a new understanding of the Spirit's ways. The practice of attentive listening has been called 'hearing into speech' so that people might 'bear witness to God's presence' in others.[31] As people 'listen' to these stories of call, they might also 'hear' God speaking to them about something burning within their hearts. It can be called 'the hearing of empowerment and Pentecost'.[32] Attentive listening – *being fully present to the other* – opens up space for people to tell their stories as they have been moved by the Spirit. Is the gift of hearing or listening also a product of Pentecost?[33]

---

[30] See near the end of Amos Yong's story/testimony: 'I have been attempting to testify "about God's deeds of power" (Acts 2.11) as a Pentecostal believer and theologian in a world of many faiths. In that sense, I may not be a traditional evangelist or missiologist, but I can no longer deny there is a very real, even if subtle, evangelical and missiological aspect to my work' (p. 217).

[31] Denise Dombkowski Hopkins and Michael S. Koppel, *Grounded in the Living Word: The Old Testament and Pastoral Care Practices* (Grand Rapids: Eerdmans, 2011), p. 30.

[32] Hopkins and Koppel *Grounded in the Living Word*, p. 30.

[33] 'The usual connection of Gen. 11:1-9 and Acts 2 is "speaking in tongues." But the accent of Acts 2 would seem to lie not on *speaking*, but on *hearing*: "... each one *heard* them speaking in his own language" (v. 6); "... how is it that we

In a modern society built around frantic activities of work, social networking, emails, television, web surfing, family life, and entertainment-oriented church life, believers are plagued by distractions and an inability to focus and concentrate, a kind of 'continuous partial attention'.[34] According to Hunter, '… the context of contemporary life, by its very nature, cultivates a kind of absence in the experience of "being elsewhere"'.[35]

> When the Word of all flourishing – defined by the love of Christ – becomes flesh in us, in our relations with others, within the tasks we are given, and within our sphere of influence – absence gives way to presence, and the word we speak to each other and to the world becomes authentic and trustworthy. This is the heart of a theology of faithful presence.[36]

Finding mentors to help young potential Pentecostal scholars sort out their growing sense of God's call to Pentecostal scholarship might be difficult. The ministry of practicing faithful presence for budding scholars will require wise elders who demonstrate the embrace of the possibility of such a call to Pentecostal scholarship and a committed intentionality to help the younger ones find clarity and spiritual witness to what God might be doing in their lives. Believers can receive mentors as gifts of the Spirit, Christians who practice faithful presence with and for earnest seekers as their faith seeks understanding. Wise mentors who believe a call to scholarship is possible in God's kingdom will need a measure of courage to confirm such a call. The attitude of anti-intellectualism persists in Pentecostal circles.[37] I am hoping this volume itself can serve as a kind of courageous mentor to believers; it can be considered a form

---

hear … them telling in our tongues the mighty works of God" (v. 11); "… give *ear* to my words" (v. 14); "Now when they *heard* this, they were cut to the heart" (v. 37). Perhaps the miracle of Pentecost concerns a new gift of speech. But we should not miss the hint of the text. The newness concerns *a fresh capacity to listen* because the word of God blows over the chaos one more time' (Walter Brueggemann, *Genesis* [Interpretation: A Commentary for Preaching and Teaching; Atlanta: John Knox/Westminster, 1982], pp. 103-104) (emphasis in original).

[34] Found in James Davison Hunter, *To Change the World: The Irony, Tragedy, & Possibility of Christianity in the Late Modern World* (New York: Oxford University Press, 2011), p. 252.

[35] Hunter, *To Change the World,* p. 252.

[36] Hunter, *To Change the World,* p. 252.

[37] Nañez, *Full Gospel, Fractured Minds?,* p. 227.

of practicing faithful presence through the testimonies/stories of call contained herein.

Finally, I hope these stories of call will inspire others to express their stories, too. Learning to tell our stories helps to give form and meaning to them. A speaking (testifying) and listening (discerning) community is a spiritually healthy community ready to hear and do what God is calling them to do. Through speaking and listening, we engage in creative acts reflective of the creative activity of God and come to recognize the authoring power inherent in both processes. To author our stories is to give voice to them, to name and put words to that which was originally formless. Authoring places us as subject in our own stories, rather than making us objects of a story told about us.[38]

The storyteller and the listener need each other. This is called 'co-authoring' our stories.[39] We are co-authors of our stories of call with God and the listening community. The stories in this volume are a kind of invitation to you, the reader, to join this process and perhaps find ways in which God and these stories are part of the process of 'co-authoring' your own story of call, perhaps a call to Pentecostal scholarship.

---

[38] Hopkins and Koppell, *Grounded in the Living Word*, p. 30
[39] Hopkins and Koppell, *Grounded in the Living Word*, p. 32.

1

WHAT YOU SEE WRITE IN A BOOK

VINSON SYNAN*

My twin brother Vernon and I greeted the world in the winter of 1934 in a small bungalow on South Ninth Street in the town of Hopewell, Virginia. Our father, the Reverend Joseph Alexander Synan, pastor of the Hopewell Pentecostal Holiness Church and Superintendent of the Baltimore Conference, was on that day preaching a revival in a small mountain church called the Goldmine Service Station Pentecostal Holiness Church in the foothills of central Virginia. Early on the morning of December 1st, he received an urgent phone call with news of a twice blessed event – the birth of twins. In his diary he wrote, 'Dec 1, Sat: received a phone call this A.M. early –"wife sick. Come home at once!" hastened home – 90 miles in 2 hours – found twins had arrived, and wife getting along well.'

The circumstances of our birth spoke volumes about my father and his dedication to the work of the ministry. Eighteen years later, when Vernon and I were graduated from high school, my father was again absent. By that time he was the Presiding Bishop of the denomination, which had recently moved its headquarters to Memphis. On the date of our graduation he was scheduled to conduct one of the largest conferences in the Church, one so important that

---

* Vinson Synan (PhD, University of Georgia) is Dean Emeritus and Visiting Professor of Church History, Regent University School of Divinity in Virginia Beach, VA.

he felt obligated to go. Since he could not share this big day with us, he sent a letter to Vernon and me, saying, 'When four of my seven children were born, I was away preaching the Gospel, but your mother, bless her heart, was there every time'. Being born in the home of a Pentecostal preacher meant that, for better or for worse, I was destined to grow up Pentecostal.

From the day of my birth, the church and ministry practically dominated our lives. That we were born in a Pentecostal home was due to the fact that my father was converted in a Pentecostal Holiness tent meeting near his home in the Chancellorsville community near Fredericksburg, Virginia. A man who lived nearby, Alma Gayle, known locally as 'Preacher' Gayle, had previous connections with the Apostolic Faith movement founded by Florence Crawford in Portland, Oregon. Since the only Pentecostals in the area at the time were associated with the Pentecostal Holiness Church, he invited evangelists Lonnie and Hattie Edge to preach a revival near the Synan homestead. This was in the year of 1921. The revival that followed swept through the community like a prairie fire.

My father had already joined a nearby Methodist church and was called to preach. His pastor and church were talking of sending him to college to study for the Methodist ministry when the tent was erected. He was the first Synan converted in the tent meeting. This occurred on July 10, 1921, when he was 16 years old. Soon his mother and father and most of the 13 Synan brothers and sisters were converted. One of the brothers was Lindsay Synan, who also entered the ministry of the Pentecostal Holiness Church. My grandfather and grandmother Synan became charter members of the Mt. Olive Pentecostal Holiness Church which was organized out of the tent revival.

The spiritual pilgrimage taught by the Pentecostal Holiness Church was that, after conversion, the seeker should pursue the experience of entire sanctification, as taught by John Wesley. Some time after his 'born again' experience, my father received an 'instant' experience of sanctification. Then followed a time of 'tarrying' for the baptism in the Holy Spirit with the expected 'evidence' of speaking in tongues 'as the Spirit gives utterance'. This occurred on a snowy night in February 1922 while he was on his knees praying for the healing of 'Preacher' Gayle's broken arm. As he prayed, Gayle testified that his arm was instantly healed. Simultaneously, my father began to speak in tongues for the first time. The healing of the arm caused a sense of awe in the community and marked young Synan as a gifted potential spiritual leader.

My childhood years were spent in Suffolk, Virginia, where we lived during the years of World War II, and in Hopewell, Virginia. My uncle Lindsey Synan pastored the very lively and fast growing Pentecostal Holiness Church on South 12th Avenue, a few blocks from where I was born. Here I attended grammar school and high school, where I played a tuba in the marching band. I was not a good student in Hopewell High, but enjoyed the carefree life of a preacher's kid.

Even though I barely passed some classes at Hopewell High, at one point I developed a strange passion to be a writer. I well remember going into my attic where there was a small desk, grabbing paper and pencil and desperately trying to think of something to write. All I got was writer's block and a few lines of nonsense words, but the desire was there. This was to haunt me for years until I eventually found my calling in life as a historian. Growing up in Virginia, I reveled in learning about the history of the Old Dominion. Even in grammar school, any fact of history I was exposed to stuck in my mind like flies on flypaper. I always tell my students 'what you say will die away with the sound of your voice. What you write will last forever'.

Our lives were drastically changed in 1950 when our father became the presiding Bishop of the denomination. This led to a decision to establish the Church's first national headquarters in faraway Memphis, Tennessee. Thus, in 1951 we made the painful journey to Tennessee. Many years later I would make a similarly painful journey to Oklahoma when the church again moved its headquarters further west.

Saved, Sanctified, and Spirit Filled

The summer of 1951 was a sad and lonely one for the Synan children. There was little to do except sit on the large front porch and count cars or attend church every time the doors were open. The highlight of the summer was the youth camp and camp meeting that convened at the Tri-States Conference campground located just west of the city. Most of my brothers and sisters attended the youth camp and found it to be a lot of fun along with heavy doses of Pentecostal revivalism. This August in Memphis became the spiritual turning point of my life.

During the youth camp, I was seized with a terrifying conviction that I was lost and had committed the unpardonable sin and was therefore lost forever. While the other children were having a great time with youth camp pranks, I was in deep despair over the fate of my soul. It seemed that internally I was hearing conflicting messages. One said, 'You are lost forever', while a still small voice whispered, 'You can still be saved'. The youth camp ended and the main camp meeting began the next day. In the first afternoon service, I slipped into the back of the tent in tortured silence as the service continued. Harold Paul, a future history professor at Oral Roberts University, was the speaker, while Louis Gibbes was the song leader. As I sat alone on the back row, I heard Gibbes begin to lead in the hymn, 'Where He Leads Me I Will Follow'.

While the song continued, I began to wrestle with God about my salvation. Suddenly a Scripture passage on a plaque that my father had given as a Christmas present years before came flooding into my mind. I had memorized the words as a little child: Acts 16.31, 'Believe on the Lord Jesus Christ and thou shalt be saved, and thy house'. It dawned on me that in salvation, there are two things necessary to be saved: what I did and what God did. My part was to believe while God's part was to save. In a moment's time, I did my part, I believed in Jesus as my savior, and God did His part. He saved me. That day a whole new world dawned before me. I was instantly freed from the doubt and depression that had haunted me for months, and I now had assurance of salvation, that now I was a child of God. Everything in the world looked different. The trees of the field seemed to 'clap their hands' as I 'went forth in peace'. Although I had not fallen into a life of sin, this experience was for me a new birth indeed.

As wonderful as this new birth was to me, it was only the first step in the theology of the church. On the second night I went back to the altar to seek for the 'second blessing' of entire sanctification. I did not understand the theology behind the experience, but I was open to all God had for me. As I knelt at the altar my preacher brother Maurice began to pray for me to be sanctified. When I began to 'claim the blessing', I was confronted by a deep conviction that I was being called into the ministry and that this issue had to be settled before I could move any further with God spiritually. I struggled for a while since my ambitions had been to be a lawyer, a governor of the state, or even to be President of the United States. As I surrendered everything to the Lord, even to the call to preach, I felt something within me saying that a definite sanctifying work had been done in my life.

That night before going to bed, I got my father's old *Thompson Chain Reference Bible* and asked the Lord to confirm my call to preach with a clear Scripture. As I turned the pages at random, my eyes fell on Isa. 61.1:

> The Spirit of the Lord is upon me because the Lord has anointed me to preach good tidings to the poor. He has sent me to heal the brokenhearted. To proclaim liberty to the captives and the opening of prison to those who are bound. To proclaim the acceptable year of the Lord.

After this, I never doubted my call to preach; I was clear about my being set apart for the work of the ministry. I later learned that the word sanctify means to purify and to set apart for holy use. As wonderful as this was, there was one more step in our theology, the baptism in the Holy Spirit, evidenced by speaking in tongues. As I began my pilgrimage towards becoming a practicing Pentecostal, I promised God that I would never miss an altar call until I received this coveted blessing. This was even more important in that the church required that all ministers experience this, the 'third blessing'.

For nine months I was the first one in the altars seeking 'the baptism'. Many times the saints gathered around and attempted to help me 'pray through'. They would lay hands on me, shout out encouragement, and do all they could to get me through to the blessing. In classic Pentecostal style, some would say 'Hold on', while others shouted 'Turn loose'. In spite of the noise and well-intentioned efforts of the altar workers, I had many wonderful experiences in these tarrying services. At one time in a youth service, I found myself prophesying even before I had spoken in tongues.

The night I 'received my Pentecost' was in the Lamar Avenue church in a revival service. Once again I went to the altar, debating whether I should stand or kneel. After I had knelt at a front pew, a brother jumped and knocked me flat on the floor. As I lay there, I tuned out all the noise around me and began to worship Jesus in the Spirit. Suddenly I was taken out of myself into a heavenly realm where I began to praise God in a new tongue. It was effortless and lasted over one half hour. From that time forward, I knew that the gifts of the Spirit would now flow through me as I ministered. It was a truly monumental experience for me. Although I was only seventeen years old, I felt that someday I would witness to multitudes around the world. How that would happen, I did not know, but I knew in my bones that my life would be interesting indeed. Now I could testify experientially that I was 'saved, sanctified, and filled with the Holy Ghost'.

At the time all this was happening, my life was also turned around academically while I was enrolled as a student at Memphis Central High School. At the time, Central was the second highest rated college prep high school in the nation, ranking just behind Boston's Latin Grammar School. To graduate from Central High, you had to take a foreign language and pass grueling courses in English and mathematics. After graduating from Central in 1953, I attended Emmanuel College, a small church-owned junior college in Franklin Springs, Georgia, where I was shocked to graduate as salutatorian of the class.

After junior college, I attended the University of Richmond where I majored in American History. At Richmond, I was required to take two foreign languages to earn a BA degree in History. At the same time I was attending classes six days a week at Richmond, I served as pastor of the Mount Olive Pentecostal Holiness Church in Chancellorsville, Virginia, where I led in building a new sanctuary.

Soon after graduation, I was asked to return to Emmanuel College to teach American History and Western Civilization courses. It was extremely difficult to stay one day ahead of my classes in my first college teaching experience. Since I was a one person Social Sciences Department, I also taught American Government, Economics, and Art Appreciation. While at Emmanuel I planted a new church in nearby Hartwell, Georgia. These were busy years indeed.

On top of all this, I went over to nearby Athens, Georgia, in 1962 to enroll in the MA program in the Department of History. I took the necessary tests and passed them with room to spare. Indeed, my scores on the GRE went off the top of the scale for English and History. Emmanuel College and the University of Richmond had served me well.

My first graduate class was in Southern History with Dr Charles Wynes, like myself a native Virginian. As a true son of the South, I delighted in Southern history, especially the parts dealing with the Civil War. I also shared the conservative views of my family on all things Southern. I soon found out, however, that Wynes and most of the professors in the History Department were what we called 'liberals', especially on questions concerning race and religion. The University had only recently been racially integrated in 1961 when Charlene Hunter had enrolled against determined hostility from white students in her classes. One of the history professors, Dr Horace Montgomery, had been her mentor and defender. Most of the professors felt a calling to stamp out any fundamentalist beliefs in the students, many of whom were from fundamentalist Baptist backgrounds. The local fundamentalist Baptist pastor, 'Preacher' Edwards, who had kept Clark County 'dry' – free of all sales of alcohol – was a special target of professorial barbs. I was singled out for special attention because of my Pentecostal background. They assumed that I was a 'super fundamentalist'.

When I took my first mid-term exam, I felt hopelessly inferior to my fellow classmates, some of whom seemed to be brilliant in classroom discussions. I turned in my paper expecting to fail. To my utter amazement, I received an A+ on the paper and was called into the professor's office. He said, 'You can write and you have a flair for history'. He offered to serve as my major professor if I majored in Southern History. This I found to be very attractive. My future was radically changed, however, when I met Dr Montgomery on the staircase on the way to class. When he found out who I was, he also offered to serve as my major professor.

Little did I know that Montgomery was the most respected member of the faculty and was a master at developing the writing skills necessary for budding historians. His area of expertise was Social and Intellectual History or the history of ideas that affect society. Montgomery, known for his major work on Georgia politics published as *Cracker Parties*, was a careful editor of papers and gave total attention to his students. I still look up to him as the quintessential PhD advisor, editor, and dissertation chairperson. Although he was a deacon in the local Unitarian-Universalist Church, he insisted that I write a history of the Pentecostal Movement in the South. He explained to me that religious doctrines are ideas that have affected history for centuries, even leading to religious wars and major upheavals in society. When he found out that the archives of the Pentecostal Holiness Church were in the Emmanuel College library in Franklin Springs, he insisted that he visit the collection to make an inventory of sources. At first I resisted because I wanted to write on secular political or economic history and had no interest in writing on Pentecostal history. In the end, he won the argument. At his insistence, I agreed to write the history of Emmanuel College for my Masters thesis.

While this was going on, I was suddenly asked not to return to teach at Emmanuel College for the 1963 academic year. Although I never fully understood this decision, I had a growing family to support and therefore sought a teaching job in the area. I soon found a wonderful opportunity to teach in Hart County High School, which was located 15 miles from the college. I met many wonderful people in Hartwell during that year and used these relationships to plant a new church in the city.

In the meantime, I had to earn my MA degree and write a Master's thesis at the University. Every day I drove the 30 miles to Athens after teaching classes. It was a difficult work load, but I survived. It was easy to do the research on Emmanuel College since I had been on the faculty. In fact, I had known Mrs G.F. Taylor, the aged widow of the founder of the college, when I was a student in the 1950s. After I received the MA in 1964, a friend of the college, Robert Robinson, and his brothers, who worked in the U.S. printing office in DC, offered to publish my thesis as a fund-raiser for the 50th anniversary of the college in 1969. They were the sons of A.E. Robinson, one of the founders of the denomination. Thus in 1968, my first book appeared in print under the title *Emmanuel College – The First Fifty Years*. The book raised $25,000 for the College, a large sum at the time.

After earning my MA degree, I learned about a new PhD program offered by the State of Georgia for pre-doctoral assistantships at the University in Athens. Those who were accepted would get a full tuition scholarship plus a tax-free income of $4000 per year, at that time a living wage. The only condition was that after graduation, the recipients would promise to teach for two years in the state of Georgia. At first I considered studying for a Doctorate in Education (EdD) degree. However, when Ruth Tew, my former history professor and colleague, explained the case for earning the PhD degree, I agreed to do so. This was a fateful decision indeed.

Just after accepting the Georgia fellowship, I was visiting Richmond, Virginia at the time Oral Roberts was conducting a crusade in the city. Ed Boyce was chairman of the local committee for the crusade. In the service I attended I noticed a great change since I had last heard Oral. Instead of a flashy white jacket, he wore a conservative business suit. I also noticed that he wore glasses to read his text. His crowd was much smaller than I expected with about 3,000 people present. In a morning session for pastors, Boyce brought Oral to see me. Roberts offered to send me to Harvard, Yale, or Princeton to earn a PhD in theology. He offered to pay all costs if I would return to teach at ORU. It was a very tempting offer. I thanked him but did not accept the offer for two reasons. I was more interested in history and I already had the Fellowship at the University of Georgia. How different my life would have been if I had gone into theology rather than history. Later on Paul Chappell a friend from Virginia, accepted Oral's offer and went on to be dean of the Oral Roberts Graduate School of Theology.

During the summer of 1965, I was awarded a federally supported scholarship to study Asian History at Florida State University in Tallahassee. The pay seemed to be huge at the time, twice what I was making at the college. This meant two months away from my wife and family. But we felt that it was worth the effort. In these seminar sessions I had the privilege of hearing O. Edmund Clubb, the last American Consul in Peking, China before the communist takeover in 1949, and also Edwin Reischauer, the great Harvard scholar of East Asian history. Since the Vietnamese war was escalating, and I was the youngest member of the class and still liable for the draft, my fellow students dubbed me 'Vietnam Vince'. When I enrolled at Georgia that fall, Asian History was accepted as one of my six fields of specialization. Thus I began my PhD studies at the University of Georgia in LeConte Hall, the Mecca for Georgia historians.

When I returned to the University of Georgia, I entertained ideas of writing on such possible themes as labor unions, southern politics, or about other secular subjects. The last thing I wanted to do was to write about Pentecostalism. After some disagreements with Dr Montgomery, I decided he was right: I should write on the history of the Pentecostal Movement. My first topic choice was to study Pentecostalism in the American South. Since I knew my dissertation topic at the start of my program, I decided as much as possible to make every classroom term paper a chapter of my final work. One of my first papers was on the story of the Black Pentecostals in America. This later became a seminal chapter of the dissertation. Other classes in Colonial History, European History, and Asian History, further piqued my interest in the roots of American Pentecostalism. As I progressed in my program, I became something of a curiosity to the faculty members and my fellow students, especially when I explained such Pentecostal practices as speaking in tongues, healing, and prophecy. Some topics, such as snake handling and the anti-medicine beliefs of some Pentecostals, elicited snickers and a certain amount of derision among some classmates. Overall, however, I felt a sense of acceptance and some sympathy, as well as a sense of awe that a Pentecostal could even be thinking of earning a PhD degree.

This busy time also included some surprising activities in addition to all this academic work. In the summer of 1966, I drove from Georgia to Tulsa, Oklahoma, with the only aim of doing two weeks of dissertation research at Oral Roberts University. My father, Bishop J.A. Synan, had preceded me to Tulsa by only a few months. He had been invited by Oral Roberts to read the Scriptures in the program of dedication for the new university in 1965. Earlier in 1966, they were together again in the Berlin Congress on Evangelism sponsored by Billy Graham. In Berlin, Roberts had been lionized by the crowd who jammed his sessions to capacity. My father and Oral had much time together in meetings and patched up any political differences they had harbored in the previous years. When Dad told Oral that I was coming to Tulsa, he generously gave me free room and board for the entire two weeks.

Already ORU had gathered the most extensive collection of Pentecostal research materials in the world. For these days I reveled in the book stacks doing crucial research for my dissertation. I was in the collection day and night. Here I discovered a mass of valuable materials that helped me shape my dissertation project. For a Pentecostal historian it was like heaven on earth.

At the same time, I was busy planting the Hartwell Pentecostal Holiness Church. I had made many friends in Hartwell while teaching in the high school and decided to go ahead with the project. From the time of the first service in 1966 to the time of the dedication of the new building was only 11 months.

During this flurry of activities, I continued my research and the task of writing my dissertation. When I first envisioned the project the working title was 'The Pentecostal Movement in the South'. I wanted it to be a regional study and to concentrate on the most southern of the Pentecostal churches including the Church of God, the Pentecostal Holiness Church, and the Church of God in Christ. But as I submitted my chapters to Dr Montgomery, he finally decided that the story was so national in scope that I changed the title to 'The Pentecostal Movement in the United States'. From the day that I wrote the first page, I definitely planned to publish the dissertation in book form as soon as possible.

One of my major findings was that the cradle of Pentecostalism was to be found in the Holiness Movement of the late Nineteenth Century and that this movement arose out of the heart of Methodism. I spent months researching in Methodist records and archives as well as Holiness and Pentecostal sources. I was struck with the power of the movement in America and the fact that religious perfectionism had been such a powerful influence in American social and political life. As I continued to pursue this research, I felt that the religious world needed to know about the Methodist and Holiness connections that were so crucial to the birth of the Pentecostal movement in the Twentieth Century. Because of this, the first two words in the book were 'John Wesley'. I knew that my approach would be controversial, but I felt obligated to tell the story as well as I could.

When I finally defended the dissertation before several professors in the history department, I felt at ease because I realized that I knew vastly more about the subject than any one of them. Nevertheless, it seemed like an eternity before Dr Montgomery came into the office where I was waiting and greeted me with the words, 'Congratulations, Dr Synan'. I knew then that I had passed the final hurdle. In our exit conversation, Dr Montgomery startled me with the confession that as a young man he had been an avid follower of Aimee Semple McPherson's career.

Just before I received my doctorate, I was called into the office of Dr Joseph Parks, Chairman of the History Department. He was a very kind man and a renowned historian of the American South. He told me of his great concern that I 'make something of myself'. He suggested that I leave the Pentecostal Holiness Church because 'there was no future there'. He said that with my new degree and my writing ability I could do very well at a state university. As he talked, I reflected on my life and my future. I thought of what the Lord had done for me as well as what the church had meant in my life. I thanked him for his concern but told him that I would make my own decisions about my future.

Looking back now, I think of what life would have been like if I had taken Dr Parks' advice. I have never heard what happened to my fellow classmates since then. I am sure some of them had distinguished careers. I do know now that I have had a most exciting life since leaving the University of Georgia. I have traveled over most of the world, I have published 19 books and dozens of articles, and have spoken to huge audiences in churches and conferences all over the world. I am so thankful that I did not follow the advice of my good friend Professor Parks.

The Society for Pentecostal Studies (SPS)

Although I was busy and happy in my pastoral and teaching ministries, I was extremely concerned to have my dissertation published. I went first to the publishing house of the Pentecostal Holiness Church and was told that the book would never sell enough copies to justify the investment. I also sent it to Abingdon Press thinking that the Methodists might be interested in my thesis. After a long time of consideration, they also declined. I then sent it to the University of Georgia Press for them to evaluate. After a long time, I was told to meet with Ed Harrell who had been a reader for the press. Harrell lectured me for not doing complete 'runs' of the major Pentecostal periodicals. Although I had read hundreds of pages in the major magazines, I could not say that I had seen every single page. Harrell said that if I did this research and incorporated it into the manuscript I would have a good book. I determined to do just what he said.

In the summer of 1968, I took a long research trip to various Pentecostal headquarters to read their periodicals. When I arrived in Cleveland, Tennessee, I read all the copies of the Church of God *Evangel*. While there I met with Charles Conn, the great historian of the church. They freely opened all their archives to me and it was especially helpful to read the journals of A.J. Tomlinson. While in Cleveland, I met Dr Horace Ward who was serving as Dean of Students at Lee College. We became fast friends and carried on endless discussions about Pentecostal history and theology. At his invitation, I came back two times to speak to the whole student body. Horace and I felt the exhilaration and joy of discovering kindred Pentecostal spirits. We began to discuss the possibility of calling a group of Pentecostal scholars together in a colloquium in the near future.

On my trip to Springfield, Missouri, a few months later I visited the Assemblies of God archives where I did a research run of the *Pentecostal Evangel.* Again I was treated royally and given access to the inner sanctum of the archives. The first person I met on this trip was the great Assemblies of God historian William Menzies, who was a professor at Evangel College. He had already read the microfilm version of my dissertation and was anxious to discuss the history of the Pentecostal movement. According to my church teachings, the Assemblies of God people were not sanctified and were therefore 'less perfect' than we. I found Menzies to be about as sanctified as any person I had ever met. He made a tremendous impression on me. As with Horace Ward, we discussed how wonderful it would be to organize a gathering of Pentecostal scholars from the various colleges to discuss common scholarly concerns. I told about my discussions with Ward and we agreed on the spot to start making plans for a gathering at the Pentecostal World Conference which was due to convene in Dallas, Texas, in 1970. I promised that I would take the lead in planning and calling such a meeting. As a result, Ward, Menzies, and I became an ad hoc committee to plan a meeting of Pentecostal scholars to meet in Dallas in 1970.

On my return home, I wrote to the chairman of the conference, Yonggi Cho, to request a slot on the program for a banquet to organize a new Pentecostal scholarly society. He enthusiastically agreed. In the meantime, I communicated regularly with Ward and Menzies about the plans for the meeting. In preparation for the organization meeting, I wrote a draft constitution based on the existing constitutions of the Wesleyan Theological Society (WTS) and the Evangelical Theological Society (ETS). The name I suggested was accepted: The Society of Pentecostal Scholars.

When we gathered in Dallas, we did not know whether enough people would attend to pay for the room. To our happy surprise 139 persons registered and the money collected was barely adequate to pay the bill. Before we entered the room for the banquet, I heard a disparaging remark by a bishop about not being a scholar and insinuating that he was not welcome. A friend from Emmanuel College, Dr Garnet Pike, counseled us to change the name and add the word 'studies'. I immediately called an emergency meeting of the leaders and suggested that we change the name to the Society for Pentecostal Studies (SPS). This was done on the spot.

Among those who attended were the top executives of Pentecostalism around the world including Thomas Zimmerman, Yonggi Cho, David du Plessis, and others. To my surprise, Father Kilian McDonnell, a Roman Catholic scholar, was there and spoke to the assembled crowd. He was one of the first charter members of the Society. This was possibly the first time a Catholic had ever addressed a function of the World Pentecostal Conference. The main speaker was Dr Klaud Kendrick, the widely known Assemblies of God historian. In the organizational part of the session, William Menzies (Assemblies of God) was elected as the first president, Hollis Gause (Church of God) as Vice President, Rev. Edward Wood (Open Bible Standard Church) Treasurer, and I was elected to serve as the first Secretary. At this meeting I also met the great Pentecostal scholar Russell Spittler of Southern California College of the Assemblies of God. He immediately saw the possibilities in the new society and soon played an important role in its growth and development.

One of my first jobs was to publish a newsletter for the Society. This I did faithfully for several years. As Secretary, I kept all the records of the Society. The first annual meeting of the SPS after the organizational session convened in Des Moines, Iowa, on the campus of the Open Bible College in November of 1971. Only 25 registered for this first meeting that featured the reading of scholarly papers. Among these were Kilian McDonnell, Myrtle Flemming, and David du Plessis. It was a small but exceedingly motivated group of scholars. The program chairman was Dr Hollis Gause of Lee College in Cleveland, Tennessee. When the meeting was reported in the religious press, some wags said that the expression 'Pentecostal scholar' was an oxymoron. Yet this was the beginning of many meetings that were destined to bring Pentecostal scholarship into the mainstream of Christian religious life.

At the same time we were organizing the SPS, David du Plessis was beginning to make plans for a Catholic Pentecostal Dialogue which would begin talks between Catholic scholars and some Pentecostal and charismatic scholars from the mainline protestant churches. He saw the SPS as a rich source of Pentecostal scholars who could speak as theologians in these annual meetings. The big news out of the first annual meeting was the announcement by Kilian McDonnell and David du Plessis that a new Catholic-Pentecostal Dialogue would convene in Rome the following year.

I was invited to be a participant in some of the earliest meetings of this group. In the meantime we attempted to keep in the good graces of the leaders of the Pentecostal Fellowship of North America (PFNA). We therefore scheduled our sessions at the end of the annual PFNA conventions so that denominational leaders could stay over and attend our sessions. This did not work out because the very busy churchmen seldom had time to stay.

At least one time, the board of the SPS met with the Board of the PFNA to explain what we were doing. This happened in Des Moines in 1971. The major question was the meaning of our constitutional purpose of speaking authoritatively as Pentecostal scholars. We were told in no uncertain terms that we could never speak authoritatively since we were not heads of churches. Our answer was that there was such a thing as scholarly authority as well as ecclesiastical authority. This answer seemed to fall on deaf ears. Soon after this, we moved our annual sessions to meet separately from the PFNA annual meetings.

In order to speak from the Pentecostal perspective, we had adopted the PFNA statement of faith as a doctrinal requirement for membership in the Society. At our second annual meeting in Oklahoma City, Father James Connolly, a Roman Catholic member, expressed surprise that we would have a doctrinal requirement for membership which would exclude some people from other traditions from joining. As a first step, we provided for Associate members who would not have to sign but could join based on their interest in Pentecostal history and theology. As time went on, this policy became more and more untenable because it led to an artificial limit on participation and leadership of non-classical Pentecostals in the society. They felt like second-class citizens. I then reminded the SPS board that the World Pentecostal Conference had no doctrinal statement but was based on 'the things that are most surely believed among us'. We decided to adopt the WPC model and make the Society a group of people who shared the same scholarly interests but not necessarily the exact same doctrines.

The SPS ultimately grew to become the major scholarly organization in the Pentecostal/charismatic world. In 1979 The Society began publication of a truly scholarly journal titled *Pneuma: The Journal of the Society for Pentecostal Studies*. This name was suggested by Russell Spittler. In time, *Pneuma* became a major focus of ongoing research and publication in the scholarly world with subscriptions going to most major seminaries and universities. Those who served as editors over the years included Mel Robeck, Murray Dempster, and Frank Macchia. Many years later, while on a trip to Korea, I served as an advisor for the birth of the Asian Society for Pentecostal Studies, a group led by Young Hoon Lee and Wonsuk Ma, that grew to be another major forum for Pentecostal research and publications.

Throughout most of this period, I was unable to find a publisher for my dissertation which was titled, 'The Pentecostal Movement in the United States'. After revising the manuscript and adding the research gathered on my trips that had resulted in the organization of the SPS, I still had no publisher. This time I sent it to W.B. Eerdmans publishers in Grand Rapids, Michigan. Since this publisher was well known for its Calvinist leanings, I expected the usual rejection letter. To my utter shock, amazement, and joy, Eerdmans accepted the book. They explained that they had been looking for a good book on Pentecostalism and that my manuscript was just what they had in mind.

As I prepared the final manuscript for publication, I decided that I needed to make two changes. First, I changed the title to *The Holiness-Pentecostal Movement in the United States*. This was done to make the title match the content of the book. The reader was not introduced to the Pentecostal movement until the fifth chapter. The first four chapters dealt with the Methodist/Holiness movement. The publisher accepted this change.

The other change was a proposal to take two weeks to add a section on the Catholic Charismatic Renewal which had begun about the time I first wrote the book. This change was also accepted. It was not until after its publication in 1971 that I understood the reason for the four-year delay in getting the book into print. Had I published it earlier, the Catholics would have had less interest in it as a resource book. The decision to add the Catholic story was also a risk to my standing in the Pentecostal world since I included the Catholic renewal as an authentic part of the whole Pentecostal phenomenon.

Little did I know how fateful this decision would be and how my life would be changed by the publication of my dissertation. It appeared in 1971 and quickly gained a wide readership among scholars of all traditions. At first I thought that a few Pentecostals, Methodists, and holiness scholars would have an interest in it. To my utter surprise, more Catholics bought the book than any other group. Copies were obtained by the Vatican and photocopies were sent all over the Europe for Catholic bishops and scholars to read. They desperately wanted to know more about the roots of the Pentecostal movement and for some reason thought that my book was what they needed. Suddenly I was in demand to speak at Catholic charismatic events and even to participate in the Catholic-Pentecostal dialogue which had just been inaugurated by David du Plessis and Father Kilian McDonnell.

The Pentecostal Methodist Church of Chile

Another matter that began to occupy my time was the new relationship between the Pentecostal Holiness Church and the Pentecostal Methodist Church in Chile. In 1966 I was invited to address a conference of pastors in Santiago at the invitation of an interdenominational ministry representing all the evangelical churches in Chile. I was asked to read a paper on the roots of Pentecostalism. We met in the Club Italiano and there were about 500 pastors in attendance. My paper, which highlighted the Methodist roots of Pentecostalism, went over like a bombshell. Soon after I returned home I received a printed copy of my paper which was published by Bishop Chavez and sent all over Chile.

On this trip I was invited to preach in the Jotabeche Pentecostal Methodist Church on Alameda Avenue. I had never seen anything like it in my life. Over 7,000 persons jammed the church and filled all the aisles. The Pentecostals were full of joy and enthusiasm. They shouted out the three glories, 'Gloria a Dios, Gloria a Dios, Gloria a Dios' (Glory to God) throughout the service. Hundreds of the saints danced in the Spirit in a style that looked like the *queca*, the native dance of Chile. The response to my sermon was electric. I was mobbed by the crowd as I left the church with hundreds of people begging me to autograph their Bibles. I became a friend and admirer of Pastor Vasquez and his great church. It was by far the largest Protestant church in the world at that time with an estimated membership of 40,000 persons.

Two major things came out of my trips to Chile at this time. The first was an agreement of affiliation between the Pentecostal Holiness Church and the Pentecostal Methodist Church of Chile. I actually wrote the document in my hotel room at the request of Dr Corvin. Bishop Mamerto Mancilla approved of the document which we brought back to the U.S. for the Pentecostal Holiness Church to consider. Joining in the affiliation was the Pentecostal Church of Chile led by Bishop Enrico Chavez. At the time the three churches numbered almost 1,000,000 members.

After a series of meetings with all the parties involved, the affiliations were approved and signed at the Eighth World Pentecostal Conference in Rio De Janeiro in July 1967. The basic principle written into the agreements was that the Chilean churches were fully developed and indigenous denominations as was the Pentecostal Holiness Church. They would remain as self-governing bodies while recognizing each other as the same church. This meant that the Pentecostal Holiness Church would not send missionaries to Chile. The agreement was based on the common Wesleyan roots of the churches as well as the common history and theology they shared.

Speaking at Asbury Theological Seminary

A totally unexpected turn relating to my book came in the summer of 1972. One afternoon while playing tennis on the Emmanuel College tennis court, I saw two men come up to the chain fence asking for me. They were David Bundy and Donald Dayton. They were student leaders at Asbury College in Wilmore, Kentucky. They had recently read my book *The Holiness-Pentecostal Movement* and felt that I should visit Asbury to present my thesis in a student-sponsored forum. This was amazing to me since I knew that Asbury had recently adopted a policy refusing to admit Pentecostals to their student body. Being a school historically committed to the Holiness-Methodist movement, Asbury had always opposed Pentecostalism although they had admitted some Pentecostals in the past.

I went to Asbury not knowing what to expect. The student paper advertised my coming to the consternation of the faculty and administration. When I arrived at the session, there was standing room only in the room with many students sitting on the floor. The session was lively as I made my presentation and answered questions afterwards. My thesis, that Pentecostalism was born in the Holiness Movement, was considered novel and even startling at the time. I was well-treated at Asbury and met with many students who talked into the wee hours of the night. Some of them included William Faupel, Donald Dayton, and Paul Chappell. Somewhat later I was invited to read a paper at the Wesleyan Theological Society explaining and defending my thesis. When the elders of the Society found out about it, they vetoed my invitation.

This is ironic in hindsight in the light future developments. Shortly after my visit, Asbury rescinded its policy excluding Pentecostals and in 1988 invited the Society for Pentecostal Studies to meet on the Asbury campus. A decade later, in 1998, there was even a joint meeting between the Society for Pentecostal Studies and the Wesleyan Theological Society.

Pentecostal Ecumenist

In the midst of all these activities, I continued to be active in many ecumenical pursuits. For many years I attended the annual sessions of the 'Glencoe' retreats which met near St. Louis, Missouri. Here leaders of the American Pentecostal and Charismatic movements dealt with controversies that arose from time to time. The greatest of these was the discipleship/shepherding movement led by Glencoe participants Bob Mumford, Derek Prince, Charles Simpson, Ern Baxter, and Don Basham. For many years we debated the issues raised by these brothers such as public exorcisms, rebaptism of newly Spirit-filled believers, and teachings on spiritual covering. In the end, we never resolved these problems but through it all, we maintained a deep love and respect for each other.

From this group came the idea which I first proposed for a huge ecumenical conference of all Charismatics in North America which would bring the movement to the attention of the church and secular worlds. The result was the Kansas City Conference of 1977 which drew 50,000 Charismatics together in a massive show of unity. In 1984 I was chosen to lead the group which was now known as the Charismatic Concerns Committee. Under my leadership, we organized the North American Renewal Service Committee (NARSC) in 1985, which sponsored giant ecumenical congresses in New Orleans in 1986-87, Indianapolis in 1990, Orlando in 1995, and St. Louis in 2000. Over 100,000 persons from all denominations registered for these great congresses. At the same time, I led in ecumenical Pentecost Celebrations in Oklahoma City, which for 17 years drew thousands of Pentecostals and Charismatics to celebrate the birthday of the Church. For most of these years, I also served as a General officer of the Pentecostal Holiness Church.

Regent University

I had known about Regent University from its founding days when it was called CBN University. In fact, I had been inside the old studio of WYAH when it was a broken-down wreck with only one black and white camera. I had met Pat Robertson on several occasions over the years and was greatly impressed with his tremendous energy and vision. Since I was an educator as well as a churchman and ecumenist, I had always admired Robertson's quest for the highest quality in everything he attempted. In 1987, I was invited to be the convocation speaker at CBNU. Here I saw a faculty and student body that was deeply spiritual and freely moving in the gifts of the Spirit. Somehow, I felt that someday I would be part of this family.

In 1992, I attended a meeting of the Society for Pentecostal Studies in Springfield, Missouri, and shared the banquet table with Dr Rodman Williams and his wife Jo. I had first met Williams in Rome in 1973 as a fellow member of the Catholic-Pentecostal Dialogue team. I then worked with him as a member of the governing board of Melodyland School of Theology in Anaheim, California, where he served as President.

Later in the year, out of the blue, I received a call from Dr Williams about coming to the Regent School of Divinity to serve as dean. Since I had tried to avoid being an educational administrator for several years, I was not too interested, but I told Williams that I would pray about it. About six months passed and I forgot about the call, thinking that the position had been filled. Then I got a second call, and I told Williams the same thing; I was not seeking the position, but I would pray about it if indeed it was the Lord's will for me to come. Again months passed and I forgot about the whole thing.

Then, in 1993 I received a third call, asking me to come to Regent and meet with the search committee, which was led by Dr Williams. I wrote him a letter and told him that I had lately been singing 'Carry me back to Old Virginia, the state where I was born'. In fact, I had grown up during World War II in Suffolk where my father served as pastor of a Pentecostal Holiness house church. I could have never dreamed then that a Spirit-filled University would be built only twenty miles away, founded by a Southern Baptist businessman who spoke in tongues.

After meeting with the faculty, students, and local pastors, along with Conolly Phillips of the Board of Trustees, I returned home to Oklahoma City knowing that I had a big decision to make. Although it would be great to live in Virginia near my family and my wife's family, I knew that I would have to leave our three children and several grandchildren who lived in Oklahoma.

I was later informed that on a certain Monday I would have to give a final answer to Dr Williams and Pat Robertson about whether or not I would come. It was a wrenching decision, one that demanded much prayer and a clear answer from heaven. On Sunday the day before I was to call in my decision, I went to Ron Dryden's church in Oklahoma City for the morning service. I asked the Lord for a clear answer about my future.

As the service progressed, I opened my Bible and prayed, 'Lord give me clear direction'. My eyes fell at random on Isa. 65.1 which begins with the words, 'I was sought by those who did not ask for me. I was found by those who did not seek me.' Then the words leaped out at me. I said, 'Here I am, here I am'. While I was pondering these words, a complete stranger came to the pulpit and in a prophecy repeated the exact same words I had just read. Immediately after this, Pastor Dryden began to lead the congregation in singing the old altar call song, 'Where He leads me I will follow'. I had not heard that song for over 20 years.

No one there could have possibly known that this was the same hymn that was being sung at the very moment I was saved as a 16 year old boy. Under a camp meeting gospel tent in Memphis, Tennessee, I had surrendered my life to the Lord while a little morning Bible study crowd was singing the refrain, 'Where He leads me I will follow'. Afterwards this became the theme song of my life, especially in times of uncertainty and transition. Now, so many years later, as we sang the words, 'I'll go with him through the garden' and 'He will give me grace and glory', I began to weep. Through my tears I said, 'Yes, I will go to Regent – I got the message, Lord'. After the service, in the pastor's office, another stranger prophesied that the Lord was calling me to enter a new open door and that I should go.

After this, I never looked back. I knew the Lord had called me to Regent University for that season in my life. I have always been grateful that the Lord was able to make His will as plain as the nose on my face. It came at first through Scripture, then through prophecy, and then through amazing confirmations from people I did not even know. After 12 wonderful years serving as Dean of the School of Divinity, I can now look back and see the marvelous and providential hand of the Lord in bringing me to Regent University in 1994.

Seminary Dean

My tenure as dean of the Regent University School of Divinity lasted for 12 years, from 1994 to 2006. When I began my work, the

School of Divinity student body numbered about 200 students. The faculty of nine full-time teachers was exceptionally good at what they did. We offered a Master of Divinity degree and a Master of Arts degree aimed at preparing future pastors and church workers. Pat Robertson and the Board of Trustees were very supportive of the school and all the plans we made for the future. One of my first decisions was to inaugurate a Doctor of Ministries degree program which we started in 1996. It grew very rapidly under the leadership of Dr Russell West as Director. Our first class was taught by Dr David Barrett, the world famous Editor of the *World Christian Encyclopedia.*

Our goal now was to offer a PhD in renewal studies as soon as possible. With the development of online programs such as CompuServe and AOL, I got the idea of asking Dr Bill Brown, Dean of the School of Communication, to consider joining with the School of Divinity in offering a track in their PhD program in renewal studies. At that time the School of Communication offered the only PhD in the University. When he agreed, we became the first school in the world to offer a PhD online. We were truly pioneers. This was done in 1997.

Now our faculty began to discuss offering our own PhD program in Renewal Studies, a title inspired by the systematic theological works published by our own Rodman Williams. In 2003 our first cohort arrived on campus for the first class. To our astonishment, 38 students signed up for the program, leading to some of the largest PhD classes ever taught anywhere. The first teachers were outstanding scholars such as Dr Stan Burgess and Dr Frank Macchia. When the program started, I remembered that I had been brought to Oral Roberts University in 1990 to help start the first PhD program ever offered by a renewal university (with a Pentecostal/Charismatic orientation.) The reason why it never happened at ORU was that there was never enough money to start the program. At Regent, I was able to realize a long held dream, to prepare scholars on the PhD level to study, do research, and write about the incredibly fast growing Pentecostal and Charismatic movements around the world.

By the time I retired as Dean in 2006, the student body had almost quadrupled to number some 1,000 currently enrolled students in all programs. This came as the fulfillment of a prophecy given by

Oral Roberts when I asked him to pray for me and the School of Divinity. He emphatically prophesied that the school would quadruple during my tenure as Dean.

Looking back over my many years as a researcher, writer, and ecumenist, perhaps my most important accomplishment was to create a scholarly environment at Regent University where bright young students could come to learn under a great and distinguished faculty, to produce the cutting edge research, writing, and publications to help guide the renewal movement into the next century, and to become themselves distinguished professors to newer generations of Spirit-filled scholars.

2

SWIMMING UPSTREAM: MY CALL TO THE PENTECOSTAL ACADEMY

MURRAY W. DEMPSTER[*]

Swimming upstream is an apt metaphor to characterize my calling to, and my life journey in, the Pentecostal academic world of theological education. You are welcome to travel with me through the pages that follow as I attempt to reconstruct my journey in episodes from my growing up years to my calling as a Pentecostal educator committed to teaching in Christian higher education, to advancing creative academic scholarship in the service of the church and the academy, and to administrative leadership in building an institution of higher learning marked by academic excellence and spiritual vitality.

Growing up on the Margins of the Pentecostal Church

I was born on June 27, 1942 in Melville, Saskatchewan to Henry and June Dempster. Both of my parents were Pentecostal in experience and attended the Elim Tabernacle, a Pentecostal Assemblies of Canada (PAOC) church.[40] Today I can still recall attending Sunday

---

[*] Murray W. Dempster (PhD, University of Southern California) is Distinguished Professor of Social Ethics at Southeastern University in Lakeland, FL.

[40] Melville History Book Committee, 'Melville Pentecostal Tabernacle', in *The Tie that Binds: Melville '83* (Altona, Manitoba: Friesen Printers, a Division of D.W. Friesen & Sons, Ltd., 1984), p. 136.

School class in the pastor's parsonage in one of the bedrooms or the kitchen or the living room. Each week that I attended Sunday School, I experienced the dissonance between Pastor Fleming's home which was a safe haven marked by love, and my own home which was marked by repeated cycles of domestic violence. My tongues-talking father was an abuser.

My father's physical violence had accelerated to the place where my mother experienced a painful broken ear drum. The night that happened she had mustered up the courage to decide to file for a legal separation with the Court. With courage, my mother moved forward in gaining a legal separation and eventually a divorce. I say with courage because of the way the church pastor and members treated my mother as a 'divorcee'. Based on the Pentecostal interpretation of Paul's teaching on marriage and Jesus' teaching on the divorce law, my mother was scapegoated as the one who legally initiated and thereby *caused* the separation and divorce from my father, and as a consequence she was *persona non grata* in the church.

To my dismay, my mother still insisted that I continue to attend Sunday School every week. I did so to respect her wishes, but I was more than annoyed in having to attend; I was emotionally upset, and even became furious at times in my internal self-talk, because these judgmental people never lived one moment in our house. None of them heard what I heard when passing by her closed bedroom door and overheard her praying in strange languages. When I asked her about it, she told me she was praying in a language the Holy Spirit gave her so that God could hear her directly when she interceded in prayer for the transformation of our lives together as a Christian family.

When I turned sixteen, my mother remarried and she moved further downward in Dante's inferno from a 'divorcee' to an 'adulteress'. The proverbial straw that broke the camel's back for me was an incident that happened in church after she and my new dad decided that we should re-engage as a family in the life of the church, which had moved and was renamed Melville Pentecostal Tabernacle. Communion was being observed as part of the church service and my mother and I were in the back pew. When the elements were passed down the pew and the tray that held the grape juice cups and crackers came to her, the deacon reached over from behind and he took the tray and passed it around her and gave it to me clearly indicating after the Scripture the Pastor had just read that she was 'not worthy' to take communion because she was 'living in adultery'. I took the tray and passed the elements to the person next to me but I did not take the elements myself both in solidarity with my mother and in dissonance with the Pentecostal Church. I whispered to my mother that we should go. She said, 'No', that we should not make a scene. I wiggled through the rest of the communion ceremony, the sermon, and the benediction. But when we walked out the front church door together I said to my mom that I will never be back here again, NEVER!

From that point on through my high school graduation, I washed my hands from any attempts to build my Christian life in the church. I found meaning for my life outside of the church in school, in competitive sports, in drama, and in music, especially playing rhythm guitar in a 'Rock & Roll' band called 'The Black Cats'.[41] I loved playing at dances, although I always felt psychologically relieved when the dance was over and Jesus had not returned to rapture the true believers to heaven. I feared being 'left behind' if Jesus came and I would have to take the 'Mark of the Beast' on my forehead.

I was accepted into the Bachelor of Pharmacy program at the University of Alberta in Edmonton for the Fall of 1960. At this same time, my mother – to my surprise – had been to church to hear a young Pentecostal evangelist, Ken Bombay, who came to town for revival meetings. My mother asked for me to do her a favor and attend a service. She emphasized that I would really like the evangelist because he quotes Rock & Roll lyrics and plays the piano like Jerry Lee Lewis. I suspected that she was exaggerating a bit but I told her that I would go.

---

[41] 'The Need for Recreation Centre', an article in the *Melville Advance,* pasted into my scrapbook created by my mother (circa 1958) states, 'A Morgue is usually a quiet place, but not when a group of teenagers take it over for rock and roll sessions ... From the moment you step in the door your ear drums are assaulted with rock and roll music played ... by four young fellows called "The Black Cats" ... The atmosphere is one of loud youthful gaiety as young couples spin around the room, their stockinged feet beating out a muffled rhythm on the well-polished floor'.

Salvation Came to my House, and More

What my mother did not know was that I had convinced Billy, the drummer of our band, to come with me to church for moral support. As I sat in the service I realized my mother was right. The evangelist talked about Elvis Presley and his hit, 'Blue Suede Shoes', to make a point from the Bible more understandable, relevant, and evocative of emotional response. He quoted lyrics with ease from the hit parade that identified various issues of life for which 'Christ is the Answer'. I was totally engaged. That night the conviction of the Holy Spirit was so strong that I raised my hand when the altar call was given with 'every head bowed and every eye closed'. Then he asked those you raised their hands to stand up. Then he asked those who were standing to come forward.

At that point, I bent over and asked Billy if he wanted to come with me and get saved. He said, 'No'. When I walked away from his side and up to the altar it was symbolic that I was walking away from my old life and into my new life in Christ. My tears and my convulsive sobbing at the altar represented the deepest emotional experience I had ever had. I was being transformed. It was like my own tears were washing away all those deeply buried resentments that I had harbored against the church.

Two nights later on the last evening of the revival meetings, I was baptized in the Holy Spirit and spoke in other tongues. It was an experience of ecstasy and joy. The evangelist encouraged me to keep praying in tongues until I broke through and received 'liberty in the Spirit' so that in the future I could speak in tongues as part of my prayer life and deepening my devotion to God. I felt the urgency to pray alone kneeling at the front pew. The evangelist was at the piano leading the singing of the chorus, 'I'll go where you want me to go dear Lord, over mountain, or plain, or sea'. I prayed to God, surrendered my will to God's will, and I felt impressed in the deepest reaches of my inner self that God was calling me into the ministry. It was bizarre, and I knew it! I had not really prepared for this! When I told the evangelist that I felt called to 'the ministry', without hesitation he recommended that I should attend the same Pentecostal Bible School that he had attended – Canadian Northwest Bible Institute (CNBI) in Edmonton. So I applied and was accepted. I would be going to Edmonton after all, only with a different sense of mission for my life.

Spiritual Formation in a Pentecostal Bible School: Gaining a Firm Foundation for my Faith

CNBI turned out to be an exact fit for me intellectually, spiritually, and personally. The three-year Ministerial Diploma program started from ground zero so there was no presupposition that students had knowledge of the Bible, Theology, and Practics. The Bible was the basis for proclaiming the truth of the gospel in preaching and witnessing to others. It was also a devotional book and its truth could be comprehended by a common reader by the illumination of the Holy Spirit. As I look back on this experience, I do not recall that the terms 'exegesis' or 'hermeneutics' were ever mentioned in class and certainly no critical method was ever proposed for interpreting Scripture. Yet in terms of my own faith development, the common reading of the Bible provided for me an introduction to the content of Scripture that shaped my sense of inner spirituality in devotion to God.

In addition to gaining knowledge of the Bible, I loved the times when the outpouring of the Holy Spirit would happen serendipitously at the beginning of a class in response to the opening prayer, or later in response to a truth in the middle of a lecture, or in the daily chapel service. And there were the more heady academic courses as well that promoted intellectual understanding of the faith like Systematic Theology I, II, III taken sequentially in the three years of study. The 'textbooks' in those courses were the mimeographed notes written by Dr J.E. Purdie, an Anglican priest who in 1919 experienced 'an infilling of the Holy Spirit' and began praying in tongues.[42] Even though I did not know it at the time, Purdie's notes were modeled on the Reformed Anglican Theology at Wycliffe College, where he had studied for five years and viewed the Wycliffe faculty as 'champions of the Evangelical truths of the Bible

---

[42] Bruce Ed Hird, 'Dr. James Eustace Purdie: A Canadian Dennis Bennett', *Anglican for Renewal Canada* (Summer 1992), available at http://edhird.word press.com/2010/09/01/dr-james-eustace-purdie-a-canadian-dennis-bennet/).

and the Reformed faith of the Reformation'.[43] John C. Cooke, who was the Principal when I attended CNBI, taught Systematic Theology I, II, and III by providing his own theological commentary on the Purdie notes having himself studied with Purdie. Cooke was a dynamic lecturer who had the capacity to make the truths on Purdie's mimeographed pages come alive. I loved his courses and his passion. These three years at CNBI gave me a firm foundation for my personal faith.

Going into the Ministry: Satisfaction and Misgivings

A huge surprise occurred in my life as my second year at CNBI was coming to a close. Pastor Robert Taitinger of Central Pentecostal Tabernacle (known as 'the Tab') – that housed the classrooms for CNBI – invited me to become his Assistant Pastor. I joyfully accepted the invitation. I was going to be in the ministry! I fulfilled my new ministry responsibilities at the Tab, finished my third year at CNBI, and received my diploma and my ministerial license. Working with Pastor Bob Taitinger was a life changing adventure. He was an incredible mentor, an authentic Christian, and a genuine friend.

Three events happened during my ministry at the Tab that I believe were providential in making me realize that I needed a more adequate ministerial education. First, a student from the University of Alberta came to see me because his faith was being seriously challenged in a sociology course and he wanted to know how I dealt with 'cultural relativism'. At CNBI and in all my high school classes I never had heard of cultural relativism. With a mother with a grade six education and a father with a grade eight education, cultural relativism was an issue that we never discussed at the dinner table. I was tongue tied. This meeting with a Pentecostal university student in a faith crisis was a defining moment for me! I truly experienced an epiphany – I realized that I was not academically pre-

---

[43] Hird, 'Dr. James Eustace Purdie', citing James D. Craig, 'Out and Out for the Lord: James Eustace Purdie, An Early Anglican Pentecostal' (MA, University of St. Michaels' College, 1995), available at www.paoc.org/administration/arch ives/pdf/jdcraig-thesis.pdf). Cf. Peter Althouse, 'The Influence of Dr. J.E. Purdie's Reformed Anglican Theology on the Formation and Development of the Pentecostal Assemblies of Canada', *PNEUMA: The Journal of the Society for Pentecostal Studies* 19 (Spring 1996), pp. 3-28.

pared as a minister to deal with the intellectual challenges that students and others faced to their Christian faith.

Second, I met the love of my life at a Quartet Concert that we were hosting at the Tab. Her name was Coralie Erickson and I found out that she attended Faith Temple, an independent Pentecostal church in the city. I was a single Assistant Pastor at the time and the Pastor felt it best that I not date anyone from the church so I was thrilled that I finally met a Pentecostal girl who did not attend the Tab. I sensed God's providence was at work. The next afternoon I called her and asked her for a date following a Sunday night service, she agreed and the rest is history. We had our first date in January 1964, we were married in September 1964, and our son, Marlon Murray, was born in June 1965.

The third providential turn in finding stronger preparation for my calling to church ministry happened right on the heels of Marlon's birth. Wesley Steelberg had just been elected as the Senior Pastor at First Assembly of God in Long Beach, California and invited me to become his Associate Pastor. We accepted and upon acquiring our Permanent Resident Visas from the US Consulate in October 1965, we flew into LAX to meet Wes and Earlene and start our new ministry. As we were coming down in our landing, we could look over some of the rubble of the Watts Riots. Racial and social tensions were still high and we were feeling our first sense of culture shock. These images stayed with us and spurred us on to develop in time a more theological understanding of holistic church mission and ministry.

Earning a BA in Biblical Studies in a Christian Liberal Arts College: A Transformational Experience

The greatest opportunity that opened for me in the move to Long Beach, from my perspective, was that Southern California College (SCC), now Vanguard University, was only about 25 miles away down Interstate 405. The school had just received full WASC accreditation as a liberal arts college in 1964 and had put together a stellar Faculty in gaining accreditation. So the timing was perfect. They were looking for students and I was looking for an education. My competency deficit about issues like 'cultural relativism' was about to get addressed big time. After one year at the church, Pastor Steelberg responded graciously to my request for me to go back to half-time at the church so I could go full-time to SCC.

I applied, I was accepted, and as a Biblical Studies major I was given a generous transfer from CNBI. However, I had to do one-half of the Bible major requirements at SCC and all the Gen Ed requirements in humanities, arts, and sciences. The General Ed Core Curriculum expanded my horizons into areas that were intellectually stimulating and gave me a new understanding of the broader world in which relevant ministry needs to take place. My idea of ministerial education was broadening out considerably.

The academic quality of my biblical courses was an equal match to my liberal arts courses. Russ Spittler, who was finishing his PhD dissertation at Harvard, and Gordon Fee, who held a PhD in New Testament from the University of Southern California, were the 'twin powers' in Biblical Studies when I was a student. I learned about the historical-critical method, a method of biblical interpretation that blended Text Criticism, Form Criticism, and Redaction Criticism. Fee's class in synoptic Gospels opened up new vistas of understanding Matthew, Mark, and Luke as authentic theological documents – not just histories of Jesus of Nazareth – that were making the proclamation of good news of God's reign to particular audiences. I was reading the Gospels in a brand new light and I was loving every minute of it because the increase in my knowledge triggered a deepening of my faith.

I also took Pauline Literature with Dr Fee that transformed my understanding of God and God's self-revelation in Jesus Christ. Sitting in those classes was truly a life-changing experience. Both Dr Spittler and Dr Fee blended the scholarly study of the Bible with a genuine personal devotion to God. As a consequence, the most significant personalized 'truth' that I received out of their classes was that I wanted to be like them in their biblically-informed spirituality, and I wanted to be able to preach and teach in the church in the way they had done in the classroom in delivering sturdy and understandable theological and ethical content out of the Bible. So, I concluded that I needed to go on to Graduate School to gain those critical skills. The University of Southern California, Fee's *alma mater*, was only 45 minutes the other way on the interstate from Long Beach.

Going on for an MA to Become a better Minister: A Dream Come True

Before my summer courses in Pauline Literature and Shakespeare were completed at SCC I had submitted my application to USC. The MA Program in Religion-Social Ethics was a one-year 30 credit hour program with 12 credit hours (three courses) in the Fall and 12 credit hours (three courses) in the Spring and a Thesis. I realized that I would not be able to complete the program in one year if I was working. So, by faith I resigned from the church, Coralie agreed to go back to work full-time, and we arranged for the care of Marlon on the days I was at the university. We moved to a less expensive rental in a duplex behind the landlord's main house, and we believed that somehow by God's grace we would survive financially.

I graduated from SCC in the summer of 1968, so I could now enclose a transcript with a record of all my SCC classes to the USC Registrar that would verify the completion of my BA with a 4.0 GPA. Because I had unaccredited courses from CNBI that transferred toward my BA at SCC, I was admitted on probation and I needed to enroll full time for 12 credit hours, and I had to earn a grade of B or higher in each 4 credit hour course. If I was successful, then at the beginning of the Spring semester I would be advanced to regular standing in the Graduate School as a degree-seeking student. I was so elated! I made it in! I felt there was no problem about the hurdles. I was ready to swim upstream in order to take advantage of this incredible opportunity to follow in the steps of my CNBI and SCC Profs in fulfilling God's call on my life for vocational ministry.

My classroom experience at USC started with a sense of intimidation and generalized anxiety. My experience in my first class of REL 570 nearly freaked me out, although I masked my interior terror quite well. My classmates in REL 570 were all PhD students. Moreover, the colleges where the majority of them studied were top-ranked RD universities, and some of those were connected with premiere Ivy League Divinity Schools or Graduate Programs for their Masters degrees. Unfortunately, my turn came toward the end of the self-introductions. After listening to everyone else's stellar pedigree, I said I had a BA in Biblical Studies from Southern

California College. I knew from their quirky facial expressions that the question of the moment was: 'Where is that?' In this class, I felt I was in over my head when my academic preparation was compared to the members of the class. At the same time, I had a calling from God and I had an opportunity to gain a first-rate education in Theology and Social Ethics so, intimidated or not, I was staying the course and swimming upstream.

About half way through the semester, I had one of those life-affirming experiences that change your mind-set. I showed up for my Directed Reading on the History of Christian Thought in Theology and Ethics with Dr John B. Orr and he asked me to drive him over to pick up his repaired car and we could talk about this week's assignment on the way. As we drove, I waited for him to ask me about my reading and my written report but he did not. Instead, he said that he noticed that I was not speaking out in his 570 class and joining in the class discussions. He said that one of the reasons I was in the program was to add to the diversity of thought. He said that since I was a Pentecostal I needed to speak out and represent the viewpoint of Pentecostal theology on the issues the class was addressing.

In my response, I was totally honest. I told him that I did not inherit a well-developed, integrated, and comprehensive Pentecostal theology from my tradition. I told him there is no existing Pentecostal Theology that could address the Vienna Circle, A.J. Ayer, and the problem of religious knowledge or the language games of Ludwig Wittgenstein and the meaning of religious discourse. I told him that I was on my own – along with others in my generation in the same predicament – trying to develop a Pentecostal viewpoint on these issues from the angle of my Pentecostal 'faith'. So, I made it clear that the class discussions stimulated an introspective response from me and I was a work in process. Dr Orr got it, but he gave a surprising response that almost turned pastoral. He said, and I have recalled it almost verbatim over the years as part of 'my story' because it was memorable to me: 'Murray, you brought your faith with you to the university. It is the most precious possession you have. Make sure you take it with you when you go from here. I lost my faith at Yale and I have never been able to get it back'.

When we arrived at our destination and he exited the car, he told me that I should get acquainted with Karl Barth's theology because it was very compatible with the existential nature of Pentecostal faith, and it was intellectually respectable in the academy. This piece of advice I tucked away in my memory banks for the future. Unfortunately, my integration of Barth into my embryonic academic Pentecostal theology caused me no end of pain from some of my Fundamentalist faculty colleagues when I later became a full-time faculty member at SCC. That conversation with Dr Orr, however, caused a fire to ignite in my bones – I wanted to construct a theological framework for a Pentecostal social ethic so I could represent my tradition in the give and take of theological and ethical discourse in a way that made intellectual sense.

I finished the Fall semester with a composite GPA of 4.0 in my probation semester. I swam upstream for the entire Fall semester and I was now able to pursue my MA as a degree-seeking student. The Spring semester, however, was even more challenging. I had to complete a full load of 12 credit hours of coursework, and at the same time, work toward the completion of my master's thesis. It was Augustus Cerillo, Jr. who came to my rescue and suggested that I should write my thesis on Carl F.H. Henry since Henry was a recognized theologian in the areas of Theology and Ethics as well as being the founding editor of *Christianity Today*.[44] Within the time deadlines of the Graduate School I had finished all my course requirements and my 95 page Master's thesis, entitled, 'The Role of Scripture in the Social Ethical Writings of Carl F.H. Henry'.[45] It was a moment of triumph!

---

[44] Later, out of our mutual interests in Evangelical social ethics, and especially Carl F.H. Henry, I co-authored with Augustus Cerillo, Jr., 'Carl F.H. Henry's Early Apologetic for an Evangelical Social Ethic, 1942-1956', *Journal of the Evangelical Theological Society* 34 (September 1991), pp. 365-79. No individual person empowered my academic life more than Gus Cerillo. We worked together in youth leadership in the church and later as editors of *Agora: A Magazine of Pentecostal Opinion*. When I became Editor of *Pneuma* and he was the Book Review Editor, we jointly read the submitted articles to judge whether there was sufficient merit in the article to send it on to our reviewers. When I became President of Vanguard in 2000, Gus was the first Provost and Chief Academic Officer who worked with me. I was so elated when in 2009 the Society for Pentecostal Studies awarded Gus the Lifetime Service Award. From my perspective, no one was more deserving of this honor than was Gus.

[45] In my thesis, I expressed appreciation for Henry's writings but attempted to show that his ethical reasoning from a biblical proposition to a moral judgment was neither deductively axiomatic nor universally valid as he proposed. Rather, the excluded middle that connected a biblical proposition to a moral

At the Crossroads: A Call to Local Church Ministry or a Call to Christian Higher Education?

With my thesis accepted, I had completed my MA in Social Ethics from USC in 1969 after completing my BA in Biblical Studies from SCC in 1968, and I was now ready to re-engage in vocational ministry in the local church. I was in the process of interviewing for an Associate Pastor position when I received a call from Russ Spittler who told me that he had talked with the Dean of Students at SCC and he would like to offer me a position on the staff and part-time faculty at SCC. The position of Men's Head Resident was a full-time position but my contract would provide released time for me to teach the Introduction to Philosophy course each semester in the Division of Religion and Philosophy.

I found myself at a crossroad. On the one hand, I had pursued my MA to become a more academically prepared minister for the local church. On the other hand, Russ challenged me to test whether or not God was calling me to become a theological educator in Christian higher education, especially in this needed area of Pentecostal social ethics. Russ challenged me in two ways that both hit home. First, he said that I could be a minister at a local assembly and add to the church, or I could be a professor and multiply myself through the students that I educated for church ministry. Second, he admonished me to be a steward of my gifts. I had just earned my Masters degree, and I needed to use that education where it provided the greater service to the kingdom of God and to the Church. Largely due to Russ's persuasiveness, I decided I would go to work at the college.

---

judgment was the Evangelical community of shared ethical discourse which community had become rhetorically persuaded to see the fit between these two levels of ethical reasoning. Since my thesis was destined to become part of the Carl F.H. Henry collection at Syracuse University – a fact that I did not know at the time of my writing the thesis – Henry sent a letter of rebuttal to me on several points with a cc to Syracuse so that a copy of his letter would be in his collection at Syracuse. Having just earned my MA degree, I recognized I was no match for this theological giant, although I believed my fundamental thesis argument to be true. I would pick up this study of rhetorical logic again later in my PhD dissertation when it fit more coherently with the first theological rumblings about post-modernism.

One semester was all it took for me to become convinced that God was calling me to be a theological educator in the area of social ethics. The excitement and joy I experienced in the classroom gave me a tangible sense of meaning in my own life by being a difference-maker in the lives of students. Similarly to the way that I had experienced the transformative power of education when I was a student, I was now a faculty member delivering an education in my academic field that had transformative power in the lives of a new generation of students. God had confirmed my calling to teaching and scholarship and I felt an urgent need to go on and pursue my PhD in Social Ethics at USC. However, I felt I needed to take a year to study and to read so I would be better prepared in going into a PhD by filling in some gaps of knowledge that I encountered in my MA program. I read voraciously and made application to return to USC in the Fall of 1971 to pursue my PhD in Social Ethics.

Pursuing a PhD to Prepare for my Academic Calling

My psychological state of mind was much different when I returned to USC for my PhD studies. I was engaged from day one. I had a sense of mission to pursue the education that I needed to fulfill my academic calling. Also I was motivated by receiving the Layne Foundation Fellowship from the university that covered all my tuition costs, fees, and textbooks for full-time enrollment. With the agreement of Religion Chair Russ Spittler, I taught one course each semester at SCC and our family continued to live in on-campus housing in the Men's Tower until my doctoral course work was finished over a two year period. During this time period I also passed my foreign language requirements in French and German. At that point I took one year to prepare further for my comprehensive examinations. Carl F.H. Henry once said that when he was preparing for his PhD comps at Boston University he focused all his efforts in answering one question that would validate to himself that he was ready to sit for his comprehensive exams: 'Explain the universe, give one or two illustrations'. That was exactly how I felt.

My multiple day comprehensive exams reflected a broad-based knowledge to the academic field of social ethics. When I was finished with the comprehensive exams I felt my knowledge reservoir had been completely drained out on the pages that I wrote! But I had a good outcome – I passed the comps and in 1974 I was formally advanced to candidacy for the PhD. One year into my dissertation, my advisor, Dr Orr, gave me the bad news, however, that the Religion Graduate Faculty had just established a policy that the topic of doctoral dissertations could not be related to the faith tradition of the students. Unfortunately, my dissertation was establishing three ideal types on Evangelical social ethics which had a burgeoning literature at the time. I had already completed the introductory chapter and laid out my threefold ideal typology. I was using Chaim Perelman's theory of rhetorical logic to demonstrate the paradigm of moral reasoning that connected theology and ethics within three different ideal types.[46] I was going to show that Evangelical agreement on theology did not translate into Evangelical agreement on social ethics. Although Dr Orr said that I could chance it and go ahead with the Evangelical focus, he strongly advised me to develop Chaim Perelman's rhetorical theory more elaborately and then apply it in a more generalized way to Christian social ethics. I took his advice and basically started from scratch with my dissertation.[47] In March 1980, I defended my dissertation, and I was awarded my PhD in the June 1980 Commencement Exercises.[48]

Upon my completion of the PhD, Coralie said to me, 'Now it's my turn'. She had supported my education in multiple ways through three academic degrees, while she remained a high school graduate. She had sublimated her own career goals, but now I was going to learn to multi-task as a faculty member, a supporter of her education and career goals, and as 'Mr Mom' in our domestic household. She earned her Bachelor of Science degree in Accounting in the School of Business at the University of Southern California (USC), and achieved her CPA certification as an auditor with Peat Marwick Main Hurdman. She moved into the private sector as a Corporate Controller and became the main 'bread winner' in our family. During these years, faculty members in Christian higher education un-

---

46 C. Perelman and L. Olbrechts-Tyteca, *The New Rhetoric: A Treatise on Argumentation* (Notre Dame, IN: Notre Dame Press, 1969).

47 All this earlier doctoral research on Evangelical Social Ethics was not lost but was useful when Gus Cerillo and I co-authored *Salt and Light: Evangelical Political Thought in Modern America* (Grand Rapids, MI: Baker Book House, 1989).

48 Murray Wayne Dempster, 'Rhetorical Logic in Ethical Justification: A Critical Exposition of Chaim Perelman's "New Rhetoric" and its Potential Bearing on Christian Moral Reasoning' (PhD, University of Southern California, 1980).

derstood that in order to survive financially the spouse also had to work if you were married. Coralie's commitment to her own professional career gave me a gift of freedom to pursue my individual research agenda and my interest in promoting a Pentecostal tradition of critical scholarship.

Promoting a Pentecostal Intellectual Tradition: Taking First Steps in Social Ethical Commentary

After I passed the qualifying exams for the PhD in 1974 and started working on my dissertation, I received my first taste of publishing, although it was more at a popular journalistic style of publishing. Three of my academic colleagues – Gus Cerillo, Gayle Erwin, and Dennis McNutt – and I, plus 26 Contributing Editors, launched *Agora: A Magazine of Opinion within the Assemblies of God* in Summer 1977 and produced four issues each year through a fifth anniversary final issue in Summer 1981. We identified a four-point agenda for *Agora*. We made it clear that the magazine, its editors and contributing editors will be *advocating* 1) the promotion of a Pentecostal intellectual tradition; 2) the articulation of a prophetic word to our own household of faith and practice; 3) the development of charismatic models of discipleship for relevant witness within our contemporary society; and, 4) the building of bridges to the charismatic movement and the Christian world.[49]

While I believed in, supported, and helped craft, all four purposes of Pentecostal engagement in the *Agora* agenda, my own heart of hearts was with the first purpose for the magazine: 'promoting a Pentecostal intellectual tradition'. That motivation hearkened back to my discussion with an Edmonton university student about the intellectual challenge to his Pentecostal faith. That motivation also caused me to weigh in on the biblical inerrancy debate that was fueled by Harold Lindsell's *The Battle for the Bible,* which was published in 1976 the year before the first issue of *Agora*.[50] Lindsell's crusade made biblical inerrancy the litmus test for Evangelical orthodoxy at a time when the evangelicalization of the Pentecostal

---

[49] Editors, 'The Agenda', *Agora* 1 (Summer 1977), pp. 4-5.
[50] Harold Lindsell, *The Battle for the Bible* (Grand Rapids, MI: Zondervan Publishing, 1976).

tradition was in full force.[51] As a consequence, I believed the creative scholarly work by a growing number of Pentecostal academics in developing an indigenous full-fledged Pentecostal theology could be co-opted by fundamentalists like Lindsell who desired to set limits on the way that the Bible could be interpreted in constructing a Pentecostal Theology.[52] The inerrancy battle finally hit some AG colleges.[53] A very powerful member of the SCC Board of Trustees had signed on to Lindsell's position and the Chicago Statement on Inerrancy. This Board Member walked the SCC President down the hallway through the Scott Academic Center that housed the Division of Religion Faculty and challenged the President to go into everyone of our offices and ask the professors if they held to the inerrancy of Scriptures in the original autographs and if they did not then the President should fire the individual on the spot. After that encounter, the President came to me as the Division Chair and told me that the Religion Faculty needed to address this issue. To his credit, President Wayne Kraiss never suggested that we should sign on to Lindsell's view in order to take the heat off him personally.

Fortunately Clark Pinnock had just published an article that outlined 'a truce proposal' on the inerrancy issue. He articulated an irenic proposal in which inerrancy should be affirmed as a useful term for focusing on the truthfulness of the Scriptures, on the one hand, and on the other hand, Pinnock showed how the term iner-

---

[51] Russell P. Spittler, 'The Cooley Inauguration: A Celebration of Sovereignty', *Agora* 5 (Summer 1981), pp. 13-14. In Spittler's estimation, the Cooley Inauguration as President of Gordon-Conwell Theological Seminary in November 1981 'completed the evangelicalization of the Assemblies of God' (p. 14).

[52] Walter Hollenweger, 'The Critical Tradition of Pentecostalism', *Journal of Pentecostal Theology* 1 (October 1992), pp. 7-17. In this article Hollenweger noted the development of a critical tradition of Pentecostal scholars who have been making original contributions to specialized analysis on Pentecostalism and ecumenism, social ethics, pacifism, feminism, and other issues based on their Pentecostal roots and identity. This developing critical tradition does not view Pentecostalism as a movement of 'evangelicals "plus" fire, dedication, missionary success, speaking in tongues and gifts of healing'. Hollenweger states flatly that this critical tradition does not view the Pentecostal movement as a 'sub-division of evangelicalism on fire' (pp. 8-9). From my point of view, Lindsell's 'battle' over his particular view of inerrancy involving original autographs was to set the litmus test for defining evangelicalism to which Pentecostals would need to comply if they wanted to be regarded as authentic evangelicals.

[53] I addressed this inerrancy issue about Evangel College in my editorial, 'Errant Ethics and Inerrant Church Politics: A Scenario of Irony', *Agora* 2 (Summer 1978), pp. 3-4.

rancy could be made compatible with the use of critical methods of interpreting the meaning of a biblical text in its original environment when the interpretive process identified the truth-claim in the text that is to be affirmed and believed.[54] Following Pinnock's lead, the SCC Religion Faculty placed inerrancy in a broader statement on biblical inspiration. The Academic Dean, the President, and the Board of Directors approved the statement below and it was incorporated into the SCC *Faculty Handbook*.

We hold Holy Scripture to be:

1. *Inspired*: By this we mean that Holy Scripture is inbreathed by the Holy Spirit, and that, though written in the words of humans in history, is nevertheless God's witness to Himself.

2. *Authoritative*: By this we mean that Holy Scripture, as the Word of God, is to be believed in all it affirms and obeyed in all it requires.

3. *Infallible*: By this we mean that Holy Scripture as the standard for faith and practice is completely trustworthy.

4. *Inerrant*: By this we mean that Holy Scripture speaks the truth and is therefore free from error, falsehood, and deceit in all it affirms and teaches.[55]

There were two important and related lessons I learned in the early years as a faculty member on the Lindsell issue about the exercise of my academic calling within AG higher education. First, I learned that it is very important in fulfilling the responsibilities of one's academic calling that, in the words of Eli Wiesel, truth stands up and speaks to power. When powerful interests intrude into the academic freedom of faculty to pursue the truth, the academic integrity of an institution of Christian higher education is placed in jeopardy. In approving the Statement on Biblical Inspiration, I was proud of my Faculty colleagues, the President and the Administration, and the Board of Trustees, in recognizing with St. Paul that

---

[54] Clark H. Pinnock, 'Inspiration and Authority: A Truce Proposal', *The Other Side* 12 (May-June 1976), pp. 61-65.

[55] The SCC *Faculty Handbook* was amended to include the 'Statement of Inspiration' in 1983. The statement has been in every iteration of the handbook through to the Vanguard University *Faculty Handbook* that was approved by the Board of Trustees on October 10, 2008 (Article 619:001, p. 29).

you can say nothing against the truth that will prevail, because 'we cannot do anything against the truth, but only for the truth' (2 Cor. 13.8). Second, I learned the importance of being irenic as a way to receive God's benediction of blessing: 'Blessed are the peacemakers for they shall be called children of God' (Mt. 5.9). We found a way to affirm both inerrancy and the critical methods of biblical interpretation.

Working on my Three-fold Academic Agenda for Constructing a Pentecostal Social Ethic

My scholarly work in teaching and publishing reflected three major prongs of academic interest. The first area was to engage in the constructive theological task of developing a Pentecostal social ethic informed by the Word and the Spirit. The second area, close to the first, was to develop a holistic approach to Pentecostal church mission that integrated evangelism and social concern. The third area focused on identifying the theological and ethical arguments in support of Pentecostal pacifism during World War I and the factors that led to the subsequent rapid demise of Pentecostal pacifism during the Vietnam War.

The Theological Task of Constructing a Pentecostal Social Ethic Informed by the Word and the Spirit

Constructing a Pentecostal social ethic involved two basic tasks. One task was to establish a basic structure of ethical thinking within a theological framework that made sense philosophically. The other task was to identify the theological and ethical content from Scripture that would provide a conceptual understanding of the norms and virtues that would empower the people of God to cultivate character, guide conduct, show compassion for the needy, pursue social justice, and change the plight of the underprivileged and marginalized. In laying out the threefold structure for ethical thinking within a coherent Pentecostal social ethic I identified: 1) the metaethics of theological definism; 2) the normative ethics of symbolic inducement; and 3) the moral life of ambiguity and congruity.[56]

---

[56] 'Soundings on the Moral Significance of Glossolalia' (13th Annual Meeting of the Society for Pentecostal Studies, Cleveland, TN, November 4, 1983). When

Theological definism adopts a basic structure of ethical thinking that places ethical reflection in a theological context. God and the good are inextricably linked together at the definitional level in both character and conduct. Theological definism is theocentric in its approach to ethics and therefore grounds ethical reflection in the principle of the *imitatio Dei – the imitation of God*. For example, the theological indicative that states that God is just can be translated into the moral imperative that God's people ought to be just. Here is the basic ethical question that encapsulates this framework of theological thinking: 'What character and conduct is in keeping with who we are as a people of God?'[57]

Given my undergraduate major in Biblical Studies and the 'Word and Spirit' moniker that marked the theological identity of Pentecostals as a people of the Word and a people of the Spirit, I decided to work within the canons of biblical theology in constructing a Pentecostal social ethic. Then, I could enrich my exegetical and hermeneutical work with relevant points from the broader theological world. I began this sojourn into the moral content of Scripture by exploring the Old Testament theme of God's justice to nurture social concern in the Pentecostal community.[58]

Then, I moved from the Old Testament into the New Testament in charting the *imitatio Dei* and the theological indicative-moral imperative structure of Jewish ethical thinking that influenced the literature of the New Testament. I developed a template of the var-

---

I was offered an opportunity to write a chapter in honor of Russ Spittler for his *Festschrift*, I took my original piece I did for SPS in 1983 after graduating with my PhD that would not have happened without Russ's advice and encouragement, and I updated and revised it and published it in his well-deserved honor. In this piece, I emphasized the significance of Spirit baptism and glossolalia for a Christian ethic that critiques the ideology of the status quo and opens up the moral imagination of a world yet to come. See 'The Structure of a Christian Ethic Informed by Pentecostal Experience: Soundings in the Moral Significance of Glossolalia', in Wonsuk Ma and Robert P. Menzies (eds.), *Spirit and Spirituality: Essays in Honor of Russell P. Spittler* (London: T & T Clark International, 2004), pp. 108-40.

[57] Bruce C. Birch and Larry L. Rasmussen, *Bible and Ethics in the Christian Life* (Minneapolis, MN: Augsburg Press, rev. and expanded edn, 1989), p. 19.

[58] The five features in Old Testament ethical thinking that addressed social justice in this article were its theocentric foundation, its concept of the *imago Dei*, its portrayal of the covenant people, its prophetic tradition of social criticism, and its Jubilee teachings. See 'Pentecostal Social Concern and the Biblical Mandate of Social Justice', *Pneuma: The Journal of the Society for Pentecostal Studies* 9 (Fall 1987), pp. 129-53.

ious 'traditions' of New Testament ethics. The template had these four social ethical paradigms that connected Theology and Ethics: 1) the Jesus tradition: a theology of the kingdom of God and an ethics of human response to God's reign;[59] 2) the Pauline tradition: a theology of the incarnation, crucifixion, and resurrection of Jesus Christ and an ethics of character formation 'in Christ'; 3) the Petrine and Johannine traditions: a theology of the historical life of Jesus and an ethics of imitating the pattern of Jesus' behavior in what he said and did; and, 4) the Later Apostolic Tradition: a theology of sound doctrine and an ethics of godly living. Within these paradigms of theological ethics, I also was able to identify love, justice, and respect of persons as normative principles for guiding conduct and normative virtues for cultivating character. Within these paradigms of theological ethics, I was also able to identify how these principles and virtues of love, justice, and respect of persons functioned with contextual sensitivity around the situational variables of act, agent, agency, purpose, and scene in specific moral cases.[60]

The Theological Task of Developing a Holistic Approach to Pentecostal Church Mission and Ministry

The work that I did toward developing a Pentecostal social ethic was closely connected to my constructive work of developing a holistic approach to Pentecostal church mission and ministry. The social ethic focused on moral theology; the holistic approach focused on ecclesiology. My SPS Presidential Address in 1991 chronicled by name the programs of social concern in the churches of three Pentecostal denominations – the Church of God in Christ, the Church of God (Cleveland, TN), and the Assemblies of God – to demonstrate the proliferation of social ministry at home and abroad.[61] Also

---

[59] I delivered the Staley Lectureship on the 'Tradition of Jesus and Everyday Moral Life' in three sessions at Southeastern University, Lakeland FL, October 3-4, 1991, and at Northwest College, Kirkland, WA, March 3-5, 1993.

[60] This template of New Testament social ethics is the paradigm I progressively developed and revised in teaching my graduate course on 'The Church and Contemporary Moral Issues' at SCC/Vanguard on campus and in our Costa Rica Study Center in San José, as well as in my course on 'The Bible and Social Ethics' that I taught at Fuller Theological Seminary as an Adjunct and as a Visiting Professor from 1980 through 1995.

[61] The paper concluded by suggesting a reformulation of Pentecostal Eschatology along the lines proposed by Miroslav Volf in his formulation of the mate-

in 1991, I published a chapter, 'Evangelism, Social Concern, and the Kingdom of God' in *Called and Empowered: Global Mission in Pentecostal Perspective* that established the Pentecost-Kingdom paradigm from Luke-Acts to formulate a holistic approach to church mission and ministry. This chapter was designed as an integrated approach to Pentecostal ecclesiology under three rubrics: the church's kerygmatic ministry: proclaiming the kingdom in spoken word; the church's koinoniac ministry: picturing the kingdom in a social witness; and the church's diakonic ministry: manifesting the kingdom in moral deeds.[62]

When I became the North American editor for *Transformation: An International Evangelical Dialogue on Mission and Ethics*, I produced two special theme issues as a Guest Editor to advance a holistic Pentecostal ecclesiology: 'Church Mission and Social Concern: The Changing Global Face of Classical Pentecostalism' (1994),[63] and 'A Pentecostal Approach to Evangelization and Social Concern' (1999).[64] I loved playing the role of an ambassador and spreading the good news about Pentecostal holistic church mission and ministry in every venue wherever I found an opportunity from San José,

---

riality of salvation. This eschatological part of my paper was later published as a stand alone article, 'Christian Social Concern in Pentecostal Perspective: Reformulating Pentecostal Eschatology', Journal *of Pentecostal Theology* 2 (April 1993), pp. 53-66.

[62] 'Evangelism, Social Concern, and the Kingdom of God' in Murray W. Dempster, Byron D. Klaus and Douglas Petersen (eds.), *Called and Empowered: Global Mission in Pentecostal Perspective* (Peabody, MA: Hendrickson Publishers, 1991), pp. 22-43. I am indebted to Roger Stronstad, *The Charismatic Theology of St. Luke* (Peabody, MA: Hendrickson Publishers, 1984), for his study that argued that Luke's Gospel and Luke's Acts are two volumes in one single treatise linked by 'the transfer of the Spirit' from Jesus at his baptism to the disciples at Pentecost. His exegetical work triggered my development of the Pentecost–Kingdom paradigm as the way to develop a Pentecostal social ethic and a wholistic approach to church mission and ministry.

[63] Guest Editor, A Special Theme Issue on 'Church Mission and Social Concern: The Changing Global Face of Classical Pentecostalism', *Transformation: An International Evangelical Dialogue on Mission and Ethics* 11 (January/March 1994), pp. 1-33.

[64] Guest Editor, A Special Theme Issue on 'A Pentecostal Approach to Evangelization and Social Concern', *Transformation: An International Evangelical Dialogue on Mission and Ethics* 16 (April/June 1999), pp. 41-73. In the same year, Byron D. Klaus, Douglas Petersen and I edited *The Globalization of Pentecostalism: A Religion Made to Travel* (Oxford, England, UK and Irvine, CA, USA: Regnum Books International, 1999).

Costa Rica,[65] to Pasadena, California,[66] to Chicago, Illinois,[67] to Los Angeles,[68] and to my alma mater.[69]

What I thought would be my crowning work in promoting a holistic approach to church mission and ministry in the Assemblies of God came about in a four-day conference in May 1998 in Brussels, Belgium. I was commissioned, along with Doug Petersen and Peter Kuzmič, by the Strategic Planning Commission of the Division of Foreign Missions (DFM) of the AG to prepare presentations on specific themes for the consultation. My presentation, in the form of a paper distributed to all the participants, was designed to provide a theological and biblical rationale – consistent with the Pentecostal tradition – for the development of an integrated statement on evangelism and social concern. The purpose of the paper was to stimulate group discussion at the conference among AG national and missionary leaders from each geographical region in the globe, as well as local practioners involved in ministries of compassion, theologians, executive leadership, and key lay people in developing an integrated statement on evangelism and social concern which could serve missionaries internationally, especially those ministering in the two-thirds world, as the majority world was known then. After many iterations of give and take on proposed drafts in group breakout sessions, there was agreement by the participants on what was called, the 'Brussels Statement on Evangelization and Social Concern'.[70]

---

65 Address, 'The Church and Human Liberation' at the Spanish Language Institute in San José, Costa Rica, June 4, 1985.

66 Workshop, 'Social Concern in Pentecostal Perspective: Toward a Wholistic View of Church Mission', at RENOVARE, A National Conference on Personal Spiritual Renewal, Pasadena, CA, October 25, 1991.

67 Seminar Presentation, 'Pentecostalism, Evangelism, and Social Concern', Chicago Declaration II, a Conference sponsored by Evangelicals for Social Action, Chicago, IL, November 19-21, 1993.

68 Workshop, 'Christian Social Concern in 19th-century Holiness and Evangelical Traditions and in Early 20th-century Pentecostalism' at the Christians Supporting Community Organizing Workshop (CSCO), Clareton Renewal Center, Los Angeles, CA, October 30, 1998.

69 Graduate Colloquium, 'The Pentecostal Movement and the Academic Field of Social Ethics', The School of Religion at the University of Southern California, Los Angeles, CA, April 6, 1994.

70 'Brussels Statement on Evangelization and Social Concern', produced by the Brussels Consultation of the Division of Foreign Missions of the Assemblies of God, *Transformation: An International Evangelical Dialogue on Mission and Ethics* 16

I was so elated as Coralie and I flew out of Brussels. The constructive work that I had done in developing a Pentecostal social ethic and a holistic approach to Pentecostal mission and ministry in integrating evangelism and social concern was now assisting the church in understanding the biblical, theological, and ethical rationale for holistic mission and ministry. In Brussels my calling to academic work was assisting the Pentecostal church in developing a holistic approach to mission and ministry on a global scale. My bubble soon burst when I learned that the statement that was produced by the Brussels Consultation of the Division of Foreign Missions (DFM) of the Assemblies of God was stillborn. The Executive Director of DFM noted that I had cited the works of liberation theologians in my paper and therefore he would not support the distribution of the Brussels Statement. At that point my arms were really getting weary in swimming upstream. The old school status quo coupled with an anti-intellectual sectarianism seemed to be a trump card over biblical theology, holistic mission and ministry, and missiological progress.

The Theological Task of Narrating the Story of Pentecostal Pacifism

After reading a copy of Jay Beaman's MDiv thesis on Pentecostal Pacifism that he sent to me, my interest in pacifism was piqued.[71] Shortly thereafter, I received an invitation to present the Seventh Annual Pentecostal Lectureship Series in October 1988 at Regent College in Vancouver, Canada on the theme of 'Pentecostal Perspectives on Social Ethics'. My first lecture was titled, 'A Pentecostal Perspective from the Past: Reassessing the Moral Rhetoric of Early American Pentecostal Pacifism',[72] and my second lecture was titled, 'A Pentecostal Perspective for the Future: Identifying the

---

(April/June 1999), pp. 41-43. My paper is in the same issue, 'Social Concern in the Context of Jesus' Kingdom, Mission, and Ministry', pp. 43-53.

[71] Jay Beaman's thesis was published as *Pentecostal Pacifism: The Origin, Development, and Rejection of Pacific Belief among the Pentecostals* by the Center for Brethren and Mennonite Studies in 1989. The volume has recently been updated as part of the Pentecostals, Peacemaking, and Social Justice Series and published by Wipf & Stock in 2009.

[72] This lecture was subsequently published in *Crux*, see footnote 82.

Moral Contours of the Story of Pentecost'.[73] In preparing my lecture on Pentecostal Pacifism, I wanted to track down the full articles from which Jay Beaman provided a variety of quotes. In Jay's source material, I noted at times almost a Marxist flavor and a class struggle motif, and at other times a humanitarian universal theme or a primitivist feel from various quotes from different authors.[74] So I used my paradigm of rhetorical logic from my dissertation work to examine the moral argumentation of Pentecostals who advocated the connection between certain theological assertions and the moral conduct of pacifism.

Based on the writings of Arthur S. Booth-Clibborn, his son Samuel H. Booth-Clibborn, Frank Bartleman, Stanley Frodsham, and Charles Parham I constructed three major arguments for pacifism from the popular literature: 1) pacifism and the twentieth-century 'restoration' of the New Testament apostolic church; 2) pacifism and the moral critique of the existing social and political order; 3) pacifism and the moral affirmation of the universal scope of the value of human life. I concluded my lecture with the thesis that the demise of Pentecostal pacifism was also the demise of the conception of the Pentecostal church as a pilgrim people, a prophetic community, and a transnational expression of the new humanity. Without a prophetic spirit and an eschatological mentality represented by the pacifists, the Pentecostal church would soon limit its mission to preaching the good news and nurturing its own spiritual life and, as a consequence, devolve into a self-absorbed verbal community with an underdeveloped social conscience.[75]

The publication of my lecture in *Crux* seemed to have a snow ball effect. Jean-Daniel Plüss, representing the European Pentecostal Theological Association, invited me to present my work on Pentecostal pacifism at the Sixth Conference on Pentecostal and Char-

---

[73] This lecture was subsequently published under the title, 'The Church's Moral Witness: A Study of Glossolalia in Luke's Theology of Acts', *Paraclete* 23 (Winter 1989), pp. 1-7.

[74] I am indebted to Jay Beaman and his groundbreaking thesis and subsequent book on Pentecostal pacifism in leading me to primary sources for this lecture. I am also grateful to Cecil M. Robeck who gave me access to use his own incredible personal library of early Pentecostal magazines and documents.

[75] 'Reassessing the Moral Rhetoric of Early American Pentecostal Pacifism', *Crux: A Quarterly Journal of Christian Thought and Opinion* 26 (March 1990), pp. 23-36.

ismatic Research in Europe in Kappel, Switzerland.[76] Richard Hughes from Pepperdine University invited me to share my work on Pentecostal pacifism in a conference hosted by Goshen College on 'Pacifist Traditions in American Churches (other than historic Peace Churches)'.[77] Jeffrey Gros, FSC, who was associate director of the Secretariat for Ecumenical and Interreligious Affairs, National Conference of Catholic Bishops asked me if I would present my research on Pentecostal Pacifism at a consultation on 'The Fragmentation of the Church and its Unity in Peacemaking', sponsored by the Faith and Order Working Group of the National Council of Churches/USA and by the Joan B. Kroc Institute for International Peace Studies at Notre Dame to be held at the University of Notre Dame in June 1995.[78] Each of these engagements identified my three arguments but utilized them to make a concluding point germane to the theme of the conference.

At the Notre Dame ecumenical consultation – representing ten major faith traditions – John Howard Yoder, who was a Fellow in the Joan B. Kroc Institute for International Peace Studies and a faculty member at the University of Notre Dame, gave some opening remarks in which he framed our ecumenical discussion through his own Mennonite-oriented question. The challenging question of our consultation, according to Yoder, was to dialogue on this main inquiry: Could a Christian church fragmented into ten major faith traditions find its unity in peacemaking? Shortly after the consultation I received a letter from John Howard Yoder which was addressed to Thomas Olbricht of Pepperdine University and to me, in which he thanked us for broadening out the discussion from the viewpoint of the restorationist and free church traditions. Yoder started his letter, 'I do not know how it happened that the Faith and Order planners got both of you, precisely the right people, to round

---

[76] '"Crossing Borders": Arguments Used by Early American Pentecostals in Support of the Global Character of Pacifism', *EPTA Bulletin: Journal of the European Pentecostal Theological Association* 10.2 (1991), pp. 63-88.

[77] 'Pacifism in Pentecostalism: The Case of the Assemblies of God', in Theron F. Schlabach and Richard T. Hughes (eds.), *Proclaim Peace: Voices of Christian Pacifism from Unexpected Sources,* (Champaign, IL: University of Illinois Press, 1997), pp. 31-57.

[78] 'Pacifism in Pentecostalism: The Case of the Assemblies of God', in Jeffrey Gros and John D. Rempel (eds.), *The Fragmentation of the Church and its Unity in Peacemaking* (Grand Rapids, MI: Eerdmans, 2001), pp. 137-65 (reprinted with permission from the University of Illinois Press).

out the demonstration of the fact that, and the ways in which, renewal phenomena in frontier America have recurrently been both
pacifist and ecumenical. This is a story that Faith and Order needed
and will always need to hear'. He concluded with this paragraph:
'Thank you for coming to Notre Dame. It was a considerable
achievement to win Faith and Order recognition, a few years ago
for the traditional three "peace churches", but it was your contribution that broke new ground this time.' It was signed, 'Fraternally
yours, John H. Yoder'.[79]

Reading those words: 'it was your contribution that broke new
ground this time', truly gave me an emotional rush, and more significantly a sense of fulfilling my academic calling. My mind went back
to the discussion with Dr John Orr when he asked me why I was
not representing my Pentecostal tradition in class discussion. I sat at
the table of discussion at Notre Dame with different traditions
from my own and represented my Pentecostal tradition. I had my
20 minutes at the mike and I had a story to tell. I thought of that
phrase in the benediction of Heb. 13.20-21: 'May the God of peace
… work in us what is pleasing to him'. I felt like the scholarly work
I had done – as a result of hours of research and writing in multiple
iterations – was really 'pleasing to God' in that conference room at
Notre Dame. It was a joyful moment for me. I was not swimming
upstream but laying down beside still waters.

The great irony was that my own denominational executive leadership of world missions declined adopting the Brussels Statement
on Evangelization and Social Concern that was produced by the
Brussels Consultation of the Division of Foreign Missions of the
Assemblies of God and thereby marginalized my academic work
while the Faith and Order NCC Consultation embraced my academic work as significant to the broadening out of the ecumenical
discussion of the church's mission in peacemaking. Go figure!

My Changing Roles in the Academy

From 1969 to 1995 I served as a faculty member at Southern California College. From 1995 to 2000, I was the Chief Academic Officer, first as the VP for Academic Affairs and later as Provost.

---

[79] Letter dated June 27, 1995, and mailed July 7, 1995.

From 2000 to 2008, I served as President of Vanguard University, and from 2008 to 2009 I was appointed Chancellor. In my Faculty service, my academic calling focused on providing solid academic classroom teaching in philosophy, theology, and ethics and producing creative scholarly work in my academic field. When I became the VPAA and Provost my academic calling expanded to exercising leadership for the entire academic house in strengthening the academic quality of programs, expanding new programs, promoting student learning and its assessment, and investing in the professional development of the Faculty. I also continued to serve as the Editor of *Pneuma: The Journal of the Society for Pentecostal Studies* to keep abreast with the academic developments in Pentecostal studies by reading and editing the research of other scholars.

Upon my appointment as President my academic calling expanded again to provide leadership for the university as a whole in integrating the major silos of the university – academics, advancement, business and finance, enrollment management, and student life – into a unified effort to fulfill our institutional mission 'to pursue knowledge, cultivate character, deepen faith, and equip each student for a life of leadership and service'. As an academic President I had the good fortune from 2000-2008 to lead the university to new levels of student enrollment,[80] financial contributions,[81] facility expansion,[82] and recognition as a 'Top Five Best Baccalaureate College in the West' by *U.S. News and World Report*.[83] However, my personal sense of good fortune came to a grinding halt as the 2007-2008 academic year progressed. Financial challenges reemerged and

---

[80] The Annual Report with Key Performance Indicators on student growth was published annually in the Fall issue of Vanguard from 2000-2001 through 2007-2008. Student enrollment increased in diversity and numbers from 1,440 students in Fall 1999 to an all-time high of 2,171 students in Fall 2007, about a 66% increase in overall enrollment of students.

[81] The Annual Report with Key Performance Indicators on total giving and a list of Vanguard Donors was published annually in the Fall issue of Vanguard from 2000-2001 through 2007-2008. The composite growth in total giving to the university over eight years from FY 2000-2001 through FY 2007-2008 reached $30,322,189.00 or an average of $3,790,294.00 per year over the eight year span.

[82] 'Heath Academic Center Opened for Fall Semester', *Vanguard* 5 (Fall 2004), pp. 22-23. The new 42,000 sq. ft. Heath Academic Center for Religion and Business featured 36 faculty offices, 10 classrooms, and two tiered lecture halls that accommodated 600 students per class hour.

[83] 'Vanguard makes high rank second consecutive year', *Daily Pilot*, August 22, 2008.

personnel changes in three vice presidential positions at the same time combined to erode my leadership by a new administrative 're-gime' who bonded with each other in alienation from me. The Chairman of the Board and I worked out an agreement that I would be appointed to the position of Chancellor and resign as President which occurred in the Board of Trustees meeting of October 10, 2008.

In the fall 2008 issue of *Vanguard* magazine, Ray Rachels, the Board Chairman, made this announcement to the constituency: 'Under Dr. Dempster's leadership, Vanguard made notable advances in the areas of community awareness and financial support for the school ... Dr. Dempster's leadership as President will be missed, but in his role as university chancellor, he will add significant momentum to the University's efforts to continue as a university of excellence'.[84] My role as Chancellor was short-lived. The new President invited me to her office on June 15, 2009. To my surprise when I entered through the door I saw the President, the new Board Chair, and the HR Director. It took me two seconds to realize I was about to be ambushed! However, what was said to me was a second surprise: the position of Chancellor itself was being terminated as of this meeting. The offer of a severance package was on a take it or leave it basis. I could resign and receive a severance package as proposed, or not resign and receive nothing. One way or another, I was gone. There would be no farewell from the community and no expression of thanks for my forty years of service. Once again, words from my mother came as solace and wisdom: 'Remember Jesus, they cried Hosanna one week and crucified him the next'. Despite the way that my time at Vanguard ended, these were 40 fulfilling years of academic service through teaching, scholarship, and institution building in which I could give back to the college and university that provided me with a superb liberal arts education and a sturdy baccalaureate degree in biblical studies that literally transformed my life and expanded my sense of calling from the local church to the Christian academy.

---

[84] Vanguard 9 (Fall 2008), p. 16.

Starting Over and Finishing Soon: Reflections on Legacy

At the time that I resigned as President, Dr Bob Houlihan, Dean of the College of Christian Ministries and Religion, called me and expressed an interest in exploring with me about coming to Southeastern University. Because I was Chancellor the timing was not right. After my June 15th meeting, however, I realized that the timing was more than right. I called Dean Houlihan and he set up an interview with Faculty members and the VPAA at Southeastern at the same time my son, Marlon, was interviewing there for a Faculty position in English as one of three final candidates. Marlon was offered and accepted the position, and his wife, Shannon, was offered a position at an Elementary School in Lakeland, and they moved with their two daughters to begin schools for the Fall semester 2009. My future was a bit more up in the air. Coralie and I were not sure how long it would take to sell our home. Until that hurdle was overcome, we could not confirm a contract with a start date. Incredibly, our home sold in three days and we began to prepare for the move to the Sunshine State to be reunited with our family and to start my position as Distinguished Professor of Social Ethics at Southeastern.

We arrived in Lakeland on December 9, 2009, and in January 2010 I started my three year Faculty contract. I returned to my first love of classroom teaching in both undergraduate and graduate programs, and to assist the Dean and Religion Faculty in the development of an MA Program in Theological Studies, a Center for the Study of Global Pentecostalism, and a Center for Hispanic Leadership. My colleagues in Religion are superb scholars, consummate professionals, and supportive and amiable colleagues of good humor. Working with Dean Houlihan is a joy. I feel like I have a new home. At the same time I hear the sound of the time clock clicking which triggers my thoughts about legacy these days.

One of my favorite hymns in the Psalter is Psalm 84, a psalm of Zion in which God's people envision their journey back from their exile to reach the holy city. Even though in exile, these sojourners have kept the highway back to the holy city alive 'in their hearts'. They never gave up hope that they would journey back to appear in Zion 'before God'. However, they must pass through the parched Valley of Baca on their way back to Jerusalem. Their heart was a highway to Zion but their feet needed to go through the parched Valley of Baca in getting to the holy city. God pronounced his benediction of blessing on those people who go on before and stop in the Baca valley to dig a well that will be filled by the autumn rains so that those who come after them will find water to sustain them to complete their journey back to Zion. The 'well diggers' left a legacy of life-sustaining water for those who came after them so that they too could 'pass through' the Valley of Baca and also arrive at the eternal city of God.

In my own journey of 'digging academic wells' on my way back home to the heavenly eternal city, I thought of these legacies created by the roles I played in the Christian academy. I thought of the institution-building in creating a new infrastructure that would facilitate the transition from a liberal arts college to a comprehensive university in order for students to 'pass through' their educational experience with a sense of academic quality.[85] I thought of three academic centers that will institutionalize for years to come the core values of the school and provide lectures, seminars, and conferences to enrich the campus community and the broader community as well.[86] I thought of a foundation that continues to raise friends and resources for the university.[87] I thought of students from all different majors who 'passed through' my General Ed course in Intro to Philosophy, Christian Ethics, or Christianity and Society and learned to integrate the life of the mind with the life of faith, and then went out to their chosen vocation to witness to their faith in Jesus Christ and contribute to society. I thought of students who felt called to the ministry whether at Vanguard, Fuller, AGTS, or SEU and 'passed through' one of my undergraduate or graduate courses in order to pastor local churches, lead para-church organi-

---

[85] Southern California College registered with the Office of the Secretary of State on July 1, 1999 as Vanguard University of Southern California.

[86] The Center for Women Studies (now named the Global Center for Women and Justice); the Jesse Miranda Center for Hispanic Leadership, and the Lewis Wilson Institute for Pentecostal Studies.

[87] 'Vanguard University Foundation Board', *Vanguard* 5 (Fall 2004), p. 24. Thirty-three influential community and business leaders, along with the University's President, VP of Advancement, VP of Business and Finance, and Associate VP of Advancement, made up the Board of Directors of the Vanguard University Foundation as a separate 501(C) 3.

zations, administrate denominational offices, or become missionaries around the world.

There is one more list of students from SCC/Vanguard that bring to me a great sense of joy and fulfillment as I continue my own academic journey at SEU. These are students who 'passed through' one or more of my courses in theological education and went on to further doctoral education in order to fulfill a call to the Christian academy. I think of Jerry Camery-Hoggatt who took four courses with me as a Biblical Studies major. He went on and received his PhD in New Testament from Boston University. Later after he returned to SCC in 1983, I team taught a course with Jerry. He had a handle on all the recent hermeneutical methods and could translate complex scholarly ideas into the world of college students with remarkable communication skills. As I sat in class and took notes with the students, I realized that my former student had outgrown his professor. Likewise, I think of Frank Macchia who took a course with me on Twentieth Century Theologians and we covered Barth, Bultmann, Bonhoeffer, the Niebuhrs, Tillich, Henry, Pannenberg, and Cobb. He went on and received his DTheol in Systematic Theology from the University of Basel. After teaching at SEU he returned to SCC in 1999 and began an incredible publication record with his two last books breaking new ground in pneumatology and ecclesiology[88] and Christology and soteriology.[89] When I read his books I realized that the student had far outgrown his professor. I was only a footnote of my former self!

If space allowed I could comment on all my former students at SCC who had a call to the Christian academy and went on to complete doctoral work. They have multiplied themselves through the education they have provided students in a variety of colleges, universities and seminaries: Sheri Benvenuti, Isaac Canales, David Cleveland, Arthur Droge, Chip Espinoza, Wayde Goodall, Daren Guerra, Kent Ingle, Peter Kuzmič, David Marley, Mark McLean, Cecile Miller, Jesse Miranda, Timothy Moyers, Matt Nelson, Alan Padgett, Sally Bruyneel Padgett, Joseph Saggio, Judd Shaver, Boyd Talbert, Jerry Ternes, and Al Tizon. Even though I played only a

---

[88] Frank D. Macchia, *Baptized in the Spirit: A Global Pentecostal Theology* (Grand Rapids, MI: Zondervan, 2006).

[89] Frank D. Macchia, *Justified in the Spirit: Creation, Redemption, and the Triune God* (Grand Rapids, MI: Eerdmans, 2010).

very minor role in shaping these former students educationally, these colleagues are my joy and I find incredible fulfillment in knowing that they are continuing a scholarly tradition within Christian higher education, and will encourage another generation of their students to respond to God's calling to the Christian academy.

When I started as a Faculty member at SCC, Pentecostal accredited liberal arts colleges were novel and developing institutions. There was a palpable underlying tension in the evolution from single purpose Bible colleges to Christian liberal arts colleges. Bible Colleges were insular institutions that focused on indoctrination for the purpose of maintaining status quo fidelity to Pentecostal truths and ministry. Christian liberal arts colleges focused on education within an open texture that investigated truth claims within all academic disciplines in order to integrate Christian faith and learning. In this tension, I had a feeling at times of 'swimming upstream' against status quo thinking of maintaining things the way they are. Yet when I think of my professors who gave me a transformative education – Gordon Fee, Albert Hoy, John B. Scott, Russell P. Spittler, and Lewis Wilson – and I think of my own Religion Faculty colleagues – Don Baldwin, David Clark, Gayle Erwin, Byron Klaus, Nancy Heidebrecht, Roger Heuser, Doug Petersen, Wally Weber, William C. Williams, and Ronald Wright – who educated in partnership with me the students listed above, then I think we can see another dimension of legacy. This legacy moves beyond the personal by banding together as colleagues over the years to transform the university itself into an institution of academic excellence and spiritual vitality.

Then, too, we must not forget that all of us 'academic well-diggers' in Christian higher education are sojourners 'passing through this Valley of Baca' heading home to the heavenly eternal city where all legacies will end at the feet of our Savior in a doxology of praise to the glory of the Father, Son, and Holy Spirit.

3

Discovering Providence: Religious Education, Pentecostalism, and Empirical Theology

William K. Kay[*]

Early Life and Education

My earliest significant memory is of an argument with my brother, Peter. It went something like this, 'My toy is better than yours'.

'No it isn't. Mine is ten times better than yours'.

'No it isn't. Mine is twenty times better than yours'. And so on until,

'Mine is a million times better than yours'.

'Mine is million, million times better than yours'.

'No' and now struggling at the limits, 'mine is a trillion, zillion, squillion times better than yours'.

And finally, we reached an impasse.

Going to school one day when I was four or five years old, I asked my father what the highest number was. I was going to beat my brother at this game.

He answered, 'The highest number is infinity'.

I replied, 'What about infinity and one or double infinity?'

---

[*] William K. Kay (PhD, Reading University; PhD, Nottingham University; DD, Nottingham University) is Professor of Theology at Glyndŵr University in Wrexham, Wales.

He replied, 'You cannot do that. Infinity cannot be added to … it is already as big as it can be'.

By this means an idea of the infinite was put into my head, an idea that was mathematically based, and the idea of a different kind of number. And I knew it was different because my dad told me that it was written like an eight on its side.

I was born in 1945 of an English agnostic doctor and a Russian mother. They had married in the Russian Orthodox Church, a small concession by my father because he thought ritual a harmless activity. His medical studies had led him to psychiatry and to research on Alzheimer's disease and eventually to an entirely materialistic view of human beings. My mother, conversely, did believe and she equipped me with a godmother from the émigré Russian community in England. More importantly, as her marriage to my father began to break up, she insisted that each night we pray and she would kneel down with me by my bed and lead me in an impromptu prayer that I had to follow.

When I was about seven years old, one summer evening I was too hot to sleep and so, against all instructions, got out of bed and began to look at the books stored in my bedroom. Among these were heavy medical textbooks my father had bought and one of them was on forensic medicine. It contained black and white photographs of corpses including, I remember, the bloated body of a man who had drowned and a close-up picture of a man who had committed suicide by shooting himself through the roof of his mouth. From that day onward I feared death.

My great grandfather had made a lot of money and so there were still sufficient resources in the family for my parents to pay for my education. My brother and I were packed off to a boarding school when I was seven and he was even younger. Before we went my mother gave me a golden crucifix to wear. The school itself was heavily biased towards languages so that, by the age of ten, we were expected to work in Latin, French, and Greek. The method of teaching was Victorian. We could be caned for poor performances or for minor infringements of rules and none of this was helped by the unpleasant discovery that my Latin master had, twenty-five years before, taught my father exactly the same lessons and kept all his marks. My marks were worse than my father's. Parsing words or trying to write Latin poetry led me on more than one occasion to ask, 'What is all this for?' and behind the frustration of a schoolboy lay the deeper question of 'What is life all about?'.

The school was Anglican and so we attended chapel each day and twice on Sundays and the most interesting parts of the services were from the Bible. A senior member of staff would walk solemnly to the lectern and announce the lesson and then read the prescribed portion.

My parents finally divorced when I was nine years old. This was a catastrophic event. We had to move to a smaller house, my mother went through three months of depression when she hardly got out of bed, our financial circumstances deteriorated, my father disappeared over the horizon and my school work plummeted. The institutional routine of school became one unchanging part of a chaotic life.

During the holidays we began attending the Orthodox church in Oxford and here we found the services incomprehensible: they were conducted in Old Church Slavonic and to make matters worse, according to Russian custom, the small church was without any seats whatever. We would stand for one or two hours while the services wound their way to a conclusion. We learnt to kiss the icons and to light a candle on coming in at the beginning. The only bit of the service in English was the sermon and this tended to be short and mystical and only occasionally biblical. There was, however, one aspect of Orthodoxy that was embarrassingly meaningful. Before taking communion, we had to go to confession and this meant kneeling down privately on Saturday afternoon in front of the priest and confessing sin. Then on Sunday we went fasting to communion and took bread and wine from the same priest.

The result of this bi-religious upbringing was to give me a respect for the authority of the Bible and a sense that I was a sinner in the presence of a mysterious God. There were times, though, when religion seemed absurd. Some of the aged Russians would kneel at unpredictable moments in the service and we could not work out whether this was because they were holier than everyone else or wished to appear so. My brother and I enjoyed a cynical laugh at their expense and yet, when my mother invited the priest home for Sunday lunch, we found him fun and worth talking to.

This was especially so when Archbishop Anthony Bloom was our guest.[90]

At the age of about 12, I was sent off to Eton College. Here at first the same pattern continued: heavy concentration on languages, corporal punishment, daily chapel services and, for the first time, bullying. We took tests more or less every week and exams at the end of the year. I won a prize for my work but was too ashamed to claim it for fear of being called a 'swat'. A period of liberation came when we embarked on science. Suddenly what we learnt made sense. I had already been given the first in the C.S. Lewis science fiction trilogy, *Out of the Silent Planet*, and loved it. When we started physics I was thrilled to escape from the drudgery of badly taught dead languages. Like many others I noticed the symmetry between the electrons that orbited the nucleus of an atom and the planets that orbited the sun. When I was told that light travelled at 186,000 miles per second and that nothing could ever travel faster than this or that absolute zero was, according the kinetic theory of temperature, minus 273 degrees, I felt that the universe was starting to make sense. There were unbreakable constants in the physical world that – though I did not articulate it this way at the time – contrasted with my inner sense of turmoil and fear.

These feelings came to a head when I was around 16. I spoke to my mother about the meaninglessness of life, especially when these feelings were exacerbated by French existentialism. We read Albert Camus and noted that suicide was seen as a legitimate act. My mother, in alarm, invited Archbishop Anthony to our home for lunch and then left me to talk with him alone. I told him that I was one person in a world population of three billion (which was about right at that time) on a little planet 93 million miles from sun and whirling about an endless universe. How could my life matter or have any significance? Perhaps it was best to 'live fast and die young'. He listened gravely and then took me by surprise by answering in a completely unscientific way. 'Your life is significant if someone loves you', he said. Moreover, he pointed out that each moment of each life can be lived with thanksgiving. 'It is like a cup filled with blessings and you must simply turn the cup upside down

---

[90] http://en.wikipedia.org/wiki/Anthony_of_Sourozh

to pour the blessings out'. He prayed for me and I was comforted for a while.

Sporting competition was built into school and consumed much of our free time. I chose science subjects and dropped the linguistic grind as soon as possible but I continued to read widely and, probably because of my Russian connections, was attracted to Tolstoy. I read *Anna Karenina* and *War and Peace* and remember the epilogue to the latter where Tolstoy gives his own philosophy of history to the reader. Events are not determined by single individuals like Napoleon in what is known as the 'Good Queen Bess and Bad King John' theory of history. Rather, as the wind blows autumn leaves, human beings are caught up in the stream of time and battles are won and lost by people who do not know or understand what they are doing. I also read John Milton. We studied *Paradise Lost* and, although I had a dim appreciation of the gigantic scale of Milton's imagination, much of what he wrote passed me by.

When I was 17, I went on a short skiing holiday and kissed a girl. Doctors later suggested that this is how I contracted glandular fever. The result was that I was laid off school for around six months and had to work on my own at home. I had by then fallen out of love with what science had become. The mass of equations we were expected to remember and manipulate drained the whole enterprise of meaning. There was, it is true, an attempt by my biology teachers to put evolution to us as a true account of the world and I recall being shown how horses used to have five toes and then evolved a hoof and, more surprisingly, that all the hairs on my arms and legs pointed backwards showing that I was descended from a fish. None of this seemed in the slightest bit probable to me ... but then neither did any other explanation. I told my tutor that I did not want to pursue 'dehumanising' science and preferred the emotional truthfulness of literature. Being a good teacher he accepted this request and simply gave me a list of 20 books to read and told me to absorb them.

So, for about six months, I lay on my back on a sofa or in a chair in the garden and worked through some of the highlights of English literature and, when I needed a rest from this, I found my father's old copy of Bertrand Russell's *History of Western Philosophy* and launched into it. Russell had one beneficial effect. His acerbic scepticism cured me of French existentialism and I veered towards

English empiricists like John Locke. Most of all I came to enjoy the Romantic Poets, especially Keats and Wordsworth. I read Keats' odes and his marvellous letters and saw the connection between the two. That autumn I came to sit the entrance papers for Oxford and my enthusiasm for the luxuriant emotion in the Romantic movement must have convinced the examiners that here was someone who cared for literature. I guess they were right. After I had gained my place, I had a gap year before starting the course and I bought myself a return train ticket from London to Rome for £28 so as to visit Keats' grave.

The course took us through English literature chronologically from Anglo-Saxon poetry onwards. We had to read Milton, including his great prose work *Areopagitica* about the freedom of the press, much of his poetry, Shakespeare, the metaphysical poets like Donne and Herbert, the Romantics, Victorian novelists, and T.S. Eliot. Although we did read a great deal, it is also true that, in those days, at the start of the 1960s, Oxford was full of students who, like me, were part of the post-war generation. Our fathers and grandfathers had put on uniform to fight in the world wars but we were free to express ourselves, and we had money to spend. It seemed generally agreed that you worked a bit in your first year and in your third year and used the second year for an excessive social life. There were no mobile phones or social networking sites and so we went to parties and our education progressed by means of heated conversations in dimly lit rooms with dance music in the background. In circumstances I do not remember, but probably to do with one of these parties, I became the film critic of the university's weekly student magazine, *Isis*.

Films were released in London first and then played a week or two later in the provinces. The film critic served his readership best if he went up to London to see the show and then wrote a review for publication to coincide with the Oxford opening. I did a lot of this in my second year and, on one visit, noticed a hoarding advertising Billy Graham's summer crusade at the arena in Earl's Court. I thought it would be fun to write a piece for *Isis* and decided to attend.

The meeting followed a well-established pattern of prayer, singing, and testimony. Above the podium from which Graham spoke was the text, 'Jesus said, "I am the way, the truth and the life"'.

Graham preached on Acts 8 about the conversion of the Ethiopian eunuch and spoke of how a brand new life in Christ was available to everyone who repented and believed. At the end of the sermon he made his appeal. 'There is a battle going on in your heart', he said, and I wondered how he knew. 'Come forward. We will wait for you.' Deeply self-conscious and embarrassed I got up from one of the upper balconies where I was sitting and made my way downstairs to the front where, as promised, the presence of Christ met me. This was a life-changing event and I am not ashamed to speak about it. My fear of death vanished.

Several months later I was tempted to turn back on the grounds that Billy Graham was a kind of father-figure, and he was indeed, born in the same year as my father. But I reasoned that if this Freudian explanation for my conversion were correct, I would still prefer to follow Christ than Freud because Christ was alive and Freud was dead. I wrote to my father to tell him of what had happened and he wrote back and for the only time ever quoted Scripture to me. 'All is vanity', he said in the words of Ecclesiastes that expressed his cynical appraisal of every ideology and religion. Yet he also implied that he did not object to my faith if it was helpful. By now my faith was functioning as an integrating intellectual force. Truth was not to be found in a scientific formula but in the person of Christ, and the proof of truth was not to be found by philosophical or scientific experiment but through the testimony of witnesses as it corresponded with personal experience. In this I may be said to have combined a kind of scientific modernism with romantic prioritization of emotion, and years later I found that John Wesley had admired Locke for his willingness to test truth against personal experience of which emotion was a part.

In my newly discovered fiery Protestantism I fell into an argument with my mother about Orthodoxy. 'Why do you worship idols?' I asked her, referring to the practice of kissing icons. We had icons in the home and, when she was ill, my mother had an icon by her bed. She was at a loss to answer me and turned for help to Uncle Dimitri. He was her half brother and a member of the Russian émigré community in Oxford. He was also Professor of Russian and Balkan History at the university and so a formidable antagonist.[91] We met over a cup of tea and he listened to my complaints and then provided a considered answer. Christ, he told me, had at the Incarnation sanctified matter and, moreover, the Orthodox did not worship icons but *venerated* them and, in this, he echoed the theological controversies between Islam and the Byzantine empire. Though I left him without a desire to return to Orthodoxy, I gained a broader sense of what the church is.

The schedule of lectures at Oxford was published in advance and students could attend whichever they wanted. Though I was not reading philosophy I went with hundreds of others to hear Isaiah Berlin on Kant. Berlin strode into the lecture hall with his academic gown flowing behind him, mounted the dais, sat on a large throne-like chair and, speaking extremely rapidly, held forth for exactly an hour.[92] We listened mesmerized, thinking that we had understood the *Critique of Pure Reason*. We heard Lionel Trilling on the liberal imagination and others on interpreting Shakespeare. I remember one lecturer comparing some interpretations of Shakespeare with Augustine's interpretation of the parable of the Good Samaritan. To say that the two pence represented the two natures of Christ was so obviously wrong that one hardly needed to dismiss it. A more cogent approach to texts was exemplified by John Carey who, that year, was giving a seminar on the metaphysical poets. I sat down next to a man in a yellow oilskin mackintosh who was engaged in writing his doctorate on dissent in the Victorian novel. He turned out to be Valentine Cunningham, who was later elected to the chair of English Language and Literature, and, surprisingly, was also the son of an Assemblies of God pastor.[93]

Cunningham invited me to a meeting at St John's College where I heard a young travelling preacher, David Petts, speak on the Holy Spirit. David took an hour to move from Genesis to Revelation and at the end prayed for those who wanted to be baptized in the Spirit. I went forward and was overwhelmed by the presence of Christ as I had been on the day of my conversion, and I joyfully spoke in tongues.

That summer I offered myself for the Operation Mobilisation summer programme. We had to read Roy Hession's *Calvary Road* by

[91] http://en.wikipedia.org/wiki/Dimitri_Obolensky
[92] http://en.wikipedia.org/wiki/Isaiah_Berlin
[93] http://en.wikipedia.org/wiki/Valentine_Cunningham

way of preparation and I became uneasy about what it taught. We had to repent continually to keep being filled with the Spirit, and a similar teaching seemed to inform Watchman Nee. During the six weeks I was with OM we learnt to pray for our finances to be met, we carried out street preaching and youth work, we learnt to work in teams, we were given a challenge to discipleship and simple living, and we heard apologetics lectures based around the fulfillment of prophecy or the evidence of the resurrection. Towards the end of the summer, we were challenged to extend our commitment for a year. I wavered and decided to pray all night for an answer. We had been taught that the way to find out the will of God was to write down what our own will was and then to put this on one side and to read Scripture and pray to see what God's will was. It might be the same as our own will or it might be quite different. I wanted to stay in the safety of an OM team with new-found friends but the Scripture in 2 Tim. 4.5, 'Make full proof of your ministry', inclined me to leave. I had no idea what to do next.

Like my secular friends, I was prone to eschatological worry. They were marching the streets in support of nuclear disarmament, especially as the near annihilation of the Cuban missile crisis and the assassination of John F. Kennedy convinced many of them they would be lucky to reach the age of 30. My faith hardly helped me here. For all I knew the Antichrist was lurking in the Middle East and ready to pounce on the church.

Starting Work

Reading *The Cross and the Switchblade* re-asserted the power of the baptism in the Spirit and led me to work with drug addicts. A British equivalent of Teen Challenge appeared on the scene, set up the apparatus of a parachurch organization, raised money from well-meaning Christians, purchased a property and opened for addicts who were just then beginning to appear on the urban streets. As far as I am aware not a single addict was actually taken into the hostel and the instigator turned out to have neither the ability nor the integrity to run a national organization. It was my first encounter with a Christian charlatan; the man later became interested in health foods and went off to run a restaurant. At a loss to know what to do next, I wrote to David Petts for advice. He outlined a series of options and then said that he was going to take on a new pastorate in Basingstoke and invited me to attend. Within a few weeks I had joined a small Assemblies of God congregation and my Christian faith moved into a new phase. It was no longer an individualistic adventure but now woven into the life of a Christian congregation complete with spiritual gifts, the weekly cycle of meetings and the requirements of financial commitment.

When I had left school, I had shaken the dust off my feet and thought, 'that's the worst over, I never want to go through the gates of a school again'. And yet, within a year of arriving in Basingstoke, I had landed a teaching job. I found myself in charge of 44 five-year-olds in a Church of England primary school and, without training, was quite unsuited to the post. Fortunately, there was a Baptist headmaster in the town and he ran one of the local secondary schools. He was on the look-out for a Christian teacher of religious education and signed me up.

Visitors to Britain are often astonished to discover the role religion has in state schools. At that time each school was obliged by law to begin the day with an act of worship and each pupil was required to receive religious education – though it is important to note that a 'conscience clause' was written into law enabling parents to withdraw their children from both worship and religious teaching if they wished; only the Jehovah's Witnesses and a few Roman Catholics bothered to do this. The churches had founded schools in the 19th century and, when the state entered the field, the two sets of schools were combined into a single 'dual system'. The 1944 Education Act defined the religious requirements for so-called maintained schools and it supported Christianity because, at that time, Britain was fighting for its life against a Nazi dictatorship which had smashed religion wherever it had conquered. Christianity was seen as an antidote to the moral vacuum which had given rise to Nazi beliefs. And so, paid by the state, I began teaching nearly all the pupils in the school a syllabus that was almost entirely biblical. There was a set of tattered Bibles in the stock cupboard and I had an endless supply of chalk. All I had to do was to make the lessons interesting to the apathetic and sometimes hostile pupils.

In those days only about 6% of the age cohort attended university. My Oxford degree was thought to be a perfectly adequate preparation for the work on which I now embarked. It was understood that one did not hold evangelistic meetings in the classroom, and that suited me. We could, however, run voluntary activities in the lunch hour and quite soon I had a Christian Union in existence and before long some of the pupils had made a commitment to Christ. Government reorganization was in the process of turning secondary schools into mammoth comprehensive institutions. After a couple of years there were about 1,800 pupils in the school where I worked and the Christian Union grew to about 200 pupils. Some of the pupils I taught needed remedial help and I remember one sad boy aged 14 asking me if Jesus would help him learn to read. Others were bright and glad to notch up another exam pass even if it was in religion. I learnt to simplify my speech so as to be acceptable to all kinds of people.

British society in the early 1970s was undergoing extensive change. Immigrant communities had brought Islam and Hinduism to the British Isles. The sheer size of the new schools made a daily act of worship impossible to arrange. We were at a point where the law addressed one reality while we were living in another. It was time to try to understand what was happening. For the previous three years the only book I had allowed myself to read was the Bible. After being fortified by the verse in Prov. 4.7 'with all thy getting get understanding', I permitted my obsessional characteristics to be turned towards further study. For the next decade I was constantly reading and obtaining new qualifications incorporating religion, sociology, psychology, and education. I took two postgraduate certificates, a master's degree and a doctorate while continuing to teach hundreds of pupils. This was one of the busiest times of my life. I married in 1971 and we had two sons. We attended around six meetings a week at the assembly (three times on Sunday, including teaching a Sunday school class, a prayer meeting, a Bible Study and assisting at a youth meeting) and we joined the staff at summer camps.

During my master's degree I visited schools in the Soviet Union and Israel to observe the impact respectively of Marxist-Leninism and Zionism on their curricula. In Moscow atheism was dinned into the heads of the children and the head teacher of one of the schools gave me an atheistic medallion as a memento of my visit. In Israel the pupils were taught Genesis the way I taught my Sunday School class, and there was not much doubt about ownership of the land. My doctorate compared the impact of religious education in three cultures: England, Northern Ireland, and the Republic of Ireland. To make the comparison precise I needed a measuring instrument and here I was fortunate in stumbling across the work of Leslie Francis who had just completed a Cambridge doctorate constructing an 'attitude toward Christianity' scale for use in secondary schools. I went to see him and he generously let me use his scale and became a life-long friend. My research required a survey of pupils and, in the end, I accumulated 3116 respondents in 33 schools and used a standard statistical package which only ran on the big university main frame machine. I would drive up and down the road to Reading University to pick up my print-outs and, examining the figures, gradually came to the conclusion that pupils' attitudes were determined more by the home than the school, though the school did have a measurable impact. The thesis led to a spate of publications and the publications led to a research post at the University of Southampton.[94] Here I carried out a national survey of school worship, helped in the training of teachers of religious education and contributed to a course on research methods.[95]

During my doctorate, and perhaps because of my interest in both arts and sciences, I first engaged with the writings of Karl Popper whose attention to the philosophy of science dated back to his days with the Vienna Circle to which Russell occasionally referred.[96] Popper developed a criterion for assessing whether a

---

[94] For instance I wrote, 'Marital Happiness and Children's Attitude to Religion', *British Journal of Religious Education* 3 (1981), pp. 102-105; 'Psychoticism and Attitude to Religion', *Personality and Individual Differences* 2 (1981), pp. 249-52; 'Subject Preference and Attitude to Religion in Secondary Schools', *Educational Review* 33.1 (1981), pp. 47-51; 'Syllabuses and Attitudes to Christianity', *The Irish Catechist* 5.2 (1981), pp. 16-21; 'Factors Bearing on Changes in Religious Education in Britain since 1944', *Journal of Christian Education*, papers 72 (1981), pp. 20-30; 'Problems with the Problem Approach', *Canadian and International Education* 10.1 (1981), pp. 5-19. W.K. Kay and J.K.P. Watson, 'Comparative Education: The Need for Dangerous Ambition', *Educational Research* 24.2 (1981), pp. 129-39.

[95] P.C. Souper and W.K. Kay, *The School Assembly Debate: 1942-82* (University of Southampton, 1982); *idem, The School Assembly in Hampshire* (University of Southampton, 1982); *idem, Worship in the Independent Day School* (University of Southampton, 1983).

[96] K.R. Popper, *The Open Society and its Enemies* (London: Routledge & Kegan Paul, 1945); *idem, The Poverty of Historicism* (London: Routledge & Kegan Paul, 1957); *idem, The Logic of Scientific Discovery*, (London: Routledge, 1959) [first published in German in 1935 as *Logic der Forschung*]; *idem, Unended Quest* (Illinois: Open Court Publishing Co, 1974).

statement was or was not scientific. If it was testable, it was scientific; if it was not testable, it was not scientific. I could see no reason to reject this conclusion and it remained important to me when a wave of post-modernistic reasoning swept through the academy some ten years later.

An immediate problem arose. My research post was funded for three years and, as the terminus approached and with a young family, I had to find another job. My old teaching post in a secondary school would have been available but at this time I was pressed by David Petts to move to the Assemblies of God college and join the faculty. He had become the principal of Mattersey Hall in 1977 and was in the process of transforming it. Reluctantly, and after prayer and fasting, I accepted the position. I was paid about half what school teachers were paid. A little later, perhaps because he knew my forthcoming destination, I received an unexpected phone call from the General Secretary of the Assemblies of God. 'Would you be prepared to write a new history of the fellowship?' he asked. 'Yes', I replied, 'if you are willing to make available to me all the minutes and other documents held by the Executive Council'. He agreed and so, sensing a providential door opening, I now entered another phase of life.[97]

Saying Hello and Good-bye to Biblical Studies

I gave about 200 lectures per year in a variety of subjects including especially the Old Testament. We prepared students for the old London University BD as well as the Cambridge Diploma. Although we taught many pastoral topics, the academic content of the syllabuses we followed required us to cover much of the material generated by critical – and especially German – scholarship. For instance, we would teach the students about the exodus and they had to learn arguments for and against the early and the late date. In an attempt to fasten discussion around irrefutable fixed points, I focused upon archaeological evidence but found that, while the first 20th century archaeologists rebutted the textual critics,[98] the later ones appeared to prefer reconstructions of the past that were ideo-

---

[97] Later published as *Inside Story* (Stourpourt-on-Seven: Mattersey Hall Publications, 1990).

[98] E.g. W.F. Albright.

logically driven. Some Israeli archaeologists wanted to show that Israel had conquered the land and exterminated the Canaanites while others wanted to show a more gradual infiltration; the reading of the evidence depended on concealed prior (political) assumptions.

Implicated in this argumentation was the further assumption that it was possible to detect differences in authorship by close analysis of the biblical text. Given that Shakespeare had written both comedies and tragedies and that, while the majority of his corpus was in blank verse, there were rhyming couplets, songs, sonnets and pieces of prose, I found it difficult to take seriously those scholars who announced dogmatically on the basis of their textual analysis that this epistle was not Pauline and that chapter was a later interpolation.[99] Shakespeare had written in a variety of forms and his later work was unlike his earlier work. I could see no reason why the later Pastoral Epistles should be stylistically identical to the earlier epistles to the Thessalonians. I grew cynical about the pronouncements of textual critics and the consensus of scholarship began to look to me as if it were driven by the whims of fashion. Like many conservative Christians I thought it reasonable to be as critical of the critics as the critics were of the Scripture.

Every Monday during a study day I settled down to work on the history of British Assemblies of God. I constructed a database of the Executive Council minutes and the minutes of the annual General Conferences and I read through the entire set of the denominational magazine, *Redemption Tidings* (starting from 1924), databasing it as I went. I consciously followed the example of the Bible itself by aiming to give a truthful account of spiritual and moral behaviour, with all the light and shade this implied. I also deliberately followed the method used by Adrian Hastings in his *A History of English Christianity 1920-1985* and divided each decade into a separate block.

The contrast between biblical scholarship and denominational history became acute. Sitting in my study in England, and using texts in my mother tongue, I sometimes found it difficult to work out what had gone on fifty years previously in the group of church-

---

[99] C.S. Lewis had made this argument with characteristic brilliance in 'Fern-seed and Elephant Grass', and it was from him I took my cue (http://orthodox-web.tripod.com/papers/fern_seed.html).

es of which I was part. It seemed improbable therefore that a German scholar sitting in his study in Tübingen or Heidelberg could work out what happened in another country and another language two or three thousand years before. My scepticism at their dogmatic pronouncements turned into rank disbelief when I read one eminent writer who told us that the birth stories in the books of Samuel had been transposed and, instead of applying to Samuel, should have been assigned to Saul. The final straw was when I read R.N. Whybray on the authorship of the Pentateuch.[100] He traced the 19th century breaking up of the Pentateuch into four sources, J, E, D, and P and then subsidiary minor sources, K, H and so on, but concluded that current scholars believed that the Pentateuch, though exilic, was actually the product of a single editorial mind. Thus a century of scholarship had ended up more or less where it started. The labour of many years had broken the Pentateuch up and then joined it all together again.

All this destroyed my confidence in the value of this kind of work. I ended by fastening onto the canonical criticism of Brevard Childs who asserted that it was impossible to get behind the canonical text to its prior sources and influences.[101] One should simply deal with the text as we have received it. Valentine Cunningham had once said something similar to me. Though there are many variants in the Shakespearean canon, the fact is that *it is there*.

While at Mattersey Hall I preached about forty times a year, usually within Assemblies of God, and in this way began to appreciate variations in Pentecostalism and the typical developmental trajectories of congregations. I interviewed veterans whose memories reached back to the 1930s and I read minute books of district councils and the missionary council. I tried to place Assemblies of God against its cultural background by noting what the poetry of the 1920s or the music of the 1960s told us. I saw the impact of the 1939-45 war and of changing educational standards. I attempted to give voice to the Pentecostals themselves rather than their subsequent interpreters.[102] Most of all I saw how a small and dedicated

---

[100] R.N. Whybray, *The Making of the Pentateuch* (Sheffield: JSOT Press, 1987).

[101] See for instance B.S. Childs, *The Book of Exodus: A Critical, Theological Commentary* (Philadelphia: Westminster Press, 1974); *idem, Old Testament Theology in a Canonical Context* (Minneapolis, MN: Augsburg Fortress, 1989).

[102] I gave the example of a Marxist account of the Reformation which interpreted it as an uprising of the working class against Rome and ignored the re-

band of men and women had, often self-sacrificially and with heroic faith, given everything they had to serve Jesus in the power of the Spirit. The missionary work of W.P.F. Burton was a case in point but there were many others who had faithfully prayed for the sick and preached the gospel.[103] I also saw how the carnality and small-mindedness of a few could damage the entire enterprise. The treatment of Donald Gee, who had for fourteen years served as Principal of the forerunner of Mattersey Hall without taking a salary, was disgraceful. The old man, at the age of 70, was turned out into the street by those of his fellow Pentecostals who wanted his job – or he would have been had not John Wildrianne stepped in to help.

My immersion in Pentecostal history was life-changing and created a perspective for evaluating my own life and the whirls and eddies of global events. I saw war as one of the great enemies of the gospel and church growth as being a natural consequence of spiritual health.[104] My history of the Assemblies of God had been completed under the supervision of the University of Nottingham and was successfully submitted as a doctoral thesis. In this way I found myself with two earned doctorates in different subjects from separate British universities. In 1993 I was offered a full-time research post at Trinity College, Carmarthen, part of the University of Wales. Its main business was training school teachers, but my research remit for the first few years relieved me of any need to lecture. Working with Leslie Francis, who had been instrumental in creating the role for me, I published a series of books and articles over the next seven years.[105]

There was a marked contrast between biblical studies and empirical theology. Biblical studies of the kind I examined was either a

---

discovery of the theological doctrine of justification by faith. The judgment of the Marxist interpreter writing several centuries later is given more weight than the view of participants like Martin Luther. Once you extend this principle, other's people experiences are no longer their own possession but are at the mercy of any manipulative theorist.

[103] Burton went out to the Congo in 1915 and, when his ministry finished in the year of his death in 1971 he left 2,100 churches and 2,500 workers.

[104] 1 Timothy 2.2 instructs Christians to pray that we may live peaceful and quiet lives, presumably for this reason.

[105] W.K. Kay and L.J Francis, *Drift from the Churches* (Cardiff: University of Wales Press, 1996); *idem* (eds.) *Religion in Education (1)* (Leominister: Gracewing, 1997); *idem* (eds.) *Religion in Education (2)*, (Leominister: Gracewing, 1998); *idem* (eds.) *Religion in Education (3)*, (Leominister: Gracewing, 2000); *idem* (eds.) *Religion in Education (4)* (Leominister: Gracewing, 2003).

critical scrutiny of the dating and authorship of texts or an attempt to use textual and extra-textual material to construct the history of Israel and the church. Empirical theology instead used specially gathered data to illuminate current practice. There is real excitement in finding a hunch confirmed by systematically collected data. I would feel like a gold prospector who had discovered a rich seam of gold. Suddenly it was no longer necessary to depend on hunches or anecdotes to describe the contours of beliefs or the internal mechanisms of churches or church schools. The empirical theologian can build an explanation through evidence of a measurably reliable kind. Indeed, he or she can work on both directions and can either start with an hypothesis and test it or start with data and generate an hypothesis. There is a delicious creative freedom here.

Living in Two Worlds

My twin foci were religious education/church schools and Pentecostalism. For the next ten years these continued in parallel. There were two sets of conferences to attend, two sets of journals to read, and two sets of papers or books to write. The first focal point resulted in an examination of the legal basis for religious education, the writing of a degree course for teachers and the construction of a syllabus for all Anglican primary schools in Wales. I took a place on the editorial board of the *British Journal of Religious Education* and supervised doctoral students, one of whom empirically tested the optimum number of religions pupils in secondary schools could learn about. It had been argued that pupils needed to learn the six religions of Christianity, Judaism, Islam, Hinduism, Buddhism, and Sikhism since these faiths were to be found among sizeable numbers of residents in the UK. It was further agued that, since the timetabling of religious education was often down to one lesson per week, the only way to cover such a broad range was to teach thematically. So one might teach about prayer in three religions, about ethics in another three, and so on, choosing topics and religions almost randomly and without seeking to show how religious beliefs and their concomitant practices cohered. My contention was that such an approach would hopelessly confuse pupils, and there was already anecdotal evidence that pupils were, for example, inclined to think Moses was a Hindu leader or Diwali was a Jewish festival. In a study of 2,879 pupils, we were able to show that, indeed, thematic approaches to religion and the insistence that six religions be learnt was counter-productive. It actually made pupils less well informed than was the case if they had not been taught at all.[106]

We were also able to show, contrary to received wisdom, that the onset of formal operational thinking at adolescence did not result in the sudden drop in pupil attitudes towards Christianity and that pupils could understand biblical texts both literally and metaphorically from quite a young age.[107] I also argued that phenomenological approaches to religion whereby pupils imaginatively entered a religious universe and then stood back from it critically were incompatible with the account of mental development given by the Swiss psychologist Jean Piaget.[108]

Soon afterwards I began a survey of ministers in the four main Pentecostal denominations in the UK. This was a large undertaking and involved mailing out over 2,000 questionnaires to the addresses in ministerial yearbooks. David Petts was by now Chairman of the Executive Council of Assemblies of God and he was supportive, with the result that other Executive Councils also gave their permission. I secured a response rate for a lengthy questionnaire of more than 50% and was able for the first time to see how well the beliefs of Pentecostal ministers corresponded with their fundamental statements of faith, to uncover generational moral shifts, and to discover the incidence of the exercise of spiritual gifts both among ministers themselves and in their congregations.[109] And all this could be done on a comparative basis that revealed how the de-

---

[106] W.K. Kay and D.L. Smith, 'Religious Terms and Attitudes in the Classroom (part 1)', *British Journal of Religious Education*, 22.2, (2000), pp. 81-90; D.L. Smith and W.K. Kay, 'Religious Terms and Attitudes in the Classroom (part 2)', *British Journal of Religious Education*, 22.3, (2000), pp.181-91; W.K. Kay and D.L. Smith, 'Classroom Factors and Attitude Toward Six World Religions', *British Journal of Religious Education*, 24.2, (2002), pp. 111-22.

[107] W.K. Kay, L.J. Francis and H.M. Gibson, 'Attitude toward Christianity and the Transition to Formal Operational Thinking', *British Journal of Religious Education*, 19.1 (1996), pp. 45-55.

[108] W.K. Kay, 'Phenomenology, Religious Education, and Piaget', *Religion*, 27 (1997), pp. 275-83.

[109] For the correspondence between denominational beliefs and actual beliefs, see 'The "initial evidence": Implications of an Empirical Perspective in a British Context', *Journal of the European Pentecostal Theological Association* 20 (2000), pp. 25-31.

nominations subtly differed from each other.[110] I was able to show that Pentecostal churches grew as they allowed their congregations to be mobilised and empowered.[111] In other words their Pentecostal distinctives were integral to their growth and it would be detrimental to Pentecostals to minimise the charismatic gifts of 1 Corinthians 12 and 14.

One of my on-going preoccupations has been with the analysis of personality. My father had ended his medical training by going on to become a psychiatrist and had left behind in our house a bound set of Freud's collected papers. Though I had not read all the volumes, my interest in the dynamics of personality had been awakened. I nearly always included items designed to measure personality in my questionnaires. I had done so when assessing pupils for my original doctorate and I did so when assessing Pentecostal ministers in Britain.[112] The extravert-introvert and the neuroticism-stability dimensions were especially interesting. The first showed that ministers who publicly exercised verbal gifts of the Spirit like prophecy tended to be extraverted and the second showed that, in comparison with general population norms, Pentecostals were more, not less, stable than men and women of similar age.[113] These findings assisted in the construction of a model of divine-human interaction of charismatic activity and showed which ministers were most likely to build charismatic congregations. With regard to neuroticism, the empirical evidence showed that Pentecostals, far from being unstable or pathological, were actually more balanced than non-tongues-speakers, a reversal of the hostile presumption that

---

[110] In some of the results of this survey I also looked at eschatology, job satisfaction, and glossolalia: e.g. W.K. Kay, 'Pre-millennial Tensions: What Pentecostal Ministers Look Forward to', *Journal of Contemporary Religion* 14.3 (1999), pp. 361-73; 'Job Satisfaction in Pentecostal Ministers', *Asian Journal of Pentecostal Studies*, 3.1 (2000), pp. 83-97; 'Speaking with Tongues: Contexts, Findings and Questions', *Journal of Empirical Theology*, 12.1 (1999), pp. 53-58.

[111] This was an extension of Margaret Poloma's thesis first published in *The Assemblies of God at the Crossroads* (Knoxville, TN: The University of Tennessee Press, 1989).

[112] See my *Pentecostals in Britain* (Carlisle: Paternoster, 2000).

[113] L.J. Francis and W.K. Kay, 'The Personality Characteristics of Pentecostal Ministry Candidates', *Personality and Individual Differences* 18 (1995), pp. 581-94; W.K. Kay and L.J Francis, 'Personality, Mental Health and Glossolalia', *Pneuma*, 17 (1995), pp. 253-63.

had dominated early 20th century psychological research on glosso-lalia.[114]

Pentecostal and Charismatic Studies

From 2001 my research interests were formalised by two concurrent half-time appointments, one in the education department at King's College, London, and the other in the theology department at the University of Wales, Bangor. This might have continued indefinitely had both departments not pressed me to go full-time. I had been ordained as an Assemblies of God minister while at Mattersey and it was this commitment that led me to accept the post at Bangor despite the fact King's was a more prestigious institution. From Bangor it was possible to serve the Pentecostal constituency in Europe by validating degrees at master's and doctoral level. I founded and directed a Centre for Pentecostal and Charismatic Studies at Bangor and argued that the academy and the church needed each other; theology, especially empirical theology, when harnessed to the church would help the church do better what only it could do.

A research grant extended my range by enabling me to map out the 12 main neo-Pentecostal groups in Britain.[115] These radical groups had mainly emerged from the charismatic movement of the 1960s. Their doctrine of the Spirit was similar to that of the Pentecostals but they were scathingly anti-denominational and often breathed rhetoric about the kingdom of God. They accepted the reality of modern-day apostles and prophets and were therefore governed without any constitutional apparatus. Consequently, they were more decisive than the older Pentecostal denominations and, on principle, they avoided voting in local churches or in conferences. They tended to be organised into networks or clusters of congregations. By the 1990s, they set the trend that classical Pentecostals attempted to follow and they were certainly more influential than Pentecostals in propagating the 'Toronto blessing'.

---

[114] See my 'The Mind, Behaviour and Glossolalia: A Psychological Perspective', in M.J. Cartledge (ed.), *Speaking in Tongues: Multi-disciplinary Perspectives* (Carlisle: Paternoster, 2006), pp. 174-205.

[115] W.K. Kay, *Apostolic Networks in Britain* (Carlisle: Paternoster, 2007).

Soon after this I wrote two books on global Pentecostalism and have recently begun to explore Pentecostal-style church growth in three major Asian cities that may well represent the future of 21st century Christianity.[116]

Reflection

Looking back on the course of my life, I notice the importance of long-standing friendships. I followed the precept that we should do whatever our hand finds to do with all our might and, whenever there were major decisions to be made, I always spent time in serious prayer. The Tolstoyan notion of history being a flow of events beyond our control was transmuted in my mind into a belief in Providence. I believe that free-will and divine foreknowledge are compatible. There is a text in 1 Kgs 22.34 where a man fired an arrow at random and fatally hit the well-armoured Ahab exactly as Elijah and Micaiah had predicted: the entirely random event fulfilled a precise prophetic prediction; one event was free and the other necessitated. There is a similar implication when Jesus says, 'Pray that your flight is not in winter or on the Sabbath' (Mt. 24.20) with the certainty that the hearers will take flight at *some* point without the exact timing of their journey being fixed. It is clear to me that a belief in the authenticity of Old Testament prophecy implies that some events (like the birth and crucifixion of Jesus) are unalterably certain while other events (like which shepherds were on the hillside or which soldiers were on duty on those days) are undetermined. For myself, then, friendships were part of God's providential provision. On two or three occasions I wrote about the importance of Providence in the construction of Pentecostal history both because Pentecostals themselves believed in it and because on the whole Christian historians have believed history is meaningfully directed towards divine ends.[117]

In Eph. 2.10 Paul tells us that we are God's workmanship fitted for works that God has prepared us in advance to do. This implied

---

[116] W.K. Kay, *Pentecostalism: Core Text* (London: SCM, 2009) and *Pentecostalism: A Very Short Introduction* (Oxford: Oxford University Press, 2011).

[117] 'Three Generations On: the Methodology of Pentecostal Historiography', *EPTA Bulletin*, (1992), X.1 and 2, pp. 58-70; 'Karl Popper and Pentecostal Historiography', *Pneuma*, 32 (2010), pp. 5-15.

to me that preparatory phases of our lives are valuable in pointing us to the right future. From my mid-twenties, I had a sense of duty that was partly contractual. Our yes should be yes and our no should be no, and this applied both in marriage and in employment. I listened to prophetic utterances in Pentecostal churches and usually found them uplifting without believing they were intended to give us guidance. I was clear that 'exhortation, edification, and comfort' were the primary functions of verbal charismata and, though there were times when dominant individuals nearly blew me off course, I also took refuge in the text that said 'in the multitude of counsellors there is safety' (Prov. 11.14) and that one should heed the advice of the godly (Ps. 1.1). I was fortunate in having David Petts as pastor during my formative Christian years. He pointed out that the Israelites received the supernatural provision of manna when they needed it, but when they entered Canaan, they had to rely on non-supernatural means by growing their own food. The powerful effects of spiritual gifts should be seen in conjunction with natural provision, and to accept the latter did not indicate a failure of faith.

Although I have spoken of my disillusionment with one type of biblical studies, that does not mean that I was disillusioned with the Bible – far from it. My friends have given me examples of exegetical preaching or 'constructive theology'. My own approach to Scripture has almost certainly been influenced by my willingness to become imaginatively immersed in literary texts and I love the moment of insight that comes after prolonged meditation on verses or passages on which I am going to preach. My quest for the empirical validation of theological descriptions comes, no doubt, from a cast of mind averse to endless unanchored speculation. I conceive of the eternal God as dwelling in 'light inaccessible' (1 Tim. 6.16) and believe that one day I shall actually see the glory of God as shown in the face of Jesus Christ (2 Cor. 4.6).

4

THE TESTIMONY OF MY CALL TO PENTECOSTAL SCHOLARSHIP

RICKIE D. MOORE[*]

I am honored by this invitation to share something of the story of how I was called to Pentecostal scholarship. I have long told my students that nothing honors older persons more than being asked to tell their stories. And now one of those former students, Robby Waddell, in partnership with his colleague Steven Fettke, has done me the honor of both following and making me (now that I am obviously old enough!) the object of that advice.

As I have considered exactly how I should respond to this present invitation, I have struggled with the thought that I have already done a version of what I am now being asked to do. Four years ago I wrote a paper, entitled, 'A Pentecostal Approach to Teaching Old Testament Introduction', which I delivered at the 2007 Society for Pentecostal Studies meeting held at Lee University, and I framed this paper essentially in terms of a narrative of how my work as a distinctively Pentecostal Old Testament scholar had unfolded. The opening paragraph of that piece introduced my story with these words:

There is a desire that can begin to stir in someone my age that, more and more these days, I take to be a worthy desire – one

---

[*] Rickie D. Moore (PhD, Vanderbilt University) is Chair of the Department of Theology, Lee University, Cleveland, TN, USA.

that the Old Testament itself would seem to commend and rein-
force (cf. Psalm 78.1-8 and Deut. 6.4-9) – and that is the desire
to pass on one's deepest, most passionately held discoveries and
deposits to the next generation. This is the spirit in which I wish
to offer this presentation, and it goes along with the context in
which I wish to offer it. Specifically, I want to give to those who
would come after me in my extended Pentecostal family, particularly those in the vocation of studying and teaching Scripture
and even more particularly in teaching the Old Testament,
something of my experience, my exploration, and my experi-
mentation in pursuing, as I have done these last 25 years, a dis-
tinctly Pentecostal approach to the Old Testament. And I want
to do this in order to help and to instigate, if not inspire, others
to find their own way forward, rather than someone else's.

In what followed, I gave it my best shot. And now this previously presented paper appears as the introductory chapter in a collection of my articles, under the title, *The Spirit of the Old Testament*.[1]
And what's more, I not only give an overview of my story in this
introductory article but I also narrate other parts of my story in several of the other articles in this collection. In all of this, I both
demonstrate and draw explicit attention to the fact that a key part
of my story of becoming a distinctively Pentecostal scholar consisted precisely in the opening up of my own story as a critical dimension of my scholarly work. While this turn toward narrative and autobiographical theology is not unique to Pentecostalism, for me,
this was crucial to my being (and becoming) true to my Pentecostal
heritage and rootage, which is where I first learned the critical importance of telling my story. At the same time, I found this to be
true to Scripture's own example of giving priority to narrative as a
method for doing theology.

These previous forays into my own story gave me the chance to
mention a good many names of teachers, mentors, and scholars
whose influence and roles in my journey of becoming a Pentecostal
scholar were profoundly deep and deeply profound. So after all of
this emphasis on and exposing of my own story, as appears in this

---

[1] R.D. Moore, *The Spirit of the Old Testament* (JPTSup, 35; Blandford Forum,
UK: Deo Publishing, 2012).

now-collected corpus of my work, I am left with the thought, 'what do I have left to say?'

What helps me as I struggle to answer this question is remembering two more things that I have frequently told my students through the years, specifically about this matter of telling our testimony: One, we never get finished telling our testimony, and two, our testimony is the story we tell when God gets us told. As these two teachings now boomerang back on this teacher, I believe I am now ready to testify – to lift up another piece of my story, one that will complement and not simply repeat the other pieces already written down and available to anyone who would care to see them, one that, no doubt, gets closer to the heart of it all than any I have yet written, one that gives prime attention to the two persons, who, more than any of the other influences, teachers, and mentors, whose impact I have deeply appreciated and previously narrated, were divinely instrumental in the genesis and development of my calling to be a Pentecostal scholar. I speak of my father and my mother, whose recent passing away, both within the past year and within two months of each other, now occasions, through the revelation that only grief and the grace that comes with it can deliver, this further and deeper piece of my story.

I have one more preliminary thought before getting on with it. The other day, I was sharing lunch with one of my students, Isaac Lutz, in the Lee University student center, and I admitted to him the struggle I was having in getting started with this present article. After listening intently to me, he posed to me a probing and prodding question that was just what I needed to hear: 'Are you writing this testimony as a son or as a father?' I believe I can now offer an answer to his question, and it is this: in telling this part of my story here, I hope both to honor my father and my mother and to bless the generation of my children, in accord with the words of Ps. 78.3-7:

Things I have heard and known,
That my ancestors have told me,
I will not hide them from their children,
I will tell to the coming generation
The glorious and mighty deeds of the LORD
And the wonders that he has done …
That the next generation might know them,

The children yet unborn,
And rise up to tell them to their children,
So that they should set their hope in God,
And not forget the works of God
But keep his commandments.

I grew up in Ypsilanti, Michigan – an automobile factory town
about a half hour west of Detroit. My father had grown up in rural
west Tennessee, the son of a sharecropper and pioneer Pentecostal
preacher, but my dad had followed several of my relatives, all part
of a mass migration of southerners, to the north soon after service
in World War II to find work in the factories around Ypsilanti and
Willow Run, Michigan – factories that had converted after the war
from making B-24 bombers to automobiles.

Moving from the south to the north was a real cross-cultural
stretch for my parents. They found 'a living' in Michigan, but in
many ways they left their heart in Tennessee. My mother lived her
life pragmatically firm about living in Michigan for the duration but
always pining for the next time she could 'go home' and see her
'mama' and the rest of the folks; my father longed for Tennessee
with a kind of wistful, romantic nostalgia that continually entertained (somewhat less than practically) the thought of 'going back
someday', akin to one's longing to revisit their past or to make it to
heaven in the bye and bye. These strong feelings in my parents always kept them from fully assimilating to the culture of the north,
in the way many of their fellow southerners, even some of our relatives, did. And they took up two powerful means of sustaining this
resistance to assimilation. First, they used every opportunity of vacation time or time off to make trips 'back home', and this was essentially two weeks every summer. In retrospect, I can now see that
these trips functioned as pilgrimages that not only kept my parents
connected to 'home' but also became for their children (me and my
three siblings) a deep conduit for our heritage and identity to seep,
almost unnoticed, into our souls.

The second means of my parents' cross-cultural 'survival' took
the form of finding and thoroughly committing themselves to a
small Pentecostal congregation, the Willow Run Church of God,
itself made up almost entirely of transplanted southerners, who like
my parents had something in their southern roots that they desperately wanted to hang onto. So church was not just a spiritual center,

but also a social shelter, a pocket of southern comfort that provided a little piece of 'home' for this group of country people who found themselves displaced in the unfamiliar, urbanized, industrial north.

I grew up shuttling back and forth between public schools, which immersed me in that northern culture, and our little Pentecostal church, which cultivated and kept guard over our southern sub-culture. It was a cross-cultural gap that I, along with all of us church kids, had to navigate, and to do so without much conscious awareness or overt acknowledgement of it. Although it was subtle and not explicit, we quickly learned in school that 'north' was better than 'south', and it was natural to associate that 'better' with the quality public education that was provided by the economic prosperity of a burgeoning automobile industry and its tax base of union wages.

I was a bright boy, and so school quickly captivated my mind. The church of my father and mother couldn't compete on that score. I was set up and tempted to feel just a little bit embarrassed about the southern, Pentecostal part of my life, and more than 'just a little bit' the further I went in school. But my parents and our church offered something else that nurtured within me a deep, almost hidden counter-weight to all of that – something that I now know, all along, was laying a claim on my heart. It's hard to describe and do justice to what that something was, but I'm going to take a swing at it here, and I will begin by saying that, in a word, it all had to do with my parents' spirituality.

My mother came from a southern Baptist family, and from it she brought her firm sense of drawing the lines between right and wrong. She knew through painful experience from a home-life bruised, though never quite broken, by the alcohol problem of her father and the enduring grace and pluck of her ever-faithful mother, that there were barriers against the chaos that needed to be made and guarded. My father, who had grown up in a Pentecostal preacher's home with 'a praying mother', was early on much less nervous about exploring and experimenting with 'the world', but the untimely death of his mother right after he came home from the war, jarred him and began to open him up to his own need for the faith that he previously had found easy to take for granted. The decisive turning point for him, however, did not come until several years later after he was married and we children came along and began making my father much more nervous when he saw us following close behind in his every footstep. That's when he made a path to that little Pentecostal church in Willow Run, Michigan – no doubt the nearest thing he could find to the Pentecostal church in which he had been raised in west Tennessee – and from there he never looked back.

My father, and especially my mother with the straight-laced Baptist standards in her background, made sure we were in church every time the doors were open, even on Sunday nights during the Walt Disney show, and even during the annual TV broadcast of the Wizard of Oz, which I consequently never got to see, at least beyond the tornado scene, until I was in college! Going to church was a given that anchored all the many other 'givens' that kept my home-life stable and steady and undergirded with the resources of renewal in the face of all our family's imperfections, skirmishes, and struggles. Yet by itself, church going did more to pose than relieve that most fundamental struggle for me, namely, that tug of war, referenced earlier, between my head and my heart.

Public education was a powerful, expanding force in my life, but, in a totally different way, so was the spirituality of my parents that was lived out and intertwined with the congregational life of that little Pentecostal church. We didn't have much of a youth program, unless you count one hayride a year, an annual Christmas play, and a group of adults that joined with my parents in loving us, owning us, and pestering us to join them in testifying and praying at the altar, where their tears and shouts over us could sometimes convince us that we were significant beyond our wildest dreams and had a destiny and a calling that far transcended any career.

Sometimes these altar experiences could be well nigh apocalyptic in intensity, where 'being saved, sanctified, and filled with the Holy Ghost' became more than just hackneyed phrases. I can remember riding home from church in the back seat of the family car, looking into the night sky and feeling almost weak and awash with the wonder and afterglow of those encounters divine, knowing in those moments that there was a vision greater and an insight more brilliant than anything on the intellectual plane. But I also remember how those exceptional moments did not seem to hold up very well when I ventured a few times to try to bear witness to them outside my church circle, particularly at school – like the time one of my junior high teachers asked the class to describe the Christian view of what happens to us in the afterlife. All she wanted was the simple answer, 'If we're good we go to heaven, and if we're bad we go to hell', but I mistakenly thought the teacher and my classmates were waiting to hear about the rapture, the tribulation, and the whole apocalyptic scenario that had been my church's best way of trying to come to terms with that apocalyptic spirituality that had been stoked in the fires of those altar experiences. But that day, the only thing that burned was my face with embarrassment before their confounded stares that let me know that I had been caught speaking in an unknown tongue.

I grew up within 5 miles of the University of Michigan, where my high school teachers, supportive of my academic potential, would have wanted to see me go. But one of the youth leaders in my church, who was one of the only members of my church who had graduated from college, had had a life-changing experience attending Lee College (now Lee University), our Pentecostal denomination's main school, and he enthusiastically lobbied me to consider going to Lee. He even took the time to drive me there, all the way from Michigan to east Tennessee, for a recruitment weekend. I was hooked, and looking back on it now, I think the main appeal of this place for me involved something deeper than anything on a conscious level. I'm sure I was aching for something that could address that inner conflict that had defined my life up to that point, and so I was drawn to this place that held out the promise of bringing my heart and my mind together in a single place and into a coherent integration.

During my college years at Lee I received and experienced many things that fed and fueled both sides of the inner conflict that I scarcely knew was even there. On the one hand, I climbed the ladder of human learning and, probably out of a desire to know my own inner self, chose psychology as a major. But on the other hand, my chosen path of study took an unexpected turn through a certain sequence of events, which at the time seemed merely coincidental but I now see in terms of an in-breaking of the Spirit, in line with what the spirituality of my parents had long promised.

After my college sophomore year, I was at home for the summer with an armful of books that my Lee biology teacher had enthusiastically been promoting to his students – books by C.S. Lewis and

Francis Schaeffer. While working through these books, something slowly began to be awakened inside me, and a clear and distinct conclusion settled down upon me, and it amounted to this: when I returned to Lee that Fall, I needed to change my major to Bible. When I arrived on campus, my first stop was the campus post-office where I expected to collect a packet of cards that would correspond to the psychology courses for which I had pre-registered right before summer break. I knew I would have to switch all these cards with new ones for the Bible major. But when I opened the packet, I found that a mistake had somehow been made. Alongside the cards for my psychology courses, which I would no longer need, there were three cards for Bible courses that I ended up needing and keeping. I was mildly amused by the coincidence and scarcely mentioned it to anyone. In fact, I don't ever remember telling anyone about it, until the day in the Lee student center when I met and had my very first conversation with Jean Hamilton, the woman who would become my wife. A little story about how I had arrived at my major would only later disclose not just one but two of the major moments of my life.

I worked my way through to graduation from Lee, with mind and heart expanded but not graduated, I must confess, to any higher degree of integration. Like two different gears that didn't mesh, these separate parts of me kept on grinding forward. Sometimes I wonder: was my failure to recognize, much less overcome, the fragmented state of my life at this time simply reflecting something of the conflicted state of the denominational context that surrounded me, as it too was trying to find its way between its Pentecostal heart and its increasingly educated mind? All I know is that after leaving Lee, Vanderbilt University was waiting for me, ready to offer *its* perspective on how this conflict could once and for all be resolved.

At Vanderbilt I entered into the rigors of the curriculum in biblical historical criticism, first for my MA and then for my PhD in Old Testament Studies. I was now a long way from 'home', although, ironically, I had chosen to pursue my graduate studies at Vanderbilt primarily because it was in Nashville, where my parents would be regularly driving through from Michigan on their continuing trips to west Tennessee. Something in me was still reaching to keep these worlds on the same map, even though at Vanderbilt they began to grow worlds apart. This was well illustrated in an incident that I narrated in a previously published part of my story, which went like this:

> I was secretly embarrassed about the uncredentialed heritage and humble status of my uneducated Pentecostal elders. Notwithstanding the fiery 'mountain top' experiences to which my elders bore witness, and perhaps more and more *because* of them, it was a past I wanted to forget and one which I was desperately trying to 'rise above'. As far as fear, I was afraid of scholars and smart people. I was constantly intimidated by them and in awe of them, never realizing at the time that this was the fear of which worship is made. I had a chance to recognize the power with which both of these passions were acting upon me one day when a friend and fellow graduate student, a Lutheran who had turned down an offer to study at Yale, asked me what church I attended. My face flushed with shame as he identified my denomination as Pentecostal and even asked me about speaking in tongues. I was so afraid of my friend's 'educated' opinion of me that I could do little more than stammer and grope for an awkward escape from the encounter. I shook off the potential self-revelation of this moment and went right back to my study carrel that day, suffering no loss of faith in my critical access to how the ancient authors came to compose the biblical writings, even though I was completely out of touch with the decisive factors at work behind *my* scholarly writing, right there in front of my nose.[2]

I remember another incident that also happened during my Vanderbilt days that witnesses to another facet of that same self-revelation. It goes like this: my father and mother, while on one of their trips to west Tennessee, came to visit me and my wife in our apartment in Nashville. I remember sitting with my father and mother and trying to talk with them. My mind was occupied with all my graduate assignments and research, which always, *always* during those years, seemed like a mountain that I secretly doubted I would ever be able to climb. Looking back on this now, I can still feel the

---

[2] R.D. Moore, 'Deuteronomy and the Fire of God', *Journal of Pentecostal Theology* 7 (October 1995), pp. 20-21. This article has now been published as Chapter 3 in my *Spirit of the Old Testament*.

profound loneliness into which this doubt plunged me. So there I was sitting with my parents, who were just wanting to be with their son, and it was as if I were a million miles away. There I was, enrolled in one of the top graduate programs in the land studying the Bible, the Scriptures on which they had raised me. Yet I couldn't think of anything to say to them. For me it was like killing time, knowing they would soon leave and I could get back to my studies, to my mountain of books, to all those zillions of words that ironically left me with no words to communicate with my own parents. They asked me the simple question, 'How's school going?' I remember saying to them after a halting pause, 'Well, it's hard'. And then I remember fighting back tears with no idea of where they were coming from. Vanderbilt was teaching me how to interpret texts, but the skills for how to interpret myself were not part of the curriculum.

My completed masters degree, together with my PhD candidacy from Vanderbilt, was validation (on the human level) that I was ready to teach. The Church of God School of Theology, young as it was at that time, was ready to have me as a teacher. The school did not yet have any faculty member with an Old Testament degree, and I was the only Church of God person in sight with these credentials. So I was signed on as a teacher, although in my early years at the Church of God School of Theology, I was, in truth, more of student. I have already presented elsewhere my testimony concerning these years and the second phase of graduate training that they represented for me. I was surrounded by a team of colleagues and scholars who already had started to envision and to chart the way forward for a thoroughgoing integration of Pentecostal faith and academic study. They invited me into this dynamic, constructive theological conversation and schooled me in the possibilities they were seeing and inviting me to see for myself in relation to my own specialization in Old Testament studies. It was like a new language I had long wanted, without knowing it, to speak. A tongue that could articulate the profound truths found in the deep wells of the Pentecostal spirituality that had been bequeathed to me by my parents, translating these truths into terms that fully engaged the categories of higher academic learning across the spectrum.

This was a radical turn in my academic journey, indeed literally *radical* (meaning back to the *radix* [Lat.] or *root*). It was no less radical than a turning of my heart back to the Pentecostal root and heritage of my elders and a turning of my mind[3] to the deep, untapped wisdom in their wells. I was part of an excavation project that was happening in this Cleveland school, where a new community and new generation of Pentecostals were re-digging the wells that their mothers and fathers had dug.

If I could interrupt my story for a moment, I would offer a little sidebar for those who might be getting a bit nervous at this point, those who have a Pentecostal background, over which they are much more vexed and with which they feel much more disaffection than affection. They might be able to manage some appreciation for their Pentecostal background as a *back*ground, but not a *fore*ground. They might have trouble seeing what I am describing here as anything other than a regressive step backward, a mere reactionary retreat back to some conservative, romanticized, pre-critical embrace of Pentecostalism, a move that ignores or forgets or denies all of *the sins of our fathers,* including the anti-intellectualism, sensationalism, materialism, racism (especially in its most virulent southern forms), sub-ordination of women and much more. To you I would want to say, with all the conviction that is within me, however bad you think all of this was, I believe it was much worse, and not just *was,* for it's not as if all of this is just in the past.

Yet I also believe that the push away from our past on those grounds can cause us to lose more than the bitter root of our fathers' sins. It can cause us to lose also the *tap*root of our identity from God, who is the One most aware of the lines of shame amid which our spiritual lineage is always to be found. This is the God who commands his people in his top-ten list, 'Honor your father and your mother', while embedding this command forever in a story of how the fathers and mothers acted *dis*honorably to the point of total failure in the wilderness. I have come to believe that the children themselves will ever be lost and will not find a way out of the wilderness of that lost-ness apart from finding a way to honor their father and their mother.

Thus, my story of becoming a Pentecostal scholar has everything to do with a radical turn, like the prodigal son, back to my father (and my mother). I could tell (or perhaps more accurately, *mis*-tell)

---

[3] I learned that *heart* and *mind* are the same word (*lev*) in Hebrew.

my story in a way that merely follows the progression of my re-sume: moving from my humble, pre-critical Pentecostal back-ground toward ever-expanding educational sophistication and criti-cal enlightenment. But such a story of the expansion of my mind would hide the very heart of my story and the story of my heart. The latter is a very different kind of story that hinges on a *post-critical* turn, where all of my investment and faith in academic scholarship and higher criticism got radically criticized by the *highest* (indeed the *ultimate*) *critic*. It's a story I can now tell only because God got me told.

So in this light, my story continues. That first year I taught at the Church of God School of Theology was, as I indicated earlier, a time of integrating my Pentecostal faith with my academic work, but not just at the level of scholarly discussion and critical study. It was much more critical than that. It included a searching, *self-critical* process of prayer and spiritual confession – a process that led me to the admission that I had a glaring need, and there was only one way adequate to describe it: *I needed to be filled with the Holy Spirit*. That's not an easy admission for an academic, especially one who is al-ready on the teaching staff of a Pentecostal school. But I learned something critical about confession at that time. The main thing that keeps us from being healed is that we can't confess that we're sick; the main thing that keeps us from being whole is that we can't confess that we're broken; and the main thing that keeps us from being filled is that we can't admit that we are empty. And I was empty. But I reached the point through that process with the Holy Spirit of wanting more than anything else to be full, to be a *full* pro-fessor.

I could have put it in other terms than *'I need to be filled with the Holy Spirit'*, but those were the terms that somehow seemed re-quired of me by the Holy Spirit, the terms I had learned from my father and mother, terms that at once terminated my long quest to have life on and through *my* terms, but that now somehow prom-ised life beyond my terms, life far better than all the terms and word-skills that I had compiled through all my academic study.

I remember confessing to my wife as we were taking a walk one afternoon down the street from our home. I said, 'Jean, there's something I have come to realize before God. I need to filled with the Holy Spirit'. She was pregnant at that time with our first child, and in that moment of confession, it was as if I became pregnant as well, strangely filled with an expectancy that it was now only a matter of time. I would be filled with the Spirit, *the promise of the Father.*

Later that summer my parents arranged a trip to west Tennessee, and it happened to be the same weekend that my wife's twin sister and her husband were traveling to the same town in west Tennessee, because my brother-in-law had been invited to preach that weekend at the Piney Grove Church of God in McNairy County. So I hitched a ride over with them to see my parents. They drove me to where my parents were staying and dropped me off. And then my parents and I decided to take a drive out through the country, visiting some of the places they had known from their childhood. Those kind of drives would invariably wind up taking us to the little country church, the Center Ridge Pentecostal Church, that had been planted and pastored by my late grandfather, Ernest P. Moore. Right beside the church building was the old cemetery where my grandfather and grandmother, Suvella, had been buried. We parked and walked to their graves and stood before their matching tombstones, each of which carried the inscription of the words of the Apostle Paul, 'I have kept the faith'.

As I stood there with my father and my mother, I knew that it was time to confess some things to them, related to all that had been going on in my life in the previous several months. I told my parents that, if I were to die right then, it would not be right to have that inscription on *my* tombstone, for I could not truly say at that moment, 'I have kept the faith', but this is what I could say, 'the faith has kept me'. I went on to confess that I had been ashamed of the faith of my grandparents, of them, of my own Pentecostal heritage with all of its humble, un-credentialed simplicity. I was then able to tell them that in recent days I had come to the discovery that this had been tantamount to being ashamed of the God who is not ashamed of any of these, the God, I would here add, who indeed chooses the weak and foolish things of this world to overrule the powerful and confound the wise.

I then directed this question to my father: 'Dad, were you ever afraid when I was at Vanderbilt that I would forsake the faith?' With a solemnity that still grips me, my father said, 'Son, I put that in God's hands'. Later my father's words connected with what I heard Peter Kuzmič say at a Society for Pentecostal Studies meeting in the early 1990's about his own father who was a humble minister in the underground Pentecostal church in the former Yugoslavia when Peter, as a brilliant young student, was being promoted and swayed by the Communist leaders to join their cause. He said that, when it came to all of his intellectual questions, his father was not academically competent, but he was spiritually competent. In the case of the most pivotal struggle of my life, my father and my mother were spiritually competent.

After that time, what I now consider sacred time, with my parents in that cemetery in front of the graves of my grandparents in the golden light of the setting sun, we drove to the Piney Grove Church of God where my brother-in-law was scheduled to preach that evening. I had never been to this church, because our family, understandably, had always gone to my grandparents' church on our visits. But here I was, going to the Piney Grove Church of God for the first time in my life, when my father thought to tell me that this church as well had been planted by my grandfather from a brush-arbor revival meeting that he had conducted. As I sat in the church service beside my mother and father, in the church that my grandfather had planted long before I was born, I suddenly realized, like someone who had figured out that a surprise birthday party had been planned for him, that this was the night and this was the place that God had chosen to fill me with the Holy Spirit.

When my brother-in-law finished his message, I could scarcely wait to go down to the altar. I stood at the altar for only a moment, then my brother-in-law came and stood before me, and the gentlest voice I ever heard said, 'Just ask me'. And I remember saying, 'Lord, would you please fill me with ...' That was as far as I got. What happened next was an experience that's too much for my words. It would take something in tongues unknown to express it. It did for me that night. I've never gotten over it. That night, in one accord with my parents, my mind, my Vanderbilt-educated mind, was blown away and back again. And it is simply and utterly the truth, as I look back on my life from this vantage point, that this is the heart of the testimony that I have been asked on this occasion to give – the defining moment of my call to be a Pentecostal scholar.

I would finally just want to say that I am deeply honored by this invitation to offer another piece of my story, which gives me the opportunity, as I expressed at the outset, to honor my parents, to bless the generation of my children, and to glorify the One who called me and is calling me still to this very day.

5

THIS PLACE IS TOO SMALL: JOURNEYS INTO UNCHARTED SPACE

CHERYL BRIDGES JOHNS*

This autobiographical reflection is an exercise in remembrance, but more than that, it serves as a testimony of the faith of others. I live and work as a Pentecostal scholar because there were those brave souls who first journeyed into the uncharted territory of Spirit-filled scholarship, paving the way for others to follow. These elders would often say to me that they sensed God's hand upon my life. They were willing to walk with me. Moreover, they were willing to send me into a place that they themselves could not go.

Living out one's calling – staying under the hand of God – is a journey filled with many twists and turns in the road. For me, that journey has often meant defying the barriers or the small places found within the Pentecostal movement. Many times I have uttered the words 'this place is too small', and, venturing into roads less traveled, I have discovered the unexplored lands to be the most sacred of all spaces. Hopefully, I, like those before me, can leave a large space for others.

---

* Cheryl Bridges Johns (PhD, Southern Baptist Theological Seminary) is Professor of Discipleship and Christian Formation at the Pentecostal Theological Seminary in Cleveland, TN, USA.

Breaking Out of the Small Space: The Legacy of Sarah McNeely

In 1907 my great grandmother, Sarah (Sally) McNeely, traveled from the upstate area of South Carolina to visit relatives in Georgia. While there she attended a camp meeting where she was baptized in the Holy Spirit. Returning home to family and to her local Methodist congregation, Sally was not reluctant to share this new-found 'third blessing'. It seemed however, that the local Methodist church would not contain her shouting and speaking in tongues, and it was not long before they asked her to leave. Breaking away from this restrictive space, Sally hosted prayer meetings in her home, and before long others joined her in receiving the baptism of the Holy Spirit.

In 1911, Sally's husband, John George Washington McNeely donated land for a church to be built. It was in this place that a congregation was organized, and Rev. Paul F. Beacham, who followed N.J. Homes as President of Holmes Bible College, served as the congregation's first 'official' pastor.

In was in this church, the 'McNeely Memorial Pentecostal Holiness Church', that I was reared and was nurtured in the Pentecostal faith. Like a sacred icon, Sarah McNeely's portrait hung in the vestibule of our country church. It was given a prominent place right over the doors leading into the sanctuary. I would often look up at her portrait and wonder about her life. Part of me wished to have known her and the other part was glad I did not. She seemed formidable, strong, and serious. No smile parted her lips. However, I can truthfully say that my great grandmother provided a much-needed sacred feminine image. I received her messages loud and clear: Women were pioneers. Women did not remain in closed space. Women of God leave restricted areas and pave new roads. Just look at Sarah McNeely, who after being filled with the Holy Ghost, had the strength and courage to raise eleven children, help manage a farm, host prayer meetings and plant a church. Sally McNeely was a tough image to follow.

The Nurturing Space of the Local Church

Around 1954 the McNeely Pentecostal Holiness church suffered a bitter split leaving five members in the original church, two of the five being my parents. My mother called her brother, Rev. Simpson Merritt, and asked him to come and help restore the church. At that time my uncle was in California helping the Pentecostal Holiness Church organize Sharon Bible College. After prayer, he felt led by the Holy Spirit to return home. He served as pastor of the church until 1965, helping it to grow numerically and leading the people in a building project. Simpson Merritt was a graduate of Holmes Bible College and Wofford College and was ABD at the University of South Carolina. He modeled a Spirit filled ministry that valued education.

While a student at Holmes, my uncle traveled to Oklahoma where he joined with a young man by the name of Oral Roberts in conducting evangelistic services throughout the state. My uncle told us that he had to write Oral's first sermon for him. Of course, in the 'official' biography Roberts' noted that my uncle was a great encouragement for this first sermon!

My family had respect for and commitment to the ministry of Oral Roberts. They were proud that my uncle helped him in the early days of his ministry. And, in the family lore my birth is related to an 'Oral Roberts miracle'. My mother had been told she would never have children, but in desperation she prayed and sent for an Oral Roberts 'healing cloth'. In the folder that contains my birth certificate there is a faded small prayer cloth stamped with the words: 'Healing Waters Blest Cloth – Acts 19:12 – Apply After Prayer'.

When Roberts' decided to leave the Pentecostal Holiness Church for his 'Methodist roots', there was no small discussion in our extended family. Questions abounded, but no one dared to say that Roberts was entirely in the wrong. They left him to the grace of God, but looking back I believe they felt somewhat betrayed and abandoned.

The McNeely Memorial Pentecostal Holiness Church was a safe and sacred space. It was a good place for my early spiritual development. Whenever I walked through the doors I knew that I had entered a place where I belonged. It was here that my early sense of calling into ministry took shape. Being told 'the hand of God is on your life', carried with it the assumption that you would serve in the ministries of the church. I played saxophone in the church orchestra, played the piano, taught Sunday School, and at the age of sixteen, preached my first sermon.

When I was twelve, my uncle Simpson left the McNeely Church. He worked as a high school guidance counselor and school principal, so he asked to be appointed to smaller, struggling churches. Often I would spend the weekends in his company and he would take me with him on visitation, door to door witnessing, and other such pastoral duties. Sometimes he would ask me to speak on the Sunday night service. There were never more than a handful of people present, but these times served as 'apprenticeship in ministry' for me. Apprenticeship is something I find missing in today's discipleship.

The Enlarging Space of Higher Education

When I graduated from high school I was torn between attending Holmes Bible College and Emmanuel College. I never even considered other options. Holmes seemed way too restrictive, so in the fall of 1973 I enrolled at Emmanuel College in Franklin Springs, Georgia. My two years at Emmanuel (it was a junior college at the time) were transformative in many ways. I am especially grateful for the professors who invested in my academic and spiritual development. In particular, Vinson Synan had a great impact on me. He was my professor for American History and guitar. (I performed miserably as a guitar student.) Synan provided my first Pentecostal ecumenical model. I was fascinated by his 'first contact' with the rising Catholic Charismatic movement and was enthralled by his stories of the large gathering of Charismatics where thousands were being filled with the Holy Spirit.

One of the most transformative experiences of my life took place between my freshman and sophomore years of college. I was part of team of young people ministering in Chile and Argentina. This trip was my first cross-cultural exposure, and it was life changing. In 1972 Chile had recently elected the socialist Salvador Allende as President. Visiting the Jotebeche Methodist Church in Santiago, one of the world's first true mega churches, I encountered Spirit-filled Christians who not only drank wine but were supporters of their socialist president. Such things created a great deal of dissonance for a nineteen year old from rural South Carolina! These good people even took us on a 'field trip' to President Allende's office. (I have a picture of me sitting in his chair!)[121]

It was in Chile where I first struggled with encountering 'the other'. Analyzing this experience in terms of James Fowler's faith development paradigm, one could say that Chile offered me opportunity to move from the comforts of stage three faith, which is faith that is held within the arms of the assumed 'we', to a more individuative-reflective stage four. Transition from stage three to stage four is often quite painful, but it offers the grand opportunity of defining the self apart from one's family and community of origin. It forces a person to systemize and reflect upon her own beliefs, and it helps one form an ideology that goes beyond the narrative of the community.

The experiences in Chile and Argentina birthed in me a love for Latin America. Moreover, the seeds for later discussions on the issues of justice, liberation, and equality were planted in my heart. In 1972 there were few Pentecostals who were taking on these issues. However, those seeds planted in my heart that summer would later be watered and flourish in my own academic and spiritual journey.

I returned from Latin America with a sense that one day I would live there as a missionary. While in Argentina I spent time with June Carter, a long-term missionary. She became my new role model. After graduating from Emmanuel, I sought appointment as a short-term missionary for the Pentecostal Holiness Church and was informed that after college I would be sent to Costa Rica. Lee College and a double major in Spanish and Christian Education became the path I chose toward this missionary work.

It took me a while to adjust to the Church of God ethos, but I found Lee to be a place of continuing growth and development. Professors like John Sims (who would later serve on my dissertation committee) stretched me toward dialoguing with the larger Chris-

---

[121] After the CIA backed assassination of Allende, Chile was ruled by the military dictator Augusto Pinochet, the leadership of the Jobeteche Church shifted their support to Pinochet, and in doing so, lost credibility in Chile's long struggle for justice. For an insightful analysis of this period of the church's history see Edward L. Cleary, *The Struggle for Human Rights in Latin America* (Westport, CT: Praeger Publishers, 1997).

tian tradition. His seminar in Contemporary Theology brought me into contact with the writings of theologians such as Paul Tillich, H. Richard and Reinhold Niebuhr, Teilhard de Chardin, and Harvey Cox. This course served as a helpful base for graduate work.

Meeting my future husband, Jackie, helped change the plans to be a career missionary. His not so humorous assessment, that I did not 'have what it takes to be single missionary' proved to be true! Jackie and I met while students in a philosophy course, and I found him to be the most engaging dialogue partner. We would argue for hours over educational philosophy. Thirty-seven years later we continue the conversations and lively debates. Most importantly, we share a common passion for the kingdom.

I realize that there are marriages that work well in which one spouse is a scholar and the other spouse has another vocation, but I cannot imagine life without extended theological conversations, debates, and joint writing projects. Jackie is a mentor, friend, companion, and his life as a scholar-pastor serves as an ongoing example of servant leadership. His analytical skills and his ability to carefully nuance the details of doctrine, polity, systems, etc. help to balance my more global, large picture worldview. And, I like to think that at times I can pull him out of the details. We are a ministry partnership, scholarly soul mates, and co-adventurers.

Shortly before graduating from Lee, Jackie and I sensed that God was calling us toward more education. And, specifically, we both felt led toward Wheaton Graduate School. In those days there were not many places where Pentecostals were welcomed. Asbury Seminary made Pentecostal students sign a written statement that while attending Asbury they would not speak in tongues. Many Evangelical schools would not even admit Pentecostals.

When we were interviewing for Wheaton, Jackie and I met with the New Testament scholar Merrill C. Tenney. On the occasion of our interview Tenney told us to 'come to Wheaton not for what you will learn but for how you will learn'. Those words were a significant foreshadowing of a life-long quest to unify method and content. In January 1975 we enrolled at Wheaton. We were there during what Jackie and I call 'the classical years'. At this time Wheaton was a centrist institution (as opposed to Dallas Seminary or Moody Bible Institute). During this period Pentecostals, Mennonites and others who were 'mainstream' Evangelical found Wheaton to be a warm and gracious institution.

Tenney's words regarding our attending Wheaton for the 'how' as well as the 'what' proved to be prophetic. His classes were taught with a unique combination of the Socratic and inductive approaches. Trained in classical Greek, Tenney embodied the ideal of the teacher as one who 'leads out' the learner toward truth. (As opposed to the teacher filling the heads of the students with pre-packaged knowledge). Tenney's inductive approach forced students to dig into texts to discover truth for themselves.

Moreover, Jackie and I took a class on inductive Bible study and learned the approach developed by Wilbert White. We have never been the same and we both share a passion for helping others to learn how to study Scripture inductively.[122]

The inductive spirit permeated Wheaton's entire program in Christian Leadership. The LeBar sisters (Mary and Lois) were significant in helping us discover a biblical approach to teaching. They mentored Jackie and me into a model of Christian discipleship that sought to be biblically and theologically grounded. Our time with the LeBars, Tenney, Earl Cairns, Wilbert Norton helped Jackie and me sort through our Pentecostal identity in the midst of an Evangelical ethos.

There are life-changing classes, life-changing professors and then there is the category of life changing books. I will never forget the day when Jackie came home with a new book, *All We're Meant to Be*.[123] The authors, Letha Scanzoni and Nancy Hardesty were two of the first Evangelicals to tackle the issue of feminism. Reading their book, I found my spirit resonating with the authors. They provided a biblical framework for what had already been incipient in my journey as a Pentecostal. I had never questioned the status of women as equal to men, and I had grown up in a church where I was affirmed as a minister. However, by now I had learned the hard truth that my vocation and calling was not going to be affirmed by everyone, not even those within my own tradition.

---

[122] My first book, *Finding Eternal Treasures* (Cleveland, TN: Pathway Press, 1985), and my forthcoming book, *Encountering the Living Word: Bible Study for a New Generation* (Cleveland, TN: Pathway Press), are examples of my passion for leading others to discover inductive Bible study.

[123] Letha Dawson Scanzoni and Nancy Hardesty, *All We're Meant to Be: A Biblical Approach to Women's Liberation* (Nashville: Word Books, 1975).

In 1975 I joined the Church of God, and at the time, it seemed the best thing to do. My husband was a minister in this denomination. However, looking back, I do not think I realized how the paradoxical treatment of women in the Church of God would affect me. On the one hand, the Church of God has given me free space to grow and develop as a minister and as a scholar. On the other hand, I soon discovered this denomination to be one of the most restrictive of all Pentecostal denominations in regards to women. In 1975 I did not realize the battles that were ahead and how these battles would wound my soul. In spite of these wounds, the hand of God presses me toward covenant in the Church of God.

The Wide Open Spaces of North Dakota

After graduation from Wheaton, Jackie was offered a teaching contract at Northwest Bible College in Minot, North Dakota. I taught part-time that first fall semester, but was later hired to teach full time. The three years that Jackie and I were at Northwest proved to be a time of stretching academically and professionally. They were good years. It seemed that if the Dean saw a course on our transcript we would be assigned to teach it the next semester. I taught Old Testament Introduction, New Testament Introduction, Psychology, many of the Christian Education courses, and piano. Jackie taught twenty-one different courses in the three years we were at Northwest!

Besides teaching, Jackie served as pastor in two different churches (at the same time): the Butte Assembly of God and the Kief Baptist Church. These churches were some of the last vestiges of life remaining in towns that were dying. We found the people to be warm and gracious and hard working. They were the second and third generation German and Russian immigrants. At the small Baptist church I was amazed that there was no indoor plumbing and that every Sunday there would be a hymn in Russian.

It was while we were in Minot that our first daughter, Alethea, was born. This daughter, whose name literally means 'truth', has filled our lives with great joy. I found teaching and parenting to be a stretch, but, as many women know, the academic calendar makes it easier to fulfill both roles.

The Year of Imploding Space

As 1979 drew to a close Jackie and I made plans to leave North Dakota and return to school. We both felt lead to complete MDiv studies at the Church of God School of Theology. Leaving North Dakota would not be easy, but we were excited to begin classes with scholars such as Hollis Gause and French Arrington.

One moment one sentence spoken by someone caused me to veer off this path. We were at camp meeting when a woman asked me about our future plans. I responded that Jackie and I would be returning to school. The woman's response was, 'really, *both* of you? So what are you going to live on, love'? Those words burned into me. And I began to doubt my decision. Perhaps I should reconsider the move toward more schooling and do 'the right thing': 'the right thing' was that I should work and put my husband through seminary. I shared this idea with Jackie who strongly objected. His words that God had provided for us while we were students at Wheaton seemed to have no effect on my determination to find a job instead of going to school.

When we moved to Cleveland, TN the housing market collapsed and our house in North Dakota did not sell as we had expected. Moreover, other than teaching part time at Lee College, I did not find a job. The weeks stretched into months and still the house did not sell and I had no job. I remember applying everywhere, including at convenience stores and factories. One day, after a particularly disappointing interview, I sat in my car and cried. And then I clearly heard God speak to my heart, 'You will not get a job here or anywhere because you are out of my will'. There, in my car, I repented for my sins of disobedience. I knew that God had called me to further my education, and I made a commitment to follow this path. Staying under the hand of God would mean that I would journey out of 'traditional' and 'expected' territory. And I had learned my lesson. It is much better to be 'out there and all alone' than confined within a space that God has not ordained for you.

Jackie and I applied to do doctoral work at Southern Baptist Theological Seminary. The day we registered for classes we also closed on our house in North Dakota. We had funds available for furthering our education. Moreover, I had peace and assurance that I was once again in God's will.

The experience of the 'black hole year' in Cleveland, TN made me aware of how easy it is for someone to be convinced that they are doing the right thing and this 'right thing' be the very 'wrong thing'. What truly matters is the fear of the Lord. Lessons learned that year were valuable for the lean years ahead in a rigorous PhD program. Knowing that you are in God's will provides strength for difficult times. For women in particular, this is an important lesson. Women are more often given culturally scripted roles and expected to fulfill them without question. Breaking out of those roles takes a deep knowledge that you have heard the voice of God.

I had no role models for the path I was taking. Women in higher theological education were few, and in 1982 they were almost non-existent within the Pentecostal movement. There was no one who could offer me a mirror of myself as a scholar, professor, and minister. And, from the awful 'black hole' year in Cleveland, I learned the painful lesson that it is often the voice of women that can be the most critical of other women.

The Time of Testing the Boundaries and Re-drawing the Lines

At Southern Seminary Jackie and I found ourselves in a situation not unlike the one at Wheaton in which there were professors, well known in their areas, who were at the edge of retirement. We were drawn to Findley Edge whose book *The Greening of the Church*[124] addressed the need for spiritual renewal and deep, justice-filled discipleship. Our seminars provided engaging dialogue and intellectual stimulation.

We had to choose a 'major' for the PhD in Christian Education. Jackie chose to focus on the early church. His seminars with Glen Hinson, Alan Culpepper, and Timothy George helped him look closely at the ante Nicene church's process of discipleship.

For my focus area I was torn between two interests: liberation studies and developmental studies. On the one hand, liberation studies, in particular liberation pedagogy, offered a unique convergence of my earlier interest in Latin America with the issues of justice, education, and full humanization. Discovering Paulo Freire's

---

[124] Findley B. Edge, *The Greening of the Church* (Nashville: Word Books, 1972).

Pedagogy of the Oppressed[125] was not unlike the experience I had with reading *All We're Meant to Be*. I devoured the works of other writers in liberation theology such as Letty Russell,[126] James Cone,[127] and Gustavo Gutierrez.[128]

On the other hand, developmental studies, in particular the work of James Fowler in faith development, offered a powerful lens through which the human being could be understood. With these choices in mind I enrolled for summer session at Boston College's Institute for Pastoral Ministry. I signed up for a class team-taught by Paulo Freire and Thomas Groome, and also a course in Developmental Studies offered by Sharon Parks, a colleague of Lawrence Kohlberg at Harvard.

The class with Freire attracted a wide assortment of students. I found myself in a strange mix of socialists, nuns who worked with the poor, and an assortment of activists. I was the only Pentecostal in the mix. One day I worked up my courage to speak with Freire after class. 'Paulo, I am a Pentecostal who is interested in your work', I said. 'A Pentecostal! You don't make history!' came the pointed response. 'Have you read *"Haven of the Masses*[129]*"*?' he asked. 'Yes', I replied. 'Have you read *Vision of the Disinherited*'?[130] 'Yes'. By this time he was all worked up about Pentecostals being 'death loving' and 'a-historical'. I let him rant, but before I walked away, I muttered the words, 'You are wrong'.

Leaving class that day I was devastated. Why was I here? Did no one understand my tradition? Did I understand my own tradition? However, walking out of the building I had a *kairos* moment in which I heard the Lord speak deeply into my heart these words: 'You are here for a purpose that you will understand later'. The 'later' understanding did come and it served as an impetus for my dissertation and the work that would come out of that research.[131]

---

[125] Paulo Freire, *Pedagogy of the Oppressed* (New York: Herder & Herder, 1970).

[126] Letty Russell, *Human Liberation in a Feminist Perspective-A Theology* (Philadelphia: Westminster Press, 1974).

[127] James Cone, *God of the Oppressed* (New York: Seabury Press, 1975).

[128] Gustavo Gutiérrez, *A Theology of Liberation* (Maryknoll, NY: Orbis, 1973).

[129] Christian Lalive d'Epinay, *Haven of the Masses* (Cambridge: Lutterworth: 1969).

[130] Robert Mapes Anderson, *Vision of the Disinherited* (Oxford: Oxford University Press, 1979).

[131] One of the most rewarding parts of my journey has been my friendship with the late Richard Shaull. Shaull was one of the grandfathers of liberation the-

My dissertation, 'Affective Conscientization; A Pentecostal Response to Paulo Freire',[132] was an opportunity to dialogue with Freire's work and with the work of liberation theologians. My thesis, namely that within Pentecostal spirituality there was an inherently liberating and humanizing element, went against the standard social deprivation material that was common decades ago. My criticism of the liberationists such as Freire was that while they advocated for the cause of the poor, they often despised the religion of the poor. Furthermore, I found the Marxist rejection of Hegel's *Geist* in favor of human praxis missing something beyond the human capacity to know the world. Praxis, human reflection, and action cannot in themselves liberate.

Conversely, I found the escapism exhibited in much of Pentecostal life to be equally troubling. Pentecostalism's ill-suited marriage with Dispensationalism and Fundamentalism had created offspring that had forgotten the primal memory of the conscientization of the Holy Spirit that enabled believers to read the world through the critical lens of the Spirit. Moreover, Pentecostals in North America had lost the vision of the Holy Spirit as a humanizing agent toward full empowerment of all people.

Writing my dissertation was, once again, an exercise of going where few people had gone. My advisor would often tell me, 'I sure hope you know what you are doing because I have no idea'. I am grateful for a dissertation committee that allowed for critical and creative constructive engagement with the Pentecostal tradition. Add to that the cross-referencing with liberationist theologians, it is amazing that I was allowed to complete the work. To be truthful, toward the end, I was not certain if the dissertation would be approved. My committee gave me what was in effect, an illegal defense, and in doing so, they put their jobs on the line. By 1987 the

---

ology and it was he who introduced the writings of Paulo Freire to the English speaking world. In the late 1990's Shaull contacted me asking for a copy of my book. He had stumbled across it on a reserve list in the library at Princeton Seminary. In the latter years of his life Shaull became fascinated with Latin American Pentecostalism. His affirmation of my critique of Freire and my assessment of Pentecostalism as transformative helped heal some of the wounds from my encounter with Freire. See Richard Shaull and Waldo Cesar, *Pentecostalism and the Future of the Christian Churches* (Grand Rapids: Eerdmans, 2000).

132 Cheryl Bridges Johns, *Pentecostal Formation: A Pedagogy Among the Oppressed* (JPTSup, 2; Sheffield: Sheffield Academic Press, 1993); reprinted by Wipf and Stock, 2010.

winds of change in the Southern Baptist Convention were beginning to blow quite strongly. The conservative coup that took over Southern Baptist Seminary was just beginning to show strength. My dissertation became caught in those first winds.

The Southern Baptist Seminary that exists today is not the same school as the one I attended. It is not a place of academic freedom where women and Pentecostals are welcomed and where students can freely dialogue with liberation theology as well as Pentecostal theology. I am grateful I was able to finish my course before the Fundamentalists purged the seminary of its academic freedom.

The Gathering of Scholars at the Church of God School of Theology

In 1984, after finishing our course work and completing Comprehensive exams Jackie was hired as Minister of Education at the Westmore Church of God in Cleveland, Tennessee. We moved to a place that I had vowed to never return. I was back to teaching part-time at Lee. Only this time I was working on a dissertation and in a much better place than when we lived in Cleveland during the 'black hole year'.

Our younger daughter, Karisa was born mid-way through my writing my dissertation. She has lived up to her name by bringing much grace to our lives. Finishing a dissertation while nursing a baby is quite a feat. Whenever I hear a male complain about his dissertation travails, I am tempted to go into the details of feeding schedules, sleepless nights, diapers, and research and writing and deadlines.

I also began teaching part-time at the Church of God School of Theology, and in 1986 was offered a full-time contract. During these years several of us 'young' scholars found ourselves called to this place. I truly believe that it was a 'gathering' brought on by the hand of God. Steven Land, Rickie Moore and Chris Thomas were already there when I arrived. And, the senior faculty, in particular, Hollis Gause, French Arrington, Robert Crick, and James Beaty, did a great job of integrating the younger faculty into their fledging community of learning.

All of us, both young and older, shared a common vision of theological education within a community of faith model.[133] This model understands theological education to be an extension of the church. In other words, while the theological school is not a church, it is an extension of the church's mission of discipleship and formation. As a community of faith the theological school should have all the marks of church: worship, fellowship, witness, and discipleship.

The Church of God School of Theology, now the Pentecostal Theological Seminary (PTS), has modeled a unique gestalt of 'Athens', with its emphasis on enculturating, 'Berlin', with its emphasis on critical reasoning skills, and 'Azusa', with its radical egalitarian, and Spirit-filled epistemology.[134] I know of no other place with this unique blending of traditional education within the framework of a pneumatological community.

Moreover, I have found PTS to be a place where the issues of global Pentecostalism can be discussed. In our early years the percentage of students from the majority world was quite high (twenty percent). This environment provided opportunities to live out kingdom ethics. It has been a place where descriptions of the pain and terror of apartheid found their way into our classes. It seemed that God would arrange things so that students from each of the racial divisions of South Africa would be sitting together in one class. Or that we would have three Palestinian students during the era of the Gulf War. And, of course, we have welcomed women into our corporate life, offering them a place to grow, express their angst with the church and its restrictions on their ministry. In these areas, and in many more, I firmly believe that PTS has served as a prophetic community within the larger Church of God and the Pentecostal world in general.

---

[133] For description of this model of theological education see Cheryl Bridges Johns, 'To Know God Truly: The Community of Faith Model in Theological Education', in Paul M. Bassett, *The Aims and Purposes of Evangelical Theological Education* (Grand Rapids: Eerdmans, forthcoming); see also Robert Banks' description and commentary on my ideas for theological education in his *Revisioning Theological Education: Exploring A Missional Alternative to Current Models* (Grand Rapids: Eerdmans, 1999), pp. 77-78.

[134] See Cheryl Bridges Johns, 'Athens, Berlin, Azusa: Reflections on Scholarship & the Christian Faith', *Pneuma* 27.1 (Spring 2005), pp. 136-47.

Perhaps the most significant grace given to gathering of scholars at the Pentecostal Theological Seminary has been our calling to re-discover the primal spirituality of Pentecostalism and to offer that spirituality for a new generation. We have understood, in the words of Steven Land, this primal spirituality not just to represent the beginning of a movement, but to reflect its heart.[135] It is this primal faith, with its radical inclusion, prophetic imagination, and peaceable vision of the kingdom to which we have been called. To be scholars of this radical tradition means that we draw deeply from those primal wells and speak creatively and clearly to contemporary theological issues. 'Pentecostal formation',[136] 'Pentecostal spirituality',[137] a 'Pentecostal worldview',[138] 'Pentecostal hermeneutics',[139] and Pentecostal readings of Scripture[140] were all part of what has come to be known as 'the Cleveland school'.[141]

The Cleveland School has produced creative scholars who are willing to engage the larger theological and biblical issues from a Pentecostal perspective. Our task, however, has been to speak from a confessional stance while at the same time acknowledging the limitations of a particular hermeneutic. Such work calls for a great deal of ecumenical humility. Otherwise, the confessional degenerates into dogma, and the creative scholars become the caretakers of ideology.

When humility is lost the confessional trumps the larger discourse. Sometimes I am fearful that this has already occurred. We have to be careful in our use of the modifying term 'Pentecostal'. It should never be a descriptor that takes precedence over the larger word of 'Christian'. Otherwise, we become Pentecostals who happen to be Christian rather than vise versa. I shall not continue to

---

[135] Steven J. Land, *Pentecostal Spirituality: A Passion for the Kingdom* (JPTSup, 1; Sheffield: Sheffield Academic Press, 1993).

[136] Cheryl Bridges Johns, *Pentecostal Formation: A Pedagogy Among the Oppressed*.

[137] Land, *Pentecostal Spirituality: A Passion for the Kingdom*.

[138] Jackie David Johns, 'Pentecostalism and the Postmodern Worldview', *Journal of Pentecostal Theology* 7 (1995), pp. 73-96.

[139] Kenneth J. Archer, *A Pentecostal Hermeneutic for the Twenty-first Century: Spirit, Scripture and Community* (JPTSup, 28; London: T&T Clark, 2004).

[140] Lee Roy Martin, *The Unheard Voice of God: A Pentecostal Hearing of the Book of Judges* (JPTSup, 32; Blandford Forum: Deo Publishing, 2008).

[141] See also Robby Waddell, *The Spirit of the Book of Revelation* (JPTSup, 30; Blandford Forum: Deo Publishing, 2006).

ramble on about these things. It is up to a new generation of scholars from the Cleveland School to make a way for the future.

Giving Witness in Wider Circles

One of the most surprising turns in my journey as a scholar has been the calling to represent the Pentecostal tradition within the larger Christian world. This vocation has been both extremely rewarding and demanding. It is rewarding because I have been immensely blessed with sacred encounters with the 'other'. It is demanding because this calling requires a careful dialectic of deep respect and appreciation for one's own tradition while reflecting respect and appreciation for the other's witness. In numerous venues I have been the 'first contact' for those outside of the Pentecostal realm. In these cases I am surprised at the lack of knowledge, the stereotypes and the fear many Christians have regarding Pentecostalism. First contact requires honesty, patience, and a special anointing of the Holy Ghost.

This ecumenical calling came somewhat out of the blue, and I am careful how I share the experience. Suffice it to say that this experience had all the marks of a Pentecostal encounter with God. It was transformative, scary, and left me face down on the floor. During this experience God clearly spoke to me through the text of John 17. The Lord allowed me to feel a small amount of his passion for the unity of his body. Such an experience was almost more than I could bear. Furthermore, the story of this experience is wrapped in the narrative of the untimely death of Jerry Sandidge, Assemblies of God theologian and early ecumenical witness. I have always had a clear sense that God placed upon me some of Jerry's burden and calling. However, I am grateful that I have not suffered the persecution and the misunderstanding that plagued Jerry's ministry and witness.

My ecumenical vocation has taken me many places: World Council of Churches, National Council of Churches, Roman Catholic–Pentecostal/Evangelical dialogues, lectures in mainline seminaries, Evangelical initiatives. There have been the surprising twists in the road such as my time as Chaplain/Preacher at the famous Chautauqua Institution. I followed Bishop John Shelby Spong, who was Preacher/Chaplain the previous week, and I have always believed that I was being set up as the counter (a.k.a. Fundamentalist, Pentecostalist). In 1993 the Culture Wars where just getting started, but I felt led to attempt to forge a 'third way' between the political right and left. It was hard, hard going and I believe many people were disappointed that I did not do my duty and take on Spong.

More recently, my ventures into Mennonite territory have been immensely enriching. Several years ago leaders from the Mennonite Church USA approached the Church of God (via Rick Waldrop) in order to pursue formal dialogue. This dialogue has produced much good fruit. I have been wonderfully received as guest lecturer at the Associated Mennonite Seminary and Eastern Mennonite Seminary. In both places I have found gracious hospitality and genuine dialogue.

Lecturing at mainline schools such as Duke Divinity (Jameson Jones Lectures in Preaching) and Columbia Theological Seminary (Smyth Lectures), has afforded opportunity to express the Pentecostal faith in a context that does not often engage our tradition. Through these experiences I have made enduring friendships and have been forced to learn how to express the Pentecostal faith in categories other than our own.

One of the greatest surprises of my journey has been my engagement in Evangelical initiatives. Being from the 'Cleveland School', the one that resists the label 'Evangelical', it has been easier not to engage Evangelical scholars or leaders. However, the Holy Spirit has not seen fit to allow me this prejudice. My work in 'Evangelicals and Catholics Together' (ECT) has been very difficult, but immensely rewarding. This group has been difficult to work with because of its conservative political agenda and the Reformed leanings among the Evangelicals. However, through the years I developed friendship with Chuck Colson, James Packer, Avery Dulles, and others. I believe that my presence has offered a different voice in an otherwise homogenous conversation.

My work with the group 'Scientists and Evangelicals Together for the Care of Creation' has been most rewarding. This group was birthed from the unique friendship between Eric Chivian, Director of Harvard's Center for Health and the Global Environment, and Richard Cizik of the National Association of Evangelicals. Their friendship stemmed from a joint passion for the environment and the care of creation. In 2006 they called a meeting of select scientists and Evangelical leaders for a three day retreat at the Melhana Plantation in Thomasville, Georgia. I was privileged to be part of this meeting. I think all of us – scientists and Evangelicals alike – arrived with concern that we would find nothing in common and that our meeting would degenerate into some sort of creation/evolution, God/science debate. But, nothing of the sort happened. We found that all of us, Christian and non-Christian, shared a deep love for the creation. We also came to a sharp awareness of the fragility of the world's global ecology. Moreover, I sensed a deep urgency, an almost palatable heaviness of spirit. It seemed that the Creator Spirit had called some of her children together in order to offer a plea for radical changes that would be necessary in order to save the planet from the tragedy of global climate change. From that meeting we issued the statement 'An Urgent Call to Action'. We released this statement at a press conference at the National Press Club in Washington, DC. Since that time this group has published material for pastors, held seminars on college campuses, and traveled to Alaska to witness firsthand the effects of global warming on the indigenous populations. My work in this group has afforded me opportunity to re-visit the whole meaning of a Pentecostal theology of creation. It seems to me that we, of all people, should develop a robust, pneumatological vision of creation care.

The Future: Conserving Space

Now that I am approaching the age of sixty I find it prudent to begin to focus on those things that matter most. Yet, even as I type this statement I realize how very hard it has been for me to focus on one or two things. I have, in the words of my loved ones, 'been all over the place'. Being all over the place has afforded a very fulfilling journey; however, perhaps it is now time to conserve space and energy. My current projects include helping a new generation discover the wonder of sacred Scripture. There is a whole generation of Christians (including Pentecostals) who are Scripturally innocent or biblically illiterate. The problem of biblical illiteracy calls for a whole new way of viewing the Bible. The issues go beyond hermeneutics into the ontological and metaphysical dimensions of the sacred text. If I can play a small role in re-capturing a love for the Bible this journey would not have been in vain.

6

BLESSED BEYOND MEASURE: AN AUTOBIOGRAPHICAL REFLECTION

FRANK D. MACCHIA[*]

When I descended the stairs of the baptismal tank of my father's Pentecostal church to be baptized, I was only eight years old. I had gone forward in response to altar calls during the previous several Sunday services. God was 'dealing with me' a number of people had said; God had a plan for me, a calling to serve one day in the ministry. Their intuitions were certainly not based on anything special in my demeanor or behavior. In fact, I was always getting into trouble or mischief (not that I necessarily broke the rules more than everyone else, but I always seemed to be the one who got caught). I think the spotlight was on me due mainly to the fact that I had a beautiful tenor voice in those years in which my mother and my Uncle Leo had trained me (my uncle had a wonderful voice which he would use on Wednesdays to sing, sometimes in Italian, while cooking for us all: me, my parents, and five siblings). I had become a favored soloist at church and for sectional youth meetings and other special occasions. I even sang for a local religious radio station. As I descended the stairs for baptism on that memorable evening, I was convinced that God was calling me to a singing ministry. I recall my father holding me firm as I stood shivering from nerves and the cool temperature of the water in the tank. Then

---

[*] Frank D. Macchia (DTheol, University of Basel) is Professor of Systematic Theology at Vanguard University in Costa Mesa, CA, USA.

came the question: 'Have you accepted Christ as your Savior and will you follow him to the best of your ability for the rest of your life?' I responded, 'I will'. He then prayed. I don't recall the prayer, only the fact his hand was raised to heaven while he prayed fervently for my soul. I felt as though I was standing between heaven and hell, reaching by God's mercy for heaven. 'I now baptize you in the name of Jesus Christ for the remission of sins, in the name of the Father, the Son, and the Holy Spirit' came the pronouncement and under I went. My eyes were open and I could see the surface of the water reflecting the lights above the church baptistery. Upon my rising from the water, the congregation burst forth in praise and clapping. I felt that I had been born anew.

About two years later, I began seeking the experience of being filled with the Holy Spirit. I didn't really know what that meant, only that others among those slightly older than I claimed to have had the experience; so, being somewhat precocious, I wanted it too. My older brother (four years my senior) claimed to have had the experience and seemed knowledgeable about most things (a real man of the world I thought then), so I quizzed him one evening about it. My major question was, 'How do I know when I get it?' 'It's simple', he replied, 'You'll know you have it when you feel it all over your body, like *electricity*'. My anticipation soared. The thought that God could draw so close as to be felt in that way both unnerved and attracted me.

The night arrived when I knew it was my time. An evangelist had given a stirring message that brought most of the congregation to the altar. I was there too, with my hands raised, crying out to God. Soon a group gathered around me to pray me through. I kept waiting for that electrical jolt but they all wanted to hear me speak in tongues. 'Say Jesus', I heard someone shout. So, I cried, 'Jesus!' Then I heard this same person shout, 'Say it again! Keep repeating it'. So I did. I kept repeating Jesus' name over and over. I felt myself being moved by the rhythm of this mantra when suddenly I got tongue-tied and I uttered something that seemed nonsensical to the human ear. 'That's it!' I heard the voice that had been guiding me shout. 'That's it, he's got it!' Before I had a chance to realize what had happened, everyone was rejoicing that I had gotten it. 'But what about the *electricity*?' I thought. 'Why did I not feel it the way others had?' I left the church that evening confused but in a strange way still convinced that God had something better in store for me. That idea kept me going.

Ours was an Italian Pentecostal church that had grown to take on a number of non-Italian families (several that were Hispanic). The Italian service in which my paternal grandmother, Antoinette, preached had been phased out and the church had come under the umbrella of the Assemblies of God. Still, few of us knew in those early years what an Assemblies of God was. Our piety was dominated by Antoinette, my 'grandma Macchia'. Stories of her prayer life and God's many answers by way of response were legendary. She was a prayer warrior who prayed daily without exception for hours with her face near the floor in the privacy of her bedroom. I recall sitting in her living room on more than one occasion and hearing her pray out loud and fervently in Italian without pause. She believed that God would answer in some way if we prayed long and hard enough. Anyone within telephone distance who had a serious need called her to pray for him, and she did so with fervor that was unmatched. She never spoke about this to others. Neither was she very emotional about her piety in public. She prayed silently in church and never joined us at the altar. Her spiritual battles were fought in the prayer closet alone with God.

My father was a successful musician, a professional accordionist who owned a few thriving music schools. He curtailed his music business considerably in order to devote himself as pastor of our growing church. But he always played his accordion in church as well as late in the evening at home. I fell asleep to that music many times, imagining sometimes as I did so that I was playing it instead. He loved that instrument and devoted his life to playing it. His theological studies consisted of Berean correspondence courses, a handful of courses taken at the nearby Valparaiso University (a Lutheran school), and an occasional book.

My father was a well-rounded and practical man who learned plumbing, electrical work, and construction just by watching other people do them. He could build a house from the ground up though he never actually worked in construction. He was likable and humble, preferring simply to be called, 'Brother Mike'. His preaching was mesmerizing. He offered a simple message but with feeling and passion. He would usually tell a biblical story in a way that made the characters come to life, punctuating his narrative with an occasional short story to illustrate the major turns in the biblical drama. His emphasis was always on God's mercy in all of life. I was reared in my understanding of the gospel through his preaching.

He was also an ecumenical spirit. His baptismal formula included Jesus' name out of sensitivity to any in our church who came from a Oneness background. I vividly recall his telling me one day over coffee not long after my first year in Bible College that it did not really matter which denomination a person belonged to so long as he or she actually experienced the truth from Scripture being embraced. His spirit was later alive in me. In many ways, I became my father's son.

My mother was the one who taught me to believe in my gifting. She worked with me in my early singing ministry, guiding me in the memorization of the lyrics to songs and in the ability to sing them with feeling. She also guided me in the memorization of the testimonies that I was to give before the songs. I memorized each one, but I never considered the performance to be routine or mechanical. With a contagious sense of humor, she was always the life of the party.

By way of contrast, my mother struggled in life with depression, but no one outside of the home ever knew it. She withdrew at times and at others became loud and difficult, lashing out at anyone in sight, as though she was fighting the pain she felt inside. When she came out of her withdrawal, she seemed to come to life in ways that made everything all right again. Her better moments (which were the longest) were so filled with life and humor that we were able to forget the difficult moments. She was the favorite aunt among my many cousins, who all affectionately called her 'Auntie Lizzy' (short for Elizabeth). My mother's mother lived with us for a while and often visited before and after. I recall 'grandma Pilla' and my mom speaking in Italian to each other for hours. I didn't understand much of what they were saying, so I simply blocked it out. I blocked it out when I heard my parents speak in Italian to each other as well, unless I heard my name in Italian being used. Then I strained to understand, but without much success.

My middle and high school years occurred in the 1960's, during a period of turbulence in American history. At 11 years old I stared at our black and white television set during the lengthy news coverage of John F. Kennedy's assassination and funeral. I recall turning sick to my stomach as I happened to witness on the news Oswald's murder only a short time later, especially as he doubled over and cried out in pain. I was frightened by the possibility that anyone can be killed at any time by someone with a gun.

Later, I was privileged to catch a glimpse of Bobby Kennedy as his convertible drove by in front of my house to cheering folks lined up at the curb as he campaigned through the streets of my town, Gary, Indiana, at that time a stronghold for the Democratic Party. I was then shocked to learn a short a while later that he was killed too. I then learned that Martin Luther King was taken in the same way. No one at my church talked about any of these events. To my mind, King's assassination was simply one in a series of national leaders struck down in the prime of life.

The morning after King's assassination, however, I noticed a large group of black students walking towards me expressing their anguish in one way or another. Some were weeping while others were shouting slogans. I stared at them as they passed by, affected by their pain. I looked directly into the face of one of the students in the group whom I knew well, hoping to get his attention, but he looked right past me as though I wasn't there. I was somewhat puzzled by the degree to which they were affected by King's murder. I didn't realize it at the time, but I was beginning to learn the difference between sympathy from the outside and feeling it on the inside. That insight would influence how I would later understand the true meaning of 'ecumenical' when it came to theology and life. The significance of glossolalia in Acts, would come to mean a great deal more to me than the experience of being tongue-tied at the altar.

My transition to teen life was difficult and my ability to stay out of trouble decreased in effectiveness. I came to rebel against the church and all that it stood for. In later teen years, I experimented with drugs. It was the late 1960's when drugs were plentiful on the streets and easily gotten by anyone who had the right (or, I should say, wrong) connections. As the middle child of six children, I found it easy to take off on my own without much supervision. We lived in a two bedroom house, so my older brother and I took up residence in the basement. We didn't mind, since that little cement dwelling became our hideaway. We wrestled, boxed, and lifted weights that we had 'borrowed' from the local Boy's Club.

When I turned 18, I awakened my father from a sound sleep one midnight to inform him that I was leaving home to 'find myself' in the world. His one request was that I give him the opportunity to talk me out of it. We ended up talking through the night. He shared stories with me about what God had done in my life and in the lives of my family. He opened the Bible and read relevant texts about the love of God revealed in Christ. We were both exhausted as the dawn came. I left him to go to sleep and immediately knelt by the bed. I was overcome by the feeling that to run any further from Christ would be to flee from someone who was already deeply a part of me. Not knowing how to pray, I simply asked God to 'take my life' and fell into the first peaceful sleep that I had had in a long time. The Hymn 'Take My Life' has been a favorite of mine ever since, even being featured later at my wedding.

My father arranged for me to attend Central Bible College. My first day on campus I purchased a large, black study Bible from the campus bookstore. I sat at my desk and decided to begin reading where the Bible fell open. It fell open at the Book of Acts. I began reading and continued without a break until I had come to the end of the book. By then the sun was setting. I opened the shade and observed the red and yellow hues of the clouds. I felt tears rolling down my cheeks as I reflected on the fact that God seemed so real to these early Christians. They had a fire burning in their hearts and all of life was a grand adventure in the life and work of the kingdom of God. If I am going to be a Christian, I thought, I want to be one like they were.

My thoughts were interrupted by a knock on the door. I was invited to join my classmates for a time of prayer in the upstairs chapel. As we climbed the stairs, I felt this depth of emotion welling up in me. We entered the little chapel and I observed a bench against the wall and a small cross above it. I fell to my knees and began crying out to God to help me. My classmates laid their hands on me and cried out with me, not having any idea what my problem was. I briefly spoke in tongues, not as something forced; in fact, it seemed at the moment to be the natural thing to do. I then lay down on the floor and began to make promises to God that I have spent my life trying to keep.

The years of study and ministry at CBC that followed (1970 – 73) were formative. The entire emphasis on campus then was finding one's calling during times of prayer and ministry, something that I desperately needed. It was the years of the Jesus Movement, which provided me with a meaningful context for grabbing the attention of young people for Christ. I read the Bible daily and often in those days, memorizing key passages and meditated on them. It was all so new and exciting, a first love experience that has become a permanent part of me. During those early studies I enjoyed the lectures of people like Ben Aker and Stanley Horton. Later, I became enamored with what was happening among the 'Jesus people' in Southern California, which led me to transfer to Southern California College (now Vanguard University). I loved SCC. Cecil Robeck and Murray Dempster helped to bring much needed clarity and direction to my early thinking. My academic development was slow and gradual but they were patient with me. Murray was the first one to tell me about Schleiermacher, Barth, and Tillich. He didn't just tell me about them, he made them come to life! I trace my study of modern theology to Murray Dempster. How I appreciated the start that he and other teachers gave me in those formative years.

Not knowing what to do upon graduation, I went back home to Gary, Indiana, and decided to study a while somewhere close to home. It was time to get serious about advanced theological education. I enrolled at Wheaton College in 1974 in the MA program in theology. I had Merrill Tenney for New Testament Backgrounds. His lectures were driven by questions which he constantly placed before unsuspecting young grad students. His responses to our answers were rich in detail, much of which he read, along with an occasional joke, from a stack of 3 x 5 cards! Charles Horne was a conservative Barthian who convinced me to read Barth. What a formative beginning that was! I read only snippets back then like a little bird beginning to drink on its own. Most intriguing at Wheaton by far was Robert Webber. He was young, culturally relevant, and deeply committed to the church fathers and the wisdom of the ancient church. I could not get enough. I had three courses under him on the history of theology. We went from Origen to modern-day existentialism. He was the first professor that I had who used the term 'catholic' in a way that was positive and reverent. I knew from that day forward that I would always respect the history of theology. Even to this day, I feel the pull to leave the modern era (the era dominated by Schleiermacher and Barth) so as to go deeper into our shared roots as the people of God. This is still an area that I wish to explore with greater depth.

My years at Wheaton were paralleled and followed by my first pastorate at an Italian Pentecostal church in Chicago. What challenging years those were! Caring for a congregation at a young age stretched me in ways that I could never have foreseen. I read a lot in those days. I happened upon Harvey Cox's *Secular City* and devoured it. That little book was nothing short of a liberating experience for me. That biblical theology could have such compelling relevance for a 'secular' environment was new and exciting for me. I found and read his *Feast of Fools* and *Seduction of the Spirit* directly afterwards. I was hooked. My passion to study contemporary theology increased. I read Paul Tillich's *Dynamics of Faith, Courage to Be*, the *Protestant Era*, and most of volume one of his *Systematic Theology*. I read Bultmann's *Jesus Christ and Mythology*, several of Kierkegaard's essays, Buber's *I and Thou*, and anything that had the word existentialism in it. I was taken with the Gospel's answer to the 'dilemma of modern man'.

It was at the tail end of these formative years (1977) that I met the love of my life, Verena. She had come to Chicago from Switzerland to learn English. It was for me love at first sight (she required more time for discernment!). After a few months of dating I popped the question and to my utter amazement and lasting joy she accepted. We were married and spent six wonderful months in the church parsonage growing deeper in love. With her encouragement and support, I applied to Harvard, Garrett-Evangelical Theological Seminary (at Northwestern), and Union Theological Seminary (at Columbia) for the Master of Divinity degree. Harvard sent me the friendliest rejection I had ever received, while Garrett and Union laid out the red carpet. So, off we went to New York City in the summer of 1978 with everything we owned in the back of a good friend's pickup truck. He let us off on Riverside Drive in front of those gothic towers that graced the surrounding architecture of one of the most important seminaries in American history. It was a new beginning for me.

Union in those days was an exciting place at which to study. Teaching there were Raymond Brown, J. Louis Martyn, Geoffrey Wainwright, Robert McAfee Brown, James Cone, Roger Shinn and

Dorothee Soelle. Among the younger faculty were Gerald Sheppard, Cornel West, and Christopher Morse. I was challenged by the breadth and intensity of the work load. The ecumenical and international breadth of the student body, not to mention its intellectual preparedness, was a delightful and challenging experience for me. I recall a Tillich seminar that I had with Tom Driver in which the Japanese student seated next to me casually mentioned that he had translated all of Tillich's major works into Japanese! I invited him to dinner to discuss the *Socialist Decision* (which at first read seemed like Greek to me). I had so much to learn in those days. Liberation theology was still in its heyday then and was powerfully present at Union as an option (as North Americans we talked about a theology of 'letting go' of power).

James Cone and Cornel West challenged me to take seriously the social context of Christian worship and confession. Cone was relentless in stressing the contradiction involved among whites who did not grieve over the lynching of blacks but who claimed at the same time to serve the Christ who was unjustly crucified. He was inspired by Barth's fierce rejection of the German church's acquiescence to Hitler. Was I to be just as fierce in my rejection of the acquiescence of white churches to racism? That question has never left me. Still, Wainwright had helped me to see that the church's identity is also profoundly shaped internally by its worship and dogma (in creative interplay). I later entertained the idea of calling the church in its social witness to its true center in the crucified Christ. In straying from that center, we stray from our true social witness and in straying from our social witness we stray from that center. Bonhoeffer has been a resource for me here. Christopher Morse was regarded as a Moltmann expert in those days at Union. Theology of Liberation and Theology of Hope were terms that I began using a lot at that time. I remember playing with the idea as a Pentecostal of a 'Theology of Presence' as an alternative slogan. I cannot recall who originally placed that bug in my ear. At any rate, that impulse stayed with me over the years and ended up resurfacing in my recent book, *Justified in the Spirit: Creation, Redemption, and the Triune God* (Grand Rapids: Eerdmans, 2010), in which I proposed that soteriological categories like justification be understood within the reality of the divine indwelling of creation. I would end up drawing from Moltmann here as well.

I read Kitamori and Moltmann for the first time at Union. They both deeply impressed me with the conviction that the divine capacity to suffer has its roots in the elect will of God to love and remain faithful to an unfaithful creation (a fundamentally Barthian idea). The cross thus becomes the supreme revelation of the eternal heart of God in relation to creation. Divine impassibility, however one comes to define it, should in my view never seek to displace this fundamental insight. At any rate, Wainwright was a refreshing alternative voice for me in those days. He was ecumenical but in a way that was deeply rooted in the history of worship and dogma. What a breath of fresh air he was for me at a time when terms like dogma or tradition were not being used by many at Union in a way that had any compelling relevance for us. I read his *Doxology* at Union and even gave a presentation on it in his presence in a seminar (what audacity). By rooting theology in the worship practices of the church, Wainwright made theology actual and concrete. That idea became a permanent part of my thinking.

By far the professor who had most personally impacted me at Union was Gerald Sheppard. Jerry was brilliant and personable. He took me under his wing, determined to teach me the Old Testament and hermeneutics, delivering me in the process from my intellectual captivity to 'authorial intent'. He got me reading Hans Frei, David Kelsey, James Sanders, Paul Ricoeur, and Brevard Childs. We spent hours talking in his office and apartment. I didn't fully appreciate then the time he took pouring his mind into me. Now that I teach, I realize the depth of the sacrifice that he made. He arranged for me to do an independent study with him on biblical hermeneutics that was nothing short of brutal. He left no stone unturned in his evaluation of my papers and I understood only portions of what he was telling me in our many sessions together. I recall a lengthy discourse on the difficulties involved with von Rad's historicism in which I took notes without understanding very much at all about the meaning of the words I was hastily writing. Believe it or not, so much of what he gave me stayed with me just beneath the surface of my active memory waiting to burst forth with volcanic significance later on. Years later, I had a few colloquia on hermeneutics at Basel in which I would suddenly say to myself, 'That's what Jerry meant!'

I first read Hollenweger at Union. Pentecostalism as a movement that had relevance for contemporary theology first became apparent to me in his writings. Hollenweger gave me a way of talking meaningfully about my Pentecostal identity at Union. I was able to connect Wainwright's liturgical method for theology with how Pentecostal worship and narratives shape the Christian identity of Pentecostal congregations and nourish their theological reflection (and are guided by it). I was already connecting all of this with Frei's postliberal narrative hermeneutic. I even remember doing a paper on Kierkegaard's narrative reading of the Abraham story. I enjoyed discussing such issues with fellow students like the late Ralph Del Colle, who became a lifelong friend.

After Union, my head was swimming with new ideas. I picked up Pelikan's *Christian Tradition* (then only four volumes) and read every page with sheer delight. Verena bought me Barth's *Church Dogmatics* as a Christmas present! We were poorer than church mice in our little Chicago apartment (where we moved after my graduation from Union) but she managed to scrape the money together somehow. I worked carefully through volume one (parts 1 and 2) writing prolifically in the margins. I looked forward to my time in the *Dogmatics* every evening. I was pastoring again and Verena was working on her BA degree in education. I took several courses in philosophy at the grad school of Loyola University of Chicago. Verena and I would rummage through used bookstores in Chicago and then sit over coffee as we looked at our haul of discounted books. We would hang out at the beach near Lincoln Park and take a bus into the downtown area to window shop. I so enjoyed every moment we had together (and I naturally still do!). Those were formative days which I will always fondly remember.

The year was 1983 and it was time for me to begin thinking about doctoral programs. I explored Zürich, Birmingham, and Tübingen. Birmingham sent me an official letter of acceptance and I received a hand-written note from Moltmann accepting me as his student! Zürich also laid out the red carpet. We moved to Switzerland to consider our options. I decided that Birmingham (under Hollenweger) was not economically feasible and the strong emphasis on theology and science at Zürich in the end lost much of its appeal for me. I recall thinking, 'Should I go to Tübingen based only on a hand-written note?' The Rector's office at the University there had not yet written me anything. Confused, I wasn't sure what to do. Then my wife said, 'Go to Basel!' It was a divine illumination.

I took a train there and wandered around the stately buildings of the University wondering if this could be the place for me. I found my way to the Divinity School and just happened into one of Jan Milič Lochman's seminars. I saw him speaking at the head of the table and I was immediately certain he was to be my *Doktorvater*. After the seminar, I waited around and walked Lochman home in order to explain my situation to him. Donald Dayton had already given me a great dissertation idea, the theological links between spirituality and social liberation in the message of the Blumhardts. Since I initially spoke English with Lochman, he came around to asking me how my German was. Of course, I had to say it was lousy. With a look of utter seriousness on his face, he informed me that he was leaving on a three month speaking tour and that upon his return we would be speaking German! I rushed home in a panic and told my wife that I had three months to master German. She then informed me with equal seriousness that English was no longer allowed in our home. She began speaking German to me. I recall watching her mouth move but not knowing what she was saying. I thought, 'I am so dead!' In the weeks that followed I devoted myself full time to German, not doing anything else every waking moment of every day. I had never applied myself to anything that intensely before.

I was accepted at Basel and three months later, after Lochman returned, I attended my first seminar with him. He left a place open next to him at the seminar table for me. When I entered the room, he motioned me over to him. He then began speaking German to me. I immediately began speaking back to him with acceptable proficiency. A smile spread over his face and he said in front of everyone, 'Das Deutsch von Herrn Macchia ist mitteilbar!' (Mr Macchia's German is communicable!). The small group of students, all of whom were aware of my struggle with German, burst forth in laughter. I was on my way.

I loved my studies at Basel. Lochman and Heinrich Ott anchored the systematics courses. Bo Reiche and Marcus Barth were the two *Neuentestamentlers*. Ernst Stagemann (now well known for his social science approach to the New Testament) had just joined the faculty as well. Martin Schmidt was their key church historian.

My second year there was the centennial of Barth's birthday and the entire Divinity School celebrated it by offering numerous seminars on Barth throughout the year. I had three with Lochman and one with Stagemann. I studied the early Barth, the later Barth, Barth's ethics, and Barth's hermeneutics. I read thousands of pages by Barth in German, loving every minute of it. Barth became important to my theological development. He not only talked about what was possible in the contemporary situation theologically but also what was necessary, namely, how we *had* to talk about God if we are to be faithful to the proclamation of the church. This is the question of dogma. Yet, Barth always warned against regarding any of our penultimate judgments as ultimate. After all, the God disclosed in Christ is also the hidden God. So, we as the church were compelled by revelation to write the Nicene Creed but revelation also cautions us against regarding this Creed as the final word on the matter. This unique blend of necessity and open-endedness in our understanding of dogma intrigued me greatly, granting me both the anchor and the ecumenical openness I was looking for. The sharp eschatological (kingdom) critique of the church that I had gained from Franz Overbeck and the Blumhardts (and that influenced the early Barth) also preoccupied me in those days (I was able to connect this with Hans Küng's masterful, *The Church*, and Moltmann's ecclesiology as well). Christoph Blumhardt's critical dialectic between the Kingdom and the church also reminded me so much of Tillich's *Socialist Decision*.

Through it all, Lochman proved to be the ideal mentor, demanding but not too hands on. He gave me a lot of freedom to take my research in my own direction. His seminars were sometimes lively, marked by intriguing debates. We met once a week at his home which housed a medieval library and a seminar room. I visited him on several occasions before his death. On one such occasion we walked into that seminar room as we talked. It seemed so empty and quiet. I was still able to recall the lively debates that I had experienced there and I felt how much I missed them.

Heinrich Ott was an important mentor for me at Basel also. He was brilliant and unpredictable in his theological leanings. He would talk about what he had gained from Barth and Bultmann in the old days, how much he cherished them both and how unfortunate the rift between them was. I recall vividly my first seminar with him (on

Karl Rahner). It was during that three month period in which I was just learning German, so my ability at the language was still quite weak. I had hoped to sit at the rear of the table and stay out of sight, just listening and practicing my German. But I entered the room late on the first day and ended up seated right next to Ott. He turned to me and asked how my German was. Not entirely truthful in my response, I answered, 'Nicht schlecht' (not bad). He then asked me to come prepared the following week to give a paper on Rahner's view of the development of dogma (*Dogmenentwichlung*). I spent the following week laboring over Rahner's writings on the subject. I found Rahner's German nearly indecipherable in those days. One sentence could be the size of a paragraph! I wisely decided to write out my paper and read it to the seminar. I gave my wife a nearly indecipherable paper in the worst German imaginable and asked her to proof it for me. What a time she had doing that! She was masterful in her editing skills, however, and sent me on my way to the seminar.

It dawned on me during the tram ride to the Divinity School that I had not clearly stated Rahner's problem at the beginning of the paper. So, I scrawled at the top of the paper, '*Das Grundproblem*', I then asked Rahner's fundamental question: 'If revelation had indeed ceased with the death of the apostles, how can we speak meaningfully today of the *development* of dogma in history?' I started the seminar with this question. But before I had the chance to read my paper, Ott's face lit up and he said to me that I had indeed isolated the basic question, whereupon his assistant stated that the fundamental problem lies elsewhere. A lively debate ensued that devoured most of the seminar time! One would think that I would have been happy about this unexpected development, but I wasn't. This was my chance to show Ott something of my ability as a student. I worked hard on that paper and wanted to give it. At one point, I broke into the debate in order to steer the seminar back to my paper, but upon speaking I had used the wrong word for my verb, causing my statement to end up totally nonsensical. The group looked at me with puzzled expressions and continued arguing as though I had not even said anything! I was depressed. With only a short time left in the seminar, Ott asked me to summarize my paper (as though I had the language ability to do that!). My summary was a disaster. This was my first seminar paper at Basel and I had failed miserably. As the seminar broke up, Ott came to me and said that my presentation was *ausgezeichnet!* (outstanding!). He thanked me for it and invited me to his colloquium that met every month at his home (or at a restaurant in town). I walked home confused. Had I done well after all? I walked into the apartment and my wife asked immediately, 'How did you do?' I tossed my paper across the room and said, 'I only needed that one stupid sentence that I wrote down in the tram on the way to the University!'

Fortunately, my language skills improved significantly after that, especially since we only spoke German at home and there was plenty of opportunity to speak it among students in the seminars. In fact, just as much education took place at Basel in the local pubs as in the seminar rooms. I recall many a late night discussing issues with a circle of students. One night we were deeply involved in a conversation about Bultmann when Ott walked in. He asked us what we were talking about, whereupon we answered, 'Bultmann'. He promptly sat down and placed a thick book entitled, 'Zen' down on the table in front of us with a gleam in his eye. The conversation quickly went in that direction.

Towards the end of my program at Basel, Lochman was awarded a European academic prize (the Jacob Burckhardt Prize) which gave him the privilege of naming a doctoral student to win the student prize by the same title. Though he had 26 doctoral students at the time (several of whom were senior to me in the program), he chose me as the student prize holder. I was deeply honored by his confidence in me. The prize ceremony was memorable. The auditorium at Basel was filled to capacity and German television (not Swiss!) filmed the event for a snippet in their evening news (Basel was near the German border). The entire faculty and some of the student body were there, along with many outside guests and dignitaries. I approached the podium more nervous than I had ever been before and began speaking in German to the crowd. I started with a humorous story. When the crowd broke out in laughter, I knew that I had control of the situation. I relaxed and gave my speech. I later graduated with distinction, which gave me the right to habilitate (write a postdoctoral thesis) and then to teach at Basel as a *Privatdozent*. Privatdozents were not paid (they lived off of stipends) but could compete for a paid position once it opened. When

Southeastern College opened for me in 1991, I decided that my heart belonged to Pentecostal higher education, so I went that route. Giving up that opportunity at Basel was hard for me and I wondered more than once in the early years whether I had made the right decision. I don't ask that question anymore. There comes a time when one simply cannot keep looking back in that way.

My years of teaching at Southeastern College (1992 to 1999) were formative for me. The work load was enormous but I still found time to write. Shortly before I arrived there, I gave a paper on glossolalia ('Sighs Too Deep for Words') at the Dallas meeting of the Society for Pentecostal Studies. I wanted to finally turn my attention to something explicitly Pentecostal. I wrote about tongues as part of an eschatological theophany that bore witness to a free God who calls us to freedom, to the eschatological openness of radical hope. Later, I developed a theology of tongues in the light of its 'sacramental' function. My goal then (and now) was to bring Pentecostal concerns into conversation with the greatest voices of contemporary theology. I met Chris Thomas and Rickie Moore at the Dallas meeting. We were excited that there were so many Pentecostals finishing doctorates in biblical or theological studies at major universities. We had so much to talk about. We felt like we were at the ground floor of helping to shape a new theological conversation. I vividly recall the following AAR/SBL meeting in which Steve Land, Sam Soliván, and I spoke at length in the lobby of a hotel about the critical relationship between the kingdom and the church. Pneumatology was to be the critical voice of this dialectic, the great 'Dialectician' of the church! Those were formative days for us all. Getting to know Amos Yong not long afterwards proved to be very important for me as well. He has become a fellow traveler who has challenged and enlightened my own theological journey. He rightly saw pneumatology as the Trinitarian principle of global and eschatological diversification and expansiveness, thus challenging previous discussions of a theology of religions that had not fully respected the otherness of our conversation partners outside of the Christian faith.

The 90's also witnessed my entry into ecumenical conversations. Thanks to Cecil M. Robeck, I joined the international Reformed (WARC) Pentecostal dialogue. I recall being confronted with the Reformed charge that they had taken the first article of the Creed more seriously than we had, allowing them to connect pneumatology more meaningfully with creation and natural processes. Our pneumatology was connected with Christ as healer and coming King, but had we connected the Spirit thoroughly enough with the Father almighty, creator of heaven and earth? Had we appreciated enough Calvin's idea of creation as the theater of God's glory? During the years of that dialogue I got to know Robeck better as well as Veli-Matti Kärkkäinen, Jean Daniel Plüss, the Ma's (Wonsuk and Julie), Rich Israel (who is currently a delight to have as a colleague and department chair at Vanguard), Dan Albrecht, Harold Hunter, and Anthea Butler. Robeck has been a mentor in more ways than one. He is an insightful church historian and ecumenist, a towering figure in early Pentecostal research. He, Murray Dempster, and Russ Spittler encouraged me as a young scholar, making me feel that I had something important to give. They will never know what their encouragement has meant to me. Veli-Matti has become a valued friend and colleague. I have never had more enjoyment pursuing an intriguing theological idea or a humorous story than in the presence of VM. His scholarship is making a significant mark far outside the bounds of Pentecostal movements. I have also enjoyed my work for Faith and Order (National Council of Christian Churches). I can recall vigorous discussions with people like Jeffrey Gross, Don Dayton, Joseph Small, Terry Nichols, Arland Hultgren, and (the late) George Vandervelde (with whom I shared a love for G.C. Berkouwer). I so enjoyed participation in conciliar ecumenism. I found the discussions to be more diverse and challenging than bilateral dialogues.

The Oneness-Trinitarian Pentecostal dialogue was also enriching for me. Getting to know David Bernard, Dave Norris, and Kim Alexander better was one of the high points of the dialogue. I chaired the Trinitarian team (which also consisted of Kim Alexander and my Vanguard colleague, Ed Rybarczyk, who helped me for years when I edited *Pneuma*). Bernard chaired the Oneness team (consisting also of Bishop Johnson, [for a while] Norris, and J.L. Hall). Ralph Del Colle, though an observer, made valuable contributions at key points and David Reed, who also functioned as an observer, proved to be a virtual storehouse of knowledge about Oneness movements. I never tire of hearing him talk about such matters. Bernard made the point more than once that Oneness exegetical arguments (for example, about baptism in Jesus' name in Acts) had mainstream exegetical support. For my part, I had tried to press the issue of the tension among Oneness Pentecostals between stressing the deity of Christ (including a strong incarnational doctrine) and saying that Jesus is only a 'manifestation' of the Father in order to avoid relationality in God. I never felt that both lines of argument can be held successfully together. St. Basel thus accused Sabellianism of denying the incarnation.[142]

On a personal note, the 90's witnessed our journey to China to adopt our two wonderful daughters, Desiree (now 18) and Jasmine (now 16). They were both only about six months old when we got them (we went twice, about eighteen months apart). Raising them has been the greatest joy of my life next to being a husband to Verena. Seeing the world through their eyes has taught me so much. I went to Vanguard University in 1999 mainly because of the large Asian population there. The presence of Murray Dempster and Roger and Gayle Heuser there was a draw for me as well. Roger has become a close friend and mentor. For the past decade my family and I have attended an English-speaking Taiwanese congregation that has become an extended family to us (pastored first by my good friend, John Sim, and now by Dwayne Nordstrom). My girls have flourished here. They've grown up with a firm sense of who they are and a deep faith in Christ. I couldn't be more satisfied. I recall walking next to my elder daughter (Desiree) a few years ago when suddenly we were surrounded by a large group of Chinese tourists speaking Mandarin. When they passed, I remarked to Desiree, 'They come from the land of your birth'. She immediately replied, 'But I'm not Asian like they are'. 'So, how *are* you Asian', I asked. She thought a moment and then answered with a smile from ear to ear, 'I'm a *California* Asian!' 'Good enough', I answered. 'Good enough'.

In 2004, I began work on a primer to Pentecostal theology. Our ecumenical interlocutors (Kilian McDonnell, Ralph Del Colle, James Dunn, and Lyle Dabney) had all in different ways pointed to Spirit baptism as the key distinctive to Pentecostal theology and spirituality. Meanwhile, Simon Chan had rightly noted that this doc-

---

[142] See Frank D. Macchia, 'The Oneness-Trinitarian Pentecostal Dialogue: Exploring the Diversity of Apostolic Faith', *Harvard Theological Review* 103.3 (2010), pp. 329-49.

trine must be expanded to be ecumenically relevant. It occurred to me that the debates over Spirit baptism implied different ecclesiologies. Word ecclesiologies viewed Spirit baptism as regeneration by faith in the Gospel. Sacramental ecclesiologies saw Spirit baptism as the reception of the Spirit in the rite of baptism. Pentecostal (charismatic) ecclesiologies viewed Spirit baptism as empowerment for charismatic gifting and mission. It became clear to me in my research that Spirit baptism is a fluid metaphor in Scripture and cannot be reduced to the interests of one ecclesiological tradition. In Scripture, Spirit baptism is connected most fundamentally to the kingdom of God involving God's triune self-giving to creation. As such, Spirit baptism is many-sided and complex. I wrote *Baptized in the Spirit: A Global Pentecostal Theology* (Grand Rapids: Zondervan, 2006) in order to develop this thesis. My next major book, *Justified in the Spirit: Creation, Redemption, and the Triune God* (Eerdmans, 2010), followed. In addition, I have just put the finishing touches on a massive commentary on Revelation written for Eerdmans with my close friend and colleague, Chris Thomas (who has penned two-thirds of it, a masterful commentary for which I have written the theological reflection). Bringing Revelation into conversation with contemporary theology has been for me an enlightening experience.

As I sit in my den and type these concluding remarks I feel a sense of having been blessed. Have there been mistakes, wrong turns, and missed opportunities in my life? Most certainly. Have I been blessed beyond measure? Without a doubt. If God is gracious to me by giving me longevity, I hope in the decade ahead to spend even more time than ever before with my family and to continue to write and to teach in ways that will bless others with a measure of the abundance that I have received from the Lord. Grace beyond measure can produce a stream of living water that flows out of our innermost beings to open paths still unexplored.

7

IN MY LIFE*

JOHN CHRISTOPHER THOMAS**

I was so young when I was born
My eyes could not yet see
And by the time of my first dawn
Somebody holding me, they said

'I welcome you to Crackerbox Palace
We've been expecting you
You bring such joy in Crackerbox Palace
No matter where you roam know our love is true'[1]

On 2 September 1954 I was born into the loving home of a young
Pentecostal couple in Maryville, TN. I was named John after my
father (John Donald), and his father before him (John Daniel), and
his father before him (John Nuggent)! My middle name apparently
came from a fictional heroic figure whose name, Christopher, my
father fancied.

A pharmaceutical salesman by day, my father, known as J.D. to
friends and family, was a handsome and talented musician who
played various instruments (including saxophone and piano) and

---

* Title of Song by Lennon and McCartney.
** John Christopher Thomas (PhD, University of Sheffield) is the Clarence J.
Abbott Professor of Biblical Studies at the Pentecostal Theological Seminary in
Cleveland, TN, USA and the Director of the Centre for Pentecostal and Charis-
matic Studies at Bangor University in Bangor, Wales, UK.
[1] Lyrics from George Harrison's 'Crackerbox Palace'.

was known for composing rather complicated, intricate piano scores. Much of the rest of his spare time was spent with the electronics of his day; his movie camera, reel-to-reel tape recorder, and record player. He apparently was very, very bright, his elder brother telling me that my father had been offered membership in Mensa.

My mother, Betty Ruth King Thomas, was a beautiful young woman as well as a talented musician, playing piano and accordion, and possessed a lovely singing voice. She too was extremely bright, serving as Beta Club President at Alcoa High School, from which she and my father graduated. She was employed full-time by the telephone company.

The Alcoa Church of God, a church with roots deep in the Pentecostal movement, was the congregation in which my parents were formed and drank deeply from the well of Pentecostal spirituality. Both sets of my grandparents were faithful members of the church, each serving in various ways.

My paternal grandfather, who worked at the Aluminum Company of America (Alcoa), was a gifted carpenter and played steel guitar. In his days as a youth he was known as 'the little dancing boy'. My paternal grandmother, Dollie Christine (who preferred the nickname 'Booch'), was an avid reader who loved to travel. Many of my earliest days were spent in their home, as Booch kept me during the day whilst my parents worked. My memories of time spent in their home are very happy. My mother tells me that is because my grandparents did exactly what I wanted done!

My maternal grandfather, Charley Walter King, worked for Alcoa as well, but also lived on a farm with crops and farm animals of all sorts. With acres and acres of wood and fields to explore, life at the Kings' was always an adventure for the numerous grandchildren that always seemed to be there. My maternal grandmother, Lena Irene Tucker King, was a quintessential Pentecostal, who at one time or another served as church clerk, choir director, soloist, Sunday School teacher and superintendent, and prayer warrior in the church they called home. In her personal library could be found a range of works including E.L. Simmons' *History of the Church of God*, W.H. Turner's *Pentecost and Tongues*, and a Greek-English Interlinear New Testament.

It is difficult for me to distinguish between memories, dreams, and stories I have heard from my early years. Sadly, I have only one extraordinarily hazy recollection of my father and it is at best just a snapshot. It seems that I recall one day in the front yard of our house in Maryville, TN we were walking in opposite directions away from one another. Funny things, memories.

Our lives would be forever changed by the events of 16 September 1956, when my father, mother, and I were traveling back from visiting my father's brother in Florida. Somewhere near Perry, GA a vehicle involved in a drag race blew a tire, crossed the road, and collided head-on with our car. My father was killed instantly, my mother was thrown from the car through a tree, suffering severe injuries. I am told that when the police arrived, they found me sitting in the middle of the road. Apparently I told the officers that my father was in the ditch, where he was later found.

Having lost her husband, my critically injured twenty-three year old mother prayed to die, she tells me, until a nurse brought me into her room and slipped my little hand around one of her fingers, a gesture she credits with giving her the will to live. It amazes me still that so deep a bond could be formed by means of a tactile moment like that – but even now the depth of this bond is difficult to articulate. These dreadful events are the occasion of one of my other early memories. Sometime later, I was back in the hospital to have my broken leg reset, owing to the fact that my uncles encouraged me to walk too much! During that hospital stay I remember my paternal grandfather sitting in my hospital room near the foot of my bed, periodically asking me if I wanted any 'brand new', our code word for a new piece of Dentyne chewing gum.

Drawing on the support of family, friends, her pastor, church family, and her own extraordinary courage, Mom began to rebuild our lives over the course of the next year. It was during this time I believe that my clearest memory of that early period of my life emerges. I recall waking up to find myself lying down on a church pew, seeing through the wooden slats used for the back of the pew, as well as seeing a mason jar of water in the floor that had been brought so that I would not get too thirsty during the long hot services.

Well over a year after our lives had been changed by the fatal car crash, they would be changed again when Wayne Fritts entered our lives. A native of Lenoir City, TN, 'Daddy Wayne', as I would call him in those early days of transition, was an army veteran who had begun a career in the insurance business. He had been a very popular presence at Lenoir City High School, excelling as a basketball player and drum major. He would go on to establish himself as a local independent businessman, a gift that would serve him well later as a bi-vocational pastor. He was an exceptional father, even winning the father of the year award in those early years.

Our new life in Lenoir City consisted of four primary things: church, school, family, and sports. Our new church was the Sixth Avenue Church of God, a thriving congregation of nearly five hundred regular attendees, with a pastor, Dr R. Leonard Carroll, who had served as President of Lee College and would later be elected as the General Overseer of the Church of God. The incongruity of being part of a group as marginal as Pentecostalism was in those days, and whose pastor was the most educated man in our little town of 6,000, was something that I reflected on more than once.

When I was five years old an extraordinary thing happened to me. Dad and I had gone to a church service one Saturday night to attend a Young People's Endeavor meeting, whilst Mom stayed at home, pregnant with my future brother, Mark. That night a film was shown that included a scene of the crucifixion of Jesus. It was more than my young heart could take. As I watched, a feeling of heaviness began to come over me. I sensed that what was happening to Jesus was wrong and, though I could not articulate it, that somehow I was responsible for his suffering and death. Hiding my feelings until I got home, I confided to Mom the sense of heaviness I felt as I watched the movie. She discerned what I could not, that I was experiencing the convicting power of the Holy Spirit, and helped me come to know Jesus as my Savior.

Unbeknownst to me I was being formed by my church community in very deep ways. The sights and sounds of Pentecostal worship, glossolalic utterances and their interpretation, prophetic messages, prayer for the sick, the holy laugh, motor responses to the presence of the Holy Spirit (commonly known as 'shouting' in our community), praying through to sanctification, testimonies of triumphs and failures, anointed singing and preaching, Sunday School classes, times of fellowship, and the prayers of my mother that carried through our house all played their role in orienting me to Pentecost.

Part of the result of such formative experiences was that some-time over the course of the next two years I was consistently seeking to be baptized in the Holy Spirit. My Mom tells me that one night after a revival service she was putting me in bed, when after saying our prayers I asked that she pray with me to be baptized in the Spirit. She tells me that she 'said' a prayer, not wanting to get me stirred up about something I might not yet understand. But as she walked down the hall to her bedroom, the Spirit spoke to her saying, 'Some day you may want him to want to be filled with the Holy Spirit and he may not be interested'. The next night I was in the altar seeking the baptism and she was right behind me. Not knowing how to pray with someone so young to receive such an experience Mom asked the Lord for help and instructed me simply to praise the Lord over and over. I remember that my sincere desire resulted in frequent participation in altar services surrounded by the saints, including my Mom, and numerous conversations about the nature and purpose of this experience as I attempted to process what was going on in my developing spiritual life. When I came to know Jesus as my Spirit Baptizer I perceived a change in my young life and while I had purposed that I would not tell anyone about it once I received, I could scarcely keep it to myself, testifying to anyone I encountered, even on my way out of church that night! I came to understand that testifying, inside and outside of church, was a natural part of my Christian life. That night, in particular, I remember having a deep sense of peace and satisfaction.

During this time our family had grown to include my younger brother, Mark Wayne Fritts, a redheaded energetic dynamo. Mark too would change our lives. Though he was five years my junior, we would become good friends and companions in activities of all sorts. Our days often consisted of playing in the neighborhood that included ample woods, fields, and trails for all kinds of adventures. When confined to the indoors we would often emulate wrestling moves we had seen on TV on a variety of stuffed animals in our living room – where we won championships of various sorts! Mark would learn to play trumpet and drums and followed in our father's footsteps with regard to popularity at school and beyond. He was destined for success in his chosen profession having earned significant awards as his career has developed.

As I ventured out into the world of school I made a number of friends, often with names from the lower part of the alphabet, as that is how our seats were assigned! Buddy Walker and Steve Spears, to name a couple, but also my first African-American friends, Cecilia Smith and Daryl Johnson, as integration made its way to our little southern town. Whilst integration became a reality, I remember it seemed like a natural course of events to me for my Mother and Father had always exhibited an obvious respect for persons of color, often pointing out to me the visible accomplishments of those who were the victims of racial discrimination, pointing out the injustices in southern life. When word came about one of the civil rights marches to Washington, when I was about ten, I asked Dad what he would do if the marchers came by his place of business on Lee Highway, the main street of our little town. Unlike some of the vitriol I was hearing in the community, Dad said that the marchers had a right to march if they chose to do so. Besides that, we would on occasion worship with persons of color, indicating to me the value and equality of all peoples before the Lord and creating a certain bond, for in my way of thinking a shared relationship with the Lord superseded other ways of relating to those of other races.

Sports, too, was a regular part of my life. Although there were still some in the church who opposed involvement in athletics – I remember that Erskine Foshee had to resign from the Council at Sixth Avenue owing to the fact that he not only allowed his sons to play high school sports but even went to the games (!) – my parents encouraged me to be active in sports and it seems that every waking moment, when I was not in school or church, I was on a ball field somewhere, normally with my neighbor Billy Buck. Though I was two years his junior, Billy helped develop whatever talent I had. While I made a variety of all-star teams of one type or another I never really excelled at any one sport, normally being good enough to compete but not dominate.

At school I became aware that not everyone was a believer in Jesus and that unbelievably, not everyone was Pentecostal! In fact, there seemed to be a certain pecking order amongst religious groups, with Pentecostalism clearly near the bottom of the food chain. Such social realities affected me in a couple of ways. On the one hand, it made things like Church of God Youth Camp every summer the highlight of the year, for I knew that at least for one week a year, I would be surrounded by people of like faith. To say that I loved Youth Camp would be a gross understatement. My church friends and I lived for it! On the other hand, the social reality with which I was faced generated within me a hermeneutics of suspicion, though I was hardly able to call it by that name at the time. Rather, I learned that it was necessary to discern my way through the social and cultural terrain I encountered in my non-church life. I believe this means of cultural engagement contributed to a strong sense of self as well as equipping me to negotiate the turbulence of the 60's and 70's. Unlike some of my friends' parents, who seemed ill-prepared to assist their children with how to navigate life in the world, my parents – by this time my Dad was a pastor planting a church amongst the poor – prayerfully entertained my ethical questions, often refusing to tell me what to do but rather by means of the words of Scripture and the leading of the Spirit helped develop within me a sense of pneumatic discernment.

Part of my developing spirituality was the role of Scripture with which I had a growing sense of fascination. Scripture was, of course, part of my daily life, being encountered in Sunday School, YPE, sermons, Youth Camps, and private study. But on a few occasions I began to experience the beauty of Scripture in ways I had not before. Once, when I spent the night with my paternal grandparents, I decided for some reason to read the Gospel of Mark. I remember how I was captivated by the power of the narrative, observing how it 'all made sense' within the context of the whole story. On another occasion I remember reading the Apocalypse in my room and the interpretive questions that it generated, questions I would take up with Mom or Dad. In the midst of such encounters it also became clear to me that there was more to Scripture than simply memorizing its disparate verses and linking them together according to catch-words. For example, I learned that a fundamentalistic literalism did not always unlock Scripture's meaning, but that its meaning often had to be discerned. In point of fact, I vividly recall observing both my mother and father do just this, a discerning interpretive process that had a place for experience as well as the literal words of the text.

During my high school years I experienced a very dramatic and charismatic call to ministry. The church that my Dad planted was one where manifestations of the Spirit were a regular part of the worship services. During one such move of the Spirit, as I was praying I looked up to find that one of the prophetesses in the church, Evelyn Coffee, had made her way 'in the Spirit' across the front of the church to where I was sitting and was prophesying over me. As I recall her message included the following:

> My child, I called you while you were in your mother's womb and delivered you from the hand of death for a holy purpose.

As I tried to make sense of the enormity of the moment, I remember thinking that my life was no longer my own. As was our habit I was soon put up to 'preach' at my home church and at churches that would invite me around the area.

One afternoon during my senior year in high school I had stayed behind to assist my elderly French teacher move some supplies into her car. During the course of our small talk I asked if she enjoyed teaching. She went on and on about how wonderful it was to be a teacher and concluded by saying, 'Monsieur Thomas *you* should be a teacher. You would be very good at it'. While affirmed by her words I remember that they brought a sense of sadness as well, for I knew that I could not be a teacher for I was called to ministry and as far as I could tell that meant I either had to preach or lead singing!

Perhaps my naïveté about such matters kept me from discerning properly – from connecting the dots, with other parts of my life – for in fact I was increasingly interested in learning with history being my favorite subject. At least I could not fully discern the connection between teaching mentors placed in my life, like Gerald Augustus and Joe Spence, and the nature of my future vocation. It was Joe, in particular, who pushed me to think critically about history as well as current events and who also pushed me to think critically about issues of faith.

My senior year proved eventful owing to my family's move to Chattanooga, where my father had been appointed as pastor of the Tyner Church of God. One night he had dreamed that the Bishop had appointed him to this church, though at the time he didn't even know there was a Church of God congregation in Tyner! The following Sunday afternoon, the Bishop rang with the news that indeed my Dad had been appointed to this congregation. Needless to say, this experience taught me much about the way in which the Lord speaks though dreams! After I had been a transfer student at Tyner High School for less than two weeks, it was decided that I would live with friends of our family, Curtis and Elizabeth Fritts (no relation), in Lenoir City for the remainder of the school year. In addition to developing a growing sense of independence I was able to participate in a number of meaningful senior year events including performing in the Senior Play, *You're a Good Man, Charlie Brown*, where I played the role of 'Snoopy', not the first or last animal part I had or would play.

Of course, senior year meant decisions about the future had to be made with regard to university. Though I had always wanted to go to the University of Tennessee, having sent my ACT scores there and to Tennessee State University, a historically Black college, my Mom made clear that I could either go to Maryville College, a Presbyterian school located in our former home town, or to Lee College, our denominational college in Cleveland, TN. In the end, the decision was an easy one, so it was off to Cleveland I went. If I was to be a minister, I reasoned, it would be good to have something to preach!

College was an interesting environment for me. In some ways it reminded me socially of being at Youth Camp for it seemed that nearly everyone at the school was Church of God or at the least Pentecostal! Thus I experienced it as a delightful place within which to construct one's life as a Pentecostal young person. At the same time, college life required more study than I had been asked to do in high school. But in many respects, my life felt very much the same. The opportunity to participate in intramural sports continued at a more competitive level where I experienced similar levels of success as before, making a few all star teams and being part of several championship teams. Church services were mandatory (very much like home!), and family was only a thirty minute trip away.

My first year and a half were characterized by going to class, and though doing okay, nothing really lit my fire. Much of that time was spent in a choir called the 'Music Men' which traveled all over the USA, exposing me to a variety of churches within the tradition, again broadening my horizon, being a percussionist in the concert band – though never having been in a proper band before (!), and joining various social service clubs. During this time I met Ron Heglar and Larry Lowry, who would become very close friends.

The second semester of my sophomore year changed my life when I encountered a free-thinking biology teacher named Robert O'Bannon, who taught a course entitled 'Science and the Bible'. In content it was really an apologetics course and I was hooked – devouring the reading assignments, engaging my professor and classmates in class, and developing an intellectual sense of self that I had not known before. Among other things, Bob O'Bannon proposed an unheard of view of God, in those days, that would come to be known as 'Open Theism', regularly saying, 'God does not have to know the things that aren't, to know all things!' Though his unorthodox views set him at odds with many of his theology colleagues, such views served as a catalyst for critical and creative thinking for me and a handful of other undergrads. Little did I know that one day Bob would be my student at the seminary where we would do a directed study on miracles.

This change in my life was followed that summer by what could only be described as a transformation: taking summer school Greek with French Arrington, who was fresh off a double sabbatical leave to complete the course work for his PhD and was in the process of writing his dissertation. Though I had attempted Greek earlier my sophomore year, my many other involvements did not allow sufficient time to complete it properly. So that summer I repeated the first semester, to make sure my foundation was sufficient, and went on to complete the second semester as well. By this time, I began to sense something of my future vocation, though at that point it was not so grand as to think I could land a teaching job in some Christian college, but I thought perhaps I could at least teach Bible in a Christian high school somewhere. From that moment, whenever I could take a course with French I signed up, even commuting three hours with him one night a week to an extension of Western Carolina University where he had been asked to teach. French became my role model, guide, and unofficial advisor. He modeled for me how one could be a minister in the Church of God and a university trained bible scholar. Of course there were others who played significant roles in my development and formation, such as Bill George and Kyle Hudson, but French became my role model. From that point on I went to school year round, having an incredible love of and desire for learning more about the bible, graduating a semester early. Fellow undergrads with whom I would later develop close working relationships included Rick Moore, Lee Roy Martin, Jackie Johns, and Cheryl Bridges (who was in the band with me). But all that lay in the future.

During my last semester at the college, it was only necessary for me to take about ten hours to graduate. As it happened, the denomination would open a graduate school that very semester, the Church of God Graduate School of Christian Ministries. The Dean and Director of this new school, Hollis Gause, allowed me to begin my graduate studies whilst completing the requirements for the BA. Thus, I was present at the school's official opening and heard Dean Gause say, 'This is an historic day in the Church of God; we have a seminary!' During my undergraduate studies, I had taken the first semester of Systematic Theology with him, but completed the second semester with another instructor owing to the fact that Dr Gause left his position as Academic Dean at the college to become the first Dean and Director of the graduate school. Later I would tell him it was like a message in tongues one semester followed by the interpretation the next semester, to which Hollis quipped, 'I didn't know my colleague had that particular gift!'

In addition to working with Hollis and getting to know his strengths as a scholar, I also took classes with F.J. May, a masterful expository preacher, by whom I was introduced to the idea of the messianic secret in Mark, as well as certain literary observations about the text of Scripture. The graduate school also called on the services of French Arrington, which was fine by me, since I could take additional courses with him. Winston Elliot rounded out the adjunct faculty, offering courses in Evangelism and Renewal. He was also a gifted critical thinker and I learned a great deal from our conversations.

For my internship I developed an adult Bible institute at my home church, which is now the Woodward Avenue Church of God in Athens, TN, where my Dad had been appointed by the Bishop, after years of sensing that one day he would do a work for the Lord there. From the moment of his arrival, the church experienced phenomenal growth spiritually and numerically. Except for a two-year pastoral stint in Huntsville, AL, he would serve Woodward as pastor for close to thirty years, eventually being honored as Pastor

Emeritus. My own life would be impacted by this congregation and the ministry of my father in ways that I still am unable to account for adequately. The best of what I know of pastoral ministry has come from him.

The Athens Bible Institute consisted of courses offered once a week to people all over the Athens District at little to no charge. During this period I began to feel more strongly that the Lord was calling me to a ministry in teaching. At this point my thought was that perhaps there might be a small bible school somewhere that might hire me to teach. In fact, one such option presented itself in the form of an offer to teach at a little school in Georgetown, DE called the Harvest Bible Institute, founded by Pastor Sonny Cox of the Georgetown Church of God, who had a vision to bring in a faculty member with graduate training in bible and theology. He even invited me up a couple of times to preach and investigate the possibility of a commute to Philadelphia, PA to complete the MDiv at Eastern Baptist Theological Seminary, where Bernard Ramm taught. In the end it didn't work out for me to join Pastor Cox in this venture, but it was a great encouragement to know that there were places where the Lord might one day use my gifts.

One of the things I did in my internship was to invite a couple of the Lee College teachers to teach for us. I enlisted the help of Bill George to teach theology and brought in Charles Beach to teach a course on evangelism. It was the latter that had a profound impact on my life in a way Brother Beach never knew. At the time, one of Brother Beach's French students had agreed to tutor me as I tried to acquire the requisite language skills for further graduate study. One day he spotted the two of us sitting on a bench together on the Lee campus. Later he rang the Woodward parsonage to say that he would not be able to drive up that night to teach, but had secured a substitute and said to my mother, 'By the way, your son has a cute girlfriend!' When Mom gave me the message she insisted on seeing a picture of my 'girlfriend' and even though I told her the real story, she would not relent. So, I showed her my friend's picture in the college yearbook and as she leafed through the book she came to the picture of Barbara Diane Reckner. Pointing her out, Mom pronounced Barb to be the most beautiful co-ed at Lee and that I should date her! The next time I saw Barb on campus I told her my mother thought she was the most beautiful co-ed at Lee and asked if she wanted to meet my Mom. When she asked where I lived, I told her Hawaii! We soon began to date, on our first date going to Gatlinburg and that night to a 'Chicago' concert at the University of Tennessee in Knoxville (so much for secular music). Soon we were inseparable.

Since I was not certain where to continue my studies, Winston Elliot had worked it out for me to transfer to Fuller Theological Seminary with advanced standing and with similar opportunities at Columbia Theological Seminary (where both French and Hollis attended), my journey to Ashland Theological Seminary was unexpected and somewhat miraculous. Over the Christmas break of 1976 I had gone to Rochester, PA to see Barb and for reasons I no longer recall we broke up. That evening I left her house and began to drive, not really knowing where I was going. Eventually I made my way to my cousin's house just across the Michigan border from Toledo. My cousin Mike, three years my elder, was a Methodist pastor. During my visit we talked and prayed quite a lot as I sought to figure out my next step. Despite my emotional state I knew that I was to further my studies. So my last night at Mike's I sat up in the bed, opened the bible at random and my eyes fell on Heb. 12.12 which said, 'Therefore, strengthen your feeble arms and weak knees' (NIV). Lifting my hands I prayed the words of this verse.

The next morning I got on I-75 and headed south, not knowing where I was going. As lunch-time approached, I began to decide where to eat, and though I had little money, I felt that I should stop at a particular steak house for which I saw a sign. Having ordered my food, I looked around the restaurant and asked the Lord what I was doing there. While eating my meal I spotted a man reading a book called *Epiphany* and, taking this as a sign from the Lord, I approached his table and asked if we could chat. It turned out he was a minister and as I poured out my whole story, we began to talk about my next step. At the time, the Dean of Ashland Seminary was Joseph Schultz whom I had met at Lee during a recruiting trip. Our conversation turned to Ashland and I discerned that I should turn up there, even though I had not applied! So, late on a January afternoon I arrived at Ashland, where I was welcomed with open arms and given an efficiency apartment that very night, was admitted later that week (after filling out all of the paperwork in case any accreditation officers should be reading), and began classes!

Given advanced standing and in the light of my undergraduate major I was allowed to concentrate in biblical, theological, and language studies. In addition to book studies I took courses in textual criticism with one of Bruce Metzger's students, finished my year of Hebrew, studied Aramaic, and spent a summer studying and digging in Israel. Whilst at Ashland I was looked after by Professor Richard Allison, with whom I went to Israel, but with whom I had no other classes (!), was inspired by Jerry Flora not to leave experience behind in the doing of theology, and was encouraged by old Professor Louie Gough to apply to Princeton's ThM program to study with Bruce Metzger. His last words of advice were, 'Wear a suit and maybe get a haircut', advice for which he later offered an apology. However, I was not offended, marking it up as a generational thing. Dr Gough even went so far as to arrange an interview for me with Metzger on Good Friday, 1977. After I had a chat with Metzger in his home, which felt like the holy of holies to this kid from Appalachia, he invited me to do a course on the Sermon on the Mount with him later that summer to see what I thought! One of the other significant events at Ashland came during a convocation sermon by a Dr Paul Shin entitled, 'Do You Love Me more than These', the main point being 'do you love the gift or the giver'. I went forward to pray, confessing to God that I did not know the answer to that question but knew that I wanted to love the giver more than the gifts. When I got back that weekend from visiting my cousin Mike and his wife Suzie I had a phone call awaiting me from Barb. I went home to Tennessee the next weekend. We were engaged to be married later that year.

Completing the MDiv at Ashland in December, 1977, I arrived in Princeton on a snowy January day. Needless to say I was ecstatic to be a student in my new surroundings there. The entire experience energized me. The location was historic; up the street from Albert Einstein's old house, across the street from the university, a ten minute walk to Nassau Hall of Continental Congress fame, and across the highway from the New Jersey Governor's mansion. The campus itself was extraordinarily lovely and conducive to serious research, always inspiring me after a walk across its grounds. The seminary library seemed to have everything, and it if should not have everything it was only a short walk to the university library on its campus. And then, of course, there was the faculty. In addition to taking about half of my coursework with Metzger, I was privileged to study with Karl Froelich, Charles Fritsch, Donald Juel, as well as E. Earle Ellis and John Bright, who were brought in for special summer courses. If my experience at Ashland stretched me in moving from a Pentecostal community to a more broadly evangelical one, Princeton stretched me further still. It was whilst at Princeton that I came up with a list of things that I wanted to know more about. The list included: footwashing, sanctification, Spirit Baptism, and Jude, among other things.

Halfway through my ThM coursework, Barb and I were married (27 May 1978). She joined me in Princeton, where she worked as a receptionist for Hilton Realty and then for the Gallup Organization, actually receiving a donation from George Gallup himself for a bike-a-thon at the Bordentown Church of God, where we attended. We have fond memories of the church and especially of the Pastor and his wife, Steve and Pam Gwaltney, who became dear friends. After subletting an apartment for the summer, we were invited to housesit for the rest of our time in Princeton. The house, a mansion in which we occupied the servants' quarters, was located about a half mile from the seminary in one direction and the Gallup Organization in the other. Barb and I often met at the university library, and had lunch on its lawn. Saturday afternoons were sometimes spent at Princeton University football games, delightful experiences of which we still speak.

After completing the ThM we moved to Cleveland, TN, in order for Barb to finish her BS degree at Lee. During this period I served as a proof reader at the Church of God Publishing House, acquiring skills that would come in handy later, and I was invited by Hollis Gause to teach my first course at an extension in Birmingham, AL for the graduate school, New Testament Introduction. To say the least I was excited to no end for such a wonderful opportunity, even though I was the youngest person in the class!

That autumn would find me in Charlottesville, VA beginning PhD studies at the University of Virginia. Whilst there I worked with Harry Gamble, Dan Via, Judith Kovacs, and Martin Jaffee, being able to do additional work in the Gospels, New Testament Theology, Greek, Hellenistic Religions, Early Judaism, and Rabbinic Judaism. At UVa I made a life long friend in another graduate student, Phil Jacobs, and in the Pastor of the Crozet Church of God,

Herbert Frazier. During this period I was asked to adjunct during the summers at the graduate school in Cleveland.

Upon completion of my coursework at UVa I was invited to teach at Lee College, replacing John Sims, who was going to Princeton on sabbatical leave. In the meantime, French Arrington moved to the grad school, now known as the Church of God School of Theology, so I inherited several of French's courses upon arrival. In addition to teaching a full load, I took comprehensive exams at UVa and served part-time as the Associate Pastor at the Woodward Avenue Church of God in Athens, TN. However, the most important event that year was the birth of our daughter, Paige Diane on 28 August 1981.

The year went well and I enjoyed teaching very much indeed (Romans and Galatians, 1 and 2 Corinthians, John, Person and Work of the Holy Spirit, third year Greek, and Christian Thought being amongst the courses taught). In personal, private conversations I was being assured by the President and Board Chair that my Visiting Lecturer post would be made permanent and that I would be at Lee for a long, long time. But 1981-82 proved to be a challenging financial year for the College and it became evident to me that I should look elsewhere for a teaching post. Two opportunities presented themselves. One offer came from West Coast Christian College in Fresno, CA, inviting me to be the Dean of the four-year bible college there. When it became apparent that I was leaving Lee, the School of Theology (seminary) offered me a job; it was a sensitive issue for the School of Theology not to take biblical studies faculty members from Lee College in two successive years. During this time I called on the General Overseer, Ray H. Hughes, for direction. After explaining the situation I said, 'You are the General Overseer of the Church of God, you tell me where to go and I will go there', to which he responded, 'Brother I can't do that. Both of our schools need you'. After an excruciating period of prayer and reflection, I decided to cast my lot with the School of Theology.

At the School of Theology I was honored to become a colleague to my friend and mentor, French Arrington, former teacher F.J. May, Harold Hunter, Bob Crick, Steve Land, and my friend from undergraduate days at Lee, Rick Moore. Teaching at the graduate level brought with it the opportunity to specialize, so I settled into courses in Matthew, Mark, John, First Century Judaism, Early

Church, Hellenistic Backgrounds to the New Testament, and Life and Teaching of Jesus. Those early days saw lots of drawing of swords as we as a faculty sought to come to terms with what a distinctively Pentecostal seminary would look like and what should characterize a Pentecostal approach. It was an exciting time, but at the same time a bit disorienting as faculty members with training across the theological spectrum were involved in the dialogue. Slowly but surely a corporate vision began to emerge, and as the faculty began to expand, other insightful perspectives were added to the mix, such as those of Cheryl Bridges Johns. Though everyone made contributions to the process and to me personally, it was Rick Moore who would become my most trusted and helpful dialogue partner for years to come as we argued out a variety of points relevant to 'Pentecostal Theology' and Pentecostal approaches to biblical studies.

Since arriving at the seminary to teach full time in 1982, I had faithfully worked on my UVa PhD dissertation on John 13, a topic I had long wanted to examine, even exploring the subject in a few seminar papers along the way. Progress was slow but steady. However, real differences began to emerge with regard to methodological approach, as I was taking my first unsteady steps toward narrative criticism, becoming more and more dissatisfied with what I felt was the circularity of redactional approaches, which I was being asked to follow. It was a very stressful time for us. Barb, who had completed a Master of Education in health and physical education at the University of Tennessee at Chattanooga, was teaching at a local college; Paige was now seven and in elementary school; and our youngest daughter, Lori Danielle, had just been born on 21 June 1988. As Barb and I prayed about the future, asking questions like, 'should we perhaps be doing something else with our lives in terms of ministry', the difficulties with regard to the dissertation were starting to affect me physically.

During this time, the stress had caused the muscles in my back and neck to tighten to the point that my doctor told me it was pulling my vertebrae out of line, so I was instructed to wear a neck brace for support. One Sunday morning as I led a worship service at an extended care facility we were closing by quoting Psalm 23, with which we always closed. During that time the mouths of residents, who seemed to be completely oblivious to their surroundings until that moment, would begin to move, as they would mouth the words of this psalm. But on this occasion, when we got to the words, 'Thou preparest a table before me', the Lord spoke directly to me. He asked, 'Don't you believe I can do this for you?' To which I responded, 'No Lord, help my unbelief!'

Not long after, I wrote Earle Ellis, with whom I had studied at Princeton, seeking his advice. He worked it out for me to transfer to Southwestern Baptist Theological Seminary to complete the PhD, the caveat being that I would be unable to work with him (owing to his placement at the time in the theology department), but would need to work with a colleague named LaCoste Munn instead, and that I would need to complete some coursework and exams in order for the degree to be their own. When I chatted with Professor Munn, he noted that all I really needed to do was complete the dissertation, not redo earlier work, and suggested that I consider schools in the UK, offering to talk with Howard Marshall personally, who would be at SWBTS in a few days' time. At SBL I also arranged to visit Sheffield via contact with David Clines and to visit James Dunn in Durham.

Thus, in January 1989 I made an exploratory trip to the UK staying with my friend and former student Brian Robinson and his wife Faye in Northampton, where he served as Principal of Overstone College. Making a quick train stop in Sheffield on my way to Aberdeen, I located the department, and had a quick chat with Andrew Lincoln, who impressed me very much indeed, with a formal talk to follow the next Monday. Spending the night in Edinburgh with former teacher and colleague Don Bowdle, who was on sabbatical leave from Lee College, I arrived at Aberdeen right on time, despite waking up late and a rail breakdown in Luchars (!). Howard Marshall took me to lunch where we discussed the possibilities with regard to a transfer to Aberdeen, the caveat being that his supervisory load was full and I would need to work with a colleague. Returning to Sheffield I attended a weekly seminar and had formal talks with John Rogerson, the Head of Department, and then with Andrew. When I left Sheffield I knew that was where I was supposed to be. The meeting in Durham never took place, as Dunn's letter indicating he could not keep our appointment passed me in the air.

Having been at the School of Theology since 1982 I had a sabbatical leave coming to which the school combined a mini-term leave so that I would be able to spend a full academic year in Sheffield. Leaving Barb with the girls in the USA, though, was very difficult. But as often in our lives together, Barb rose to the occasion and I worked doubly hard for as the saying goes, 'guilt is the gift that keeps on giving'! With me, when I arrived at Sheffield, was a copy of the Vanderbilt PhD dissertation of my colleague Rick Moore, which I hand-delivered to David Clines for possible publication as part of the *Journal for the Study of the Old Testament* Supplement Series. When I next saw David, he was raving about Rick's work and did indeed accept it for publication.

The Biblical Studies Department in Sheffield was everything I heard it to be: lively, provocative, creative, energetic, and academic. Trips were arranged to the Manson Lectures in Manchester, where I met Barnabas Lindars and Richard Bauckham for the first time, visiting the John Rylands Library beforehand, seeing $\mathfrak{P}^{52}$ (the oldest extant NT manuscript [140 CE]) as well as a number of John Wesley manuscripts. From the beginning, Andrew Lincoln treated me as a colleague and I learned much about critical reflection, academic writing, and what constituted excellent supervision from him. Though he thought the outline for completion of the thesis an ambitious one, we came very close indeed to hitting it bang on the mark, submitting in April 1990 with my viva scheduled for early July. Stephen Smalley would be the external examiner. Unfortunately, the Thursday I was to fly to the UK I had emergency gall bladder surgery. Being released from the hospital on Saturday, I left on Sunday, flew all night to London, where my late flight was met by Brian Robinson, who got me from London's Gatwick Airport to Sheffield in two and a half hours! When the examining committee returned from lunch I was waiting outside the examining room. The viva proved successful and I was awarded the degree.

One of the things I discovered about myself during my sojourn in Sheffield was my own developing sense of Pentecostal theological identity and how much having a community like the one emerging at the School of Theology back in Cleveland offered orientation in a disorienting theological world. Little did I realize that I would meet someone whilst in Sheffield who would become one of the leading biblical scholars in the tradition, a Canadian named Blaine Charette. Blaine would become a close friend and co-conspirator in any number of academic ventures in the days to come. Before leaving Sheffield, David Clines asked that I submit my thesis for possible publication in the *Journal for the Study of the New Testament* Supplement Series. I was honored and delighted. It would, along with Rick's publication, serve as a nice *inclusio* around my time in Sheffield.

My experience in the UK would forever change me. I found that I quite liked England, that it felt very familiar to me. My time in Sheffield, Northampton, where I lectured fortnightly, Cambridge, where I spent considerable time at Tyndale House and the University Library, as well as time in London, created a hope in me that I would be able to return often. Little did I know that I would average one trip a year to the UK nearly every year to the present.

Within months of my return to Cleveland, we were discerning a certain critical mass in our thinking and theological reflection at the School of Theology. It seemed to us that something special was going on and we suspected elsewhere as well. For me the role and nature of the five-fold Gospel (Jesus is Savior, Sanctifier, Holy Spirit Baptizer, Healer, and Soon Coming King) within Pentecostal theology not only resonated with my own experience but also brought a great deal of clarity as to the theological heart of the movement.

At the annual meeting of the Society for Pentecostal Studies that fall at Christ for the Nations Institute in Dallas, TX, a veritable theological explosion took place in the program arranged by Murray Dempster. Presenters included Frank Macchia, Peter Kuzmič, Robert Menzies, and Roger Stronstad, among others. As I recall, Rick and I were staying in one of the dormitory rooms, designed a bit like a hotel room with two single beds and a lamp above a night stand between the beds. We had just concluded yet another late night conversation about our excitement and disappointment with what we had discovered at this meeting. In fact, we had even turned out the light and were preparing for sleep, when like a bolt out of the blue, the Lord impressed upon me an idea that seemed both realistic and unrealistic all at the same time. I immediately shared the idea with Rick in words something like, 'Rick, you know what we should do?' without giving him a chance to respond, 'We should propose to Sheffield Academic Press that they undertake the publication of an academic series of monographs on Pentecostal theology to be published in paperback, ensuring that actual individual readers could afford to purchase them'. I added, 'David (Clines) and Philip (Davies) are just crazy enough to go for it!' At that moment the lights came back on, both literally and figuratively. We knew immediately what the first volume should be, Steve Land's soon to be completed Emory University PhD dissertation on Pentecostal Spirituality, a work that in large part would chart the course for a variety of constructive engagements in the area of Pentecostal Theology, to be followed by Cheryl Bridges Johns' work on Pentecostal Formation. Other manuscript possibilities seemed to spring to us almost out of nowhere. Amazingly enough, our late night work looked as good, if not better, in the light of day the next morning.

In those days the SPS annual meeting occurred during the autumn so it would not be but a fortnight before I made a trip to New Orleans for the annual SBL/AAR meeting, accompanied by Steve Land, who had been brought on board as a collaborator. In New Orleans I was able to make an appointment with David Clines for a fortnight later, when I would be in Sheffield to receive formally my recently completed PhD degree. When I arrived in Sheffield I discovered that our carefully crafted proposal had been inadvertently left in Cambridge, where I was staying, so I had to make an oral presentation from memory. Having posted the proposal upon my return to Cambridge, back in the USA we awaited word from the Press.

On a cold, clear January day a letter from Sheffield Academic Press arrived with the long awaited (pre-email!) response. I yelled out to Rick, whose office was across from mine in the attic of a lovely old historic home, to come and hear the news first-hand. The response was all we had hoped for and more. David and Philip were enthusiastic about the series of monographs and gave us the green light to pursue our plan. But there was more. 'Would the three of us kindly agree to edit a companion journal to be called the *Journal of Pentecostal Theology*', they asked? We were simply overwhelmed by what the Lord had done. Not only had a door been opened to publish affordable academic monographs committed to the exploration of constructive Pentecostal theology, but a companion journal had also been dropped in our laps. Such a development reinforced our conviction that neither of the projects were for us, but were projects we were to hold in trust for the tradition. The positive response to our proposal offered by David and Philip is testimony to their adventurous spirit and willingness to give those on the margins a voice around the academic table. It was especially humbling that ours was the Press' first venture beyond biblical studies into 'theology'. For this kindness, foresight, and courage we are forever grateful. And so it began.

The next years would be full of excitement and affirming developments. Eventually, *JPT* and *JPTSup* would be joined by a Pentecostal Commentary Series, publishing ventures that opened doors and even launched the academic careers of numerous colleagues in and around the tradition. Thus, Rick and I would devote a not insignificant amount of time to editing the work of others, an activity that would be an education in itself.

On the writing and research front I have been fortunate to have had a sense of divine leading when it came to major research projects. Such had been the case with the Footwashing research, which sought to gain a better understanding of this rite practiced across the early Pentecostal movement. I had also felt divine leading with the Devil, Disease, and Deliverance project, which sought to bring some clarity to the whole issue of healing that had become somewhat dualistic in parts of the tradition, the commentary on 1, 2, 3 John, as well as a recently completed commentary on the Apocalypse (with Frank Macchia). I would never have dreamed that my writing projects would lead me to five continents around the globe for discerning conversations about them, invitations for which I am humbled. Each has its own story and I am grateful for the Lord's leading in such ways.

Those who would join the faculty of the seminary over the years, with whom I would interact significantly in various research projects, include Kimberly Alexander, Ken Archer, Ayo Adewuya, and last but not least my old college friend, Lee Roy Martin. Lee Roy would not only come along side me to edit *JPT*, when Rick found it necessary to resign owing to his new duties in a post he had taken up at Lee University, but with him and Steve Land would also establish the Centre for Pentecostal Theology on the campus of the Pentecostal Theological Seminary (the school's latest name). Lee Roy and I would go on to found CPT Press, a venture into which I went reluctantly but from which a great deal of affordable Pentecostal scholarship is already emerging. Perhaps the influence of David Clines and Philip Davies continues to be felt in this foray as well. For all of this I am humbled and grateful.

Amongst professional developments, my being named as the first holder of the Clarence J. Abbott Chair of Biblical Studies at the Seminary and being elected into membership of the Studiorum Novi Testamenti Societas have been extraordinary honors, as has been the offer to serve with my good friend William Kay on the staff of Bangor University in Wales, for whom I supervise PhD students in North America. This work, too, is hosted by the Centre for Pentecostal Theology and provides a warm environment in which doctoral level students and established scholars can conduct their research. Whilst the Pentecostal tradition does not yet have a Tyndale House type research facility, the CPT is a humble step in that direction.

As ever, the local church continues to inspire, inform, and support my Pentecostal scholarship. I am personally convinced that it is well nigh impossible to be a Pentecostal theologian if one is not part of a worshipping Pentecostal community. For a number of years I have taught and preached weekly, prayed for the sick, prayed with those in the altars, and been involved in ministry to the community. Despite the presence of a number of so-called 'professional people', our church is a church on the margins in many respects, with numerous poor people (and/or their children), a large Hispanic constituency, a growing African American presence, a number of individuals who have been delivered and/or seek deliverance from addictions of various sorts, the mentally challenged, as well as ex-convicts. The testimonies, prayers, and words of the saints continue to feed my own life as a Pentecostal scholar. They have made a place for me and me for them. Without them, I would be all the poorer, indeed I might not be at all.

They say that a full life is better than an empty life, if so I have a 'better' life. My wife continues to be the hardest working and most steadfast person I know, my daughters Paige and Lori serve the Lord in their respective fields of aerospace and communications, my sons-in-law David (Paige's husband) in electrical engineering and Chad (Lori's husband) in business; all choice servants of the Lord. My parents, without whom I would never have had the opportunity to pursue the academic study of the New Testament, continue as witnesses in my own life and the lives of countless others.

My advice for others who might follow is simple: follow what is in your heart, discerning and becoming what God has created you to be, and do not stop short.

As my maternal grandmother, Lena King, lay dying in the hospital, she began to cry. When my Mother asked her what was wrong she said, 'I wish I had done more for the Lord', to which my Mom responded, 'Mother, what else could you have possibly done? You did everything'. My grandmother said, 'I wish I hadn't let what people said keep me from doing the things the Lord laid on my heart'.

So may it be with me.

So may it be with you.

8

A Hopeful Journey

Lee Roy Martin[*]

The Value of Testimony

> Let the redeemed of the Lord say so,
> whom the Lord has redeemed
> from the hand of the adversary (Ps. 107.2).

Every Wednesday night at the Cumming Church of God we shared our testimonies of God's work in our lives. This witness was not considered optional. When I first came into the Pentecostal church (or 'Holiness church' as it was more commonly called in my early experience), I was immediately taught the benefit of testimony – believers are made overcomers 'by the blood of the Lamb and by the word of their testimony' (Rev. 12.11). I was taught also that if we fail to testify when given the opportunity, we are acting in disobedience to the Scriptural command, 'Let the redeemed of the Lord say so' (Ps. 107.2). Furthermore, in light of the fact that those who are full of the Spirit have 'holy boldness' (Acts 4.13, 29, 31), any fear of testifying indicates that we need to pray for our baptism in the Holy Spirit or for a 'refilling'. I am grateful, therefore, for this opportunity to offer a brief testimony of my redemption in Christ and my calling to be a Pentecostal scholar.

---

[*] Lee Roy Martin (DTh, University of South Africa) is Professor of Old Testament and Biblical Languages at the Pentecostal Theological Seminary in Cleveland, TN, USA.

Born Out of Place

> They wandered in the wilderness on a desolate path;
> They could find no city to dwell in.
> Hungry and thirsty, they were nearly exhausted (Ps. 107.4-5).

It is obvious to me now that God created me for the ministry of scholarship and teaching. My calling, however, was not always so clear in my mind; and I realize that, much like Israel in the wilderness, I needed a great deal of preparation before I would be ready to fulfill the calling to which God was moving me. In fact, until I was eighteen years of age I had no idea what direction my life should take. I wandered about with no path marked before me. Even after God called me to the ministry, my view of the future was clouded with uncertainty. I prayed for guidance as to whether I should be a pastor, a missionary, or an evangelist (the categories of teacher and scholar did not enter my mind as they were not aggressive enough to match the urgent needs of the last days). Before settling down at the Pentecostal Theological Seminary, I journeyed as a pastor through many communities, cities, and states. In our first fourteen years of pastoral ministry, Karen (my wife) and I moved nine times.

My wandering, however, started before my birth. I was born out of place, away from home, and in strange surroundings. My parents and all of my grandparents lived in northern Georgia, but I was born in Texas (a desolate country in comparison to Georgia). My father had been drafted to serve in the army during the Korean war, and while he was in Korea, his young pregnant wife waited for him at Fort Hood in Killeen, Texas. There in the army hospital, far from friends and family, alone and afraid, my eighteen-year-old mother gave birth to me on a Sunday morning in January, 1955. We were alone in the world and feeling very much in exile.

Away Down South

> The Lord delivered them from their distresses,
> And the Lord led them forth on a straight path
> That they might go to a city to dwell in (Ps. 107.7).

Upon my father's discharge from the Army, we returned to Georgia, where I remained until I left home to attend Lee College (now Lee University). We lived in the Friendship community, a rural area of Northern Georgia between the small towns of Canton and Cumming. It was a monolithic community where everyone held to the same worldview. We were white; we were Baptists; and we were conservatives. We loved Franklin Roosevelt and hated Communism. Sadly, Forsyth County had become all white as a result of the racial cleansing that began in 1912 when African-Americans were advised to leave the county or suffer violence. Throughout the twentieth century, the people in power allowed it to be known that African-Americans should not even attempt to pass through the county, much less settle there. My first conversation with an African-American occurred when I was sixteen and our high school soccer team had stopped off at a McDonald's in Atlanta. An African-American man standing beside me looked at our school bus and asked, 'You from Forsyth County?' 'Yes', I replied. 'I'll never go there again', he said; 'I drove through there last month and by the time I got out of the county my truck was shot through with holes'. Shaking my head, I apologized, 'I'm sorry; I hope you won't hold it against me'. Thankfully, my parents sheltered me from racist influences and never engaged in bigoted talk.

Like most everyone else in the community, my grandparents were hard working people who had grown up on the farm. They exemplified the Southern ethos, with its hospitality, conservative morality, and Christian underpinnings. My maternal grandfather, Roy Sanders (from whom I received my middle name), managed a chicken farm with four or five chicken houses, each one housing 3,000 to 5,000 chickens as they grew from chicks to young 'broilers'. It was later converted to an egg producing operation. Pop Sanders was an interesting man. Three of his fingers had been partially cut off in a sawmill accident. He enjoyed catching infant squirrels and raising them as pets, but they always grew wild when they reached adulthood. For a broken leg, he constructed his own cast out of sticks and mud. He trained his parakeet to whistle at passing women.

I always loved visiting with Pop Sanders and his second wife, Lillie Mae, who were young enough to be active and attentive to the grandchildren. Our cousins might also be there, and we would engage in great exploits together. Sometimes, Pop Sanders would take us fishing in the daytime and in the evening we would watch 'Gunsmoke' or 'Bonanza' on the TV. Lillie Mae was a kind woman and a great cook, who reminded me of Aunt Bea from 'The Andy Griffith Show' (though a bit quieter). She had a green thumb and grew many flowers and potted plants.

I was told that my maternal grandmother, Lucille Ingram Sanders, had suffered a 'nervous breakdown' and had abandoned her family when my mother was a small child. I regret that I was unable to know her. I remember seeing her four times, twice at my house and twice at her house after she had remarried. When I was small, she gave me a pair of shorts that I refused to wear; and when I was about twelve years old she gave me a chess set, which I enjoyed immensely. (She mistakenly thought she was giving me checkers, which she called 'checks'.)

Although my maternal grandparents considered themselves to be Christians, they rarely attended church, and did not outwardly practice religion. My paternal grandparents, however, were more devoted to church life. My father's father, Landrum Duffy Martin, whom I called 'Papaw' and others called 'Duffy', was a Baptist preacher. He had at one time pastored the small community church that we attended – Friendship Baptist. By the time I was old enough to know him, he had already suffered a stroke and was very sickly. In my memory I can see him walking around the yard with his cane, while he sang the old gospel song, 'I Feel Like Traveling On'. I also remember that he offered thanks before every meal, a ritual that we did not practice at home and which I rarely witnessed elsewhere. Because of a series of strokes and heart attacks, Papaw's health deteriorated rapidly. His 'nerves' would bother him whenever the grandchildren became too loud, so we were often told to go outside and play.

My paternal grandmother, Mary Belle Sosebee Martin, was a cheerful, optimistic, and energetic woman, though in my eyes she was old. She did eventually become very old, living to the age of one hundred five. Memaw, as I called her, always had a smile on her face, and she laughed frequently. I loved her fried chicken, biscuits, green beans, and mashed potatoes. She encouraged me at every opportunity and made it known that she was proud of my becoming a preacher.

When Memaw was in her 90's, she told me a story from her childhood. She lowered her voice to little more than a whisper and said,

> I want to tell you something that I have not told anyone. You know that our church didn't believe in miracles like your church does. But when I was just a little girl, my mother became very sick. The doctor gathered the family together and told us that mama would not live. We were all so sad and crying. I did not want to lose my mother, so I went in and knelt down beside my mother's bed, and I prayed. I told God that I had read about miracles in the Bible, and I asked him to perform a miracle and heal my mother. The next day, my mother got up out of the bed, and her sickness passed. I just wanted to tell you about it.

My father, Franklin Duffy Martin, was a tall, slim man with black hair. He was taciturn and introverted, but he knew how to be social when necessary. He was faithful to his obligations and to his family. Farming was his passion, but our little farm could not provide for all our needs. Therefore, he was employed 8 to 5 at a pants factory, and he worked our small farm on the side. He was too absorbed in his own pursuits to provide guidance and direction to his children, but I learned quite a lot by observation as we plowed the fields, planted fruit trees, built fences, raised livestock, and added rooms to the old farm house.

As might be expected, my mother was the most powerful influence in my early life. Lara Lee Sanders Martin (from whom I received my first name) is the only one of my ancestors who is living today. She is an outgoing, enthusiastic, and cheerful optimist. She cares deeply about everyone around her, and she is willing to demonstrate that care through her actions. I remember her seeking out extra employment in the weeks before Christmas so that she would have money to buy our gifts (I remember receiving over the years a very nice football, a slot car race track, a Timex watch, and a telescope with which I viewed the solar eclipse March 7, 1970).

My mother is a very creative and inventive person, always trying something new and changing old patterns. Back on the farm, when everyone else was growing mundane crops like beans and corn, she decided to plant asparagus and broccoli. Other people go to Wal-Mart to purchase their yarn, but she has raised sheep and made her own yarn. She milks goats and makes goat cheese. She produces homemade soap, and she built an outdoor mud oven in which to cook bread and pizza.

With broad interests that include art, music, and drama, she has acted in community theatre, and she has written and illustrated three children's books. Her singing and storytelling kept us children occupied and entertained constantly. She routinely addressed life situations with proverbial sayings, such as, 'Don't cry over spilt milk', 'A bird in the hand is worth two in the bush', 'Curiosity killed the cat', 'A stitch in time saves nine', and 'Don't count your chickens before they are hatched'.

I gained from my mother a fundamental inquisitiveness, a passion for knowledge, and an enthusiasm for living. Like my mother, I enjoy devoting myself fully to every endeavor. For us, nothing is done halfheartedly or perfunctorily.

I also received from my mother a love of art, music, and literature. She bought a set of record albums with the twenty-five greatest works of classical music, and she played them over and over for us to hear. Furthermore, she was my first and best teacher, the person in whom I witnessed most clearly the joy of discovery and the joy of helping others make their own discoveries.

My brothers and sisters have also taught me much over the years. My brother, Darryl, and I roamed the woods in search of adventure (always accompanied by our dogs). Each spring we would build a dam on a small creek, thus fashioning a swimming hole. However, the rocks and mud would be washed away in the first big rain storm. I always admired Darryl's determination. He was able to marshal the discipline necessary to overcome whatever obstacle stood before him. Darryl and I were once given the task of cutting down a large oak tree. We stood in the snow and pulled back and forth on a crosscut saw for two days before we cut through the trunk of that big oak tree.

My sisters, Angela and Mary, were several years younger than I; therefore, I did not spend as much time with them as I did with Darryl. I can only hope that I served as a positive influence upon my little sisters. In our adult years, I have enjoyed every moment that we have spent together during holidays, family reunions, and special occasions. All three of my siblings are now happily married, a fact that gives me great joy.

Growing up on a small farm means that I have memories of plowing with a mule (and later with a tractor), drawing water out of a hand-dug well, milking the cow, feeding the hogs, gathering eggs, dressing chickens, chasing possums, birthing pigs, shucking corn, picking strawberries and blackberries, eating apples and peaches fresh from the tree, cutting firewood, making slingshots, and learning all things having to do with the outdoors. I learned that seasons come and go. Both plants and animals live, grow, and die.

We experienced several years of weather so cold that the lakes froze over. One January night, a little pig's tail froze and fell off. We lived in an old house with only a single wood heater. The cracks in wall made the house so cold and drafty that we sometimes wore our coats inside the house. One night, the water in a glass beside my bed froze. During a snowstorm, snow blew in through a crack in the front door and made a small pile on the living room floor.

What we grew we ate – corn, beans, peas, and tomatoes. One year we grew a large crop of sweet potatoes. That winter we had them in boxes in the corner, in the closet, and under the beds. We ate sweet potatoes every day and in every form imaginable. When I left home, I never wanted to see another sweet potato (or bowl of pinto beans and corn bread either for that matter).

Growing up in the country taught me to be self-reliant and innovative. It taught me how to take whatever is available and make it work. It taught me an appreciation and respect for nature, the environment, natural resources, and animals. Living on the farm with my father, my mother, one brother, and two sisters taught me how to be part of a structure in which everyone has responsibilities and contributes to the benefit of the whole.

School Daze

Their hearts were bowed down with labor;
They stumbled, and there was none to help (Ps. 107.12).

Perhaps one of the reasons that I never considered becoming a teacher is that my first year in school was very traumatic. It was not that I found the curriculum to be too challenging. On the contrary, my mother had already taught me to read, write, add, and subtract. I was well prepared, and school was easy. In fact, I was so far ahead of the other students that the teacher appointed me as tutor to the slow learners (my first teaching assignment). Academics was not the problem; the problem was the combination of my own emotional immaturity and my teacher's stern approach. I was so terrified of being away from home that I became physically ill every day. On a few occasions, I was allowed to go home early, and for a short time I was given medication – 'nerve pills'. My father suffered from an anxiety disorder, and perhaps I inherited a bit of it myself. At the least, I was extremely shy and introverted. My fears could have been quieted by a caring, motherly teacher; but my first grade teacher was an austere woman who offered me little sympathy. I have never been incarcerated, but first grade seemed like prison to me. Once the door was shut each day, I felt abandoned and hopeless. Eventually, however, the anxiety attacks became briefer and less severe.

Outside of school my mother continued to encourage my intellectual development – she purchased a new set of the World Book Encyclopedia. I began reading through it while in the second grade, and, to the disdain of my teacher, I often brought my discoveries to class. Once I was telling about the extinct Dodo bird, and she exclaimed, 'There was no such thing as a Dodo bird', and she swatted my hand several times with her wooden paddle. This and many similar events provoked a deep distrust of authority figures.

By the fourth grade, when I was encouraged by my teacher, Mrs Groover, reading had become a daily occupation and a genuine passion for me. My natural thirst for knowledge was fueled by biographies of great personages such as Leonardo da Vinci, Thomas Jefferson, and George Washington Carver. I could enter great adventures in far away lands through novels such as The Golden Impala,[1] and Tarzan of the Apes.[2] By the sixth grade I was reading sometimes ten books in a week. I would read one book at school after I finished all my work; then I would take another book home and read it that night. I was disappointed when it took me three days to read David Copperfield.[3] My sixth grade achievement test placed me at an eleventh grade reading level, and, consequently, I

---

[1] Pamela Ropner, *The Golden Impala* (New York: Criterion Books, 1958).
[2] Edgar Rice Burroughs wrote twenty-six Tarzan books, each over two hundred pages, and I read every one of them.
[3] Charles Dickens, *David Copperfield* (New York: The Modern Library, 1934), 923 pages.

skipped the seventh grade and went straight to the eighth. Eighth grade was a bit of a challenge, but still I scored the highest grades in the class.

Awakening

> He brought them out of darkness and the shadow of death,
> And he broke apart their bonds (Ps. 107.14).

As a child, I gave little thought to God. Of course, I knew about God. Every school day began with a Bible reading and the Lord's Prayer, and I often attended Sunday School and Vacation Bible School. But the sermons seemed incomprehensible, and the hymns were meaningless. During worship services I preferred to sit on the back row and carve my initials into the pew in front of me. Then, when I was nine years old, everything changed suddenly.

Our church, Friendship Baptist, held a week-long revival meeting in August of each year, with a service in the morning and another in the evening. The evening services were a popular community event and were well-attended, while the morning services consisted mostly of women and children. The weather was hot, and the church was not air conditioned; therefore, we opened the windows and hoped for a breeze. We also utilized cardboard fans that featured a picture of Jesus on the front and an advertisement for Ingram funeral home on the back.

On the first evening of the revival, my family was sitting on the second pew of the small church. I have no recollection of the preacher or the sermon, but during the invitation I began to weep. I did not know why I was weeping, and, being a very private person, I was embarrassed to be weeping in public. I was especially embarrassed when a minister came over to me and asked, 'Are you lost?' I had no idea what he was talking about. He continued, 'Do you want to be saved?' The terms 'lost' and 'saved' made no sense to me. I do not remember my answer, but they led me out of my seat and over to the center pews where people were kneeling to pray. As I knelt with my face down in the pew, my grandfather came over and exhorted me, 'Just believe and confess'. Then he asked, 'Do you believe that Jesus died for your sins?' As I continued to weep, I responded weakly, 'I don't know'. Others came over to help me.

They asked me the same questions, and I kept on saying, 'I don't know'. After half an hour or so, the service ended, and I had not made a confession of faith.

The next day we returned for the morning service (absent my father, who was at work), and the same scenario played out again. The third day of the revival came, and again I cried with my face in the pew, with people asking, 'Do you believe that Jesus died for your sins?' Once again, I mumbled through my tears, 'I don't know'. After a long while, I saw in my mind a vision of Jesus as he hung on the cross, and I could hear him say, 'I did this for you'. As I viewed the scene in my mind, I said to Jesus, 'Yes, I believe'.

Oddly, I did not sense an immediate relief from the heaviness that had rested upon me. Perhaps I was so emotionally spent from the three days of struggle that I was a bit numb. As soon as I awoke the next day, however, I knew that everything had changed. My first thought was that I loved God and wanted to go to church and worship him. I had been changed.

Once my parents learned of my conversion, they informed the pastor, and I was baptized and joined the church. My conversion was a radical transformation of my heart. Before, the hymns were uninteresting to me, but now, I was eager to learn every song and sing praises to God. Songs that were previously meaningless were now deeply significant. They were the voicing of my newly created Godward affections. I began to pray for my friends who were not Christians, and I even daydreamed about someday preaching the message that had changed my life so dramatically. My new birth was a transformation of my affections, an awakening of my spirit to communion with God. Jesus had saved me.

For Love of the Game[4]

> The Lord turns the desert into a pool of water,
> And the dry ground into springs of water (Ps. 107.35).

At the age of twelve, I entered the first day of Little League tryouts with small expectations. I had not played baseball the previous year, choosing instead to spend the summer in the Boy Scouts. Two

---

[4] Title of the film, *For Love of the Game* (directed by Sam Raimi; Los Angeles: Universal Studios, 1999).

years earlier, I had barely made the team. The coach, J.W. Holbrook, lined us up at home plate and ordered us to race to center field and back. Winning the race easily, I was astonished to find that I was the fastest player on the field. Batting practice revealed similar, surprising results. I hit one pitch after another out of the park as the whole team gathered in left field and beyond to catch my home runs. Apparently, my hard winter of cutting firewood and clearing brush had produced more than just the callouses on my hands. That year, I hit a home run in every game except one, and I won every game in which I pitched. Our team won the county championship, and several of us were chosen for the all-star team, hoping to reach the Little League World Series. We won several games in the tournament, but finally we faltered and were eliminated. We consoled ourselves with the knowledge that we had advanced farther than any previous team from Forsyth County. For the next few years, I never tired of playing baseball. It became my second consuming passion (in addition to reading). I continued to play every year, through Little League, Pony League, Senior League, and high school.

Jesus saved me, but baseball helped. Baseball was to me an oasis in the desert land of adolescence. I was loved and affirmed at home, but at school I felt uneasy and self-conscious. I was the shy, socially awkward, smart kid who did not always fit in. Baseball turned me into a normal kid, and the team became my community, giving me a sense of belonging. Moreover, as I grew into my teen years, baseball kept me occupied and out of trouble.

Even though baseball is just a game, it demands discipline and long hours of practice. I learned to do my best at all times, to persevere in the face of setbacks, and to 'leave it all on the field'. In the movie, 'For Love of the Game', Kevin Costner plays the role of forty-year-old major league pitcher, Billy Chapel, who is pitching the last game of his long career. His catcher, Gus, warning the pitcher not to exhaust himself too quickly, advises Chapel, 'Chap, don't throw it away too early'. But the aging pitcher, wanting to give his very best effort and go out strong, says to his catcher, 'Today I'm throwing hard, Gus'.[5] Like Billy Chapel, I no longer have the

---

[5] Billy Chapel and Gus Sinski in *For Love of the Game*.

stamina of a young man, but I am trying to throw hard until my last pitch.

Welcome to Pentecost

> Let them exalt the Lord in the congregation of the people,
> And let them praise the Lord in the assembly of the elders (Ps. 107.32).

My academic success continued through high school where I placed second in the Governor's Honors Program and received an award in the eleventh grade for the highest score on the PSAT. My studies focused heavily on math and science, which helped me to score above the 98th percentile on both the SAT and ACT.

In our senior year of high school, my best friend and I joined the Future Teachers of America, not because either one of us hoped to become teachers, but because the membership consisted of thirty girls and no boys. It never occurred to me that I possessed both the gifts and the disposition to be a teacher. Even my frequent tutoring of other students did not give me a clue. My love of the outdoors caused me to look into the careers with the National Park Service. I was intrigued by the mysteries of the deep, and I considered studying marine biology. My aptitude for math coupled with my interest in astronomy made me lean toward the newly formed NASA as a future career path.

Little did I know that God was about to set me on a new path that would eventually bring me to where I am today. Just as he did when I was converted at the age of nine, God appeared when I least expected him.

Our senior English course was taught by a young woman who enjoyed creative assignments, and one of those assignments required us to work together in teams to produce an essay on a topic of contemporary interest. I was joined with Brinkley Goodson, the son of a local pharmacist. Brinkley was known to be rebellious and full of teenage angst – given to cigarettes, drinking, fighting, and smoking pot. I never socialized with him and had rarely even spoken to him. Reluctantly and apprehensively I met with him to talk about our project and soon learned, to my amazement, that he was friendly and easy to work with.

We took a ride in his car, and he proceeded to tell me that God had recently changed his life when he accepted Christ in a revival service at the Cumming Church of God. He then looked over at me and asked, 'Do you know Jesus?' The truth is that in the seven years since my conversion, my family had stopped attending church; I had drifted away from God, and I had lost my 'first love' (Rev. 2.4). I had starting to seek my teenage independence, and I was developing new interests (with names like Angie, Karen, and Patty).

Recalling my experience in the Baptist Church, I replied to Brinkley's question in the affirmative and explained that I had received Christ and was a church member. My answer would have satisfied anyone from within the typical religious community, but in light of Brinkley's affiliation with the Church of God (which was anything but typical), he pressed for more information, 'Have you been baptized in the Holy Ghost?' I was puzzled and answered, 'What is the Holy Ghost?' At that point, he presented the case for Spirit baptism, leading me through several biblical passages in support of the doctrine. I reiterated the fact that I had not been taught about the Holy Ghost. He continued, 'Did they teach you about the second coming of Jesus?' I answered, 'No, I haven't heard anything about that either'. Brinkley then shared several scriptures regarding the return of Jesus. He invited me to a revival that was going on at the Church of God. I was soon a regular attender, and within a year I had experienced sanctification and had been baptized in the Holy Spirit.

The Cumming Church of God was known locally for its external 'holiness' teachings – no jewelry, no makeup, and no worldly amusements. Unfortunately, the church's legalistic stance made it appear bizarre to some people. I soon learned, however, that underneath the external restrictions was a deep spiritual freedom that enthralled me and eventually liberated me. Although the church was best known for what it stood against, I was captivated by what it stood for. It advocated a fully formed Pentecostal spirituality that exemplified what Steve Land has called 'a passion for the kingdom'.[6] The joyful singing, exuberant shouting, and unrestrained prayer were evidence of the manifest presence of God. In every worship service we prayed at the altar; we invited sinners to be

---

[6] E.g. the subtitle of Steven Jack Land, *Pentecostal Spirituality: A Passion for the Kingdom* (Cleveland, TN: CPT Press, 2010), p. 2 and *passim*.

saved; we prayed for the sick; and we prayed for people to be baptized in the Holy Ghost. In every service we were reminded, 'Jesus
is coming soon' and he is coming for a church that is sanctified.
Revivals were frequent, and it seemed like I was in church almost
every night.

The pastor of the Cumming Church of God, Rev. Dewey F.
Miller, was a positive role model for me and always available. My
life and ministry was also influenced by two outstanding women
ministers – Rev. Chloe Miller (wife of the pastor) and Rev. Mae
Terry. Sister Terry had planted several churches in Georgia (including the Cumming church) and was well-known as an evangelist.
Both of these women loved the young people in the church, and
they devoted themselves to mentoring us in the areas of Bible
study, prayer, and preaching.

In 1970 the Pentecostal church occupied a relatively insignificant
position on the religious landscape. Pentecostal theology and practice had not yet influenced the church world to the degree that we
witness today. At that time, most non-Pentecostals considered
speaking in tongues to be aberrant behavior (or demonic). The belief in miracles was not commonplace. Prayer for the sick was practiced only in Pentecostal churches. Praise and worship music was
unheard of. Non-Pentecostal churches did not offer 'contemporary'
worship services, and Pentecostals were not yet on television – in
fact, there were no Christian TV networks at all. Furthermore,
Christian denominations (including the Church of God) were more
monolithic than they are now, and both ministers and laity were
more devoted to their denominations. The consumerist approach
had not yet come to dominate the church world.

Looking back on my first conversation with Brinkley Goodson,
I am struck by his ability to communicate the Fivefold Gospel after
having been a Christian for only a few months. His facility in the
Scriptures is evidence of that church's commitment to discipleship
and to Pentecostal doctrine. New believers were expected to learn
biblical teachings and follow Jesus wholeheartedly. For most of the
members, church attendance was not just a religious duty to be
added to their schedule of diverse activities. The church was more
than a peripheral element in their otherwise secular lives. Instead,
the church was central to their lives, the locus of their primary experience of community. It was in this quintessential Pentecostal

church that I was baptized in the Holy Spirit and formed as a Pentecostal believer and minister.

Ramblin' Wreck[7]

> They cry out to the Lord in their trouble,
> And the Lord brings them out of their distresses (Ps. 107.28).

Graduation from high school gave me little consolation because at that point I was forced to make decisions about my future, but I could not decide what I should do with my life. My love for the Lord and my involvement in the Church of God motivated me to attend Lee College, but I had received an academic scholarship to attend Georgia Tech, a highly regarded university in Atlanta. My school counselor convinced me that I should give Georgia Tech a try for at least one year. At Tech I learned a little about some things, and I learned a lot about other things. I learned a little about calculus, architecture, and American literature. I learned a lot about the world that I had read about but had never experienced. For the first time in my life, my worldview was challenged by teachers who scoffed at religion and who ridiculed anyone who believed in God. I learned a little from those professors; mostly, I learned from them that I needed more theological education.

My most valuable lessons, however, came through interaction with other students. For the first time in my life, I engaged in conversation with people who were different from me. Down the hallway in my dorm I met Chinese, Pakistani, African-American, Jewish, and Roman Catholic students. I asked them about their lives and their cultures. We watched the Vietnam War on the TV, and played football behind the dorm. I learned that reading about other cultures is one thing, but living across the hall from an orthodox Jew is something else entirely. A few of the boys loved to drink,[8]

---

[7] The term 'Ramblin' Wreck' refers to Georgia Tech students and alumni. In the late 19th century, engineers from Georgia Tech constructed makeshift vehicles in the jungles of South America. The vehicles and the engineers who made them came to be known as 'Rambling Wrecks from Georgia Tech'.

[8] Drinking is an honored tradition at Ga. Tech, where the football fight song includes the words, 'Like all the jolly good fellows, I drink my whiskey clear'. My avoidance of alcohol offended a few of my fellow students, though one of them begged me to pray for him when he became violently ill from overdrinking.

especially on weekends when I would sometimes have to step over bodies lying on the floor in the hallway. One of the worst drinkers was a Pentecostal Holiness lad who was sowing his wild oats. The only other Pentecostal student that I met at Georgia Tech was a red-headed Assembly of God boy. He rarely left his room, but kept himself in studious seclusion. Unlike him, I attempted to participate in dorm life and at the same time be a witness for Christ, but I never felt very successful in my attempts. I was only seventeen years of age and very immature.

Called to Preach

> The Lord sent his word and healed them
> And the Lord saved them out of their distresses (Ps. 107.20).

While attending Georgia Tech, I would drive home on the weekends, work on Saturday, and attend the Church of God on Sunday. During a revival service in the spring, I received from the Lord a very clear call to ministry. The altar was full of people who were praying fervently. Many of the seekers were teenagers, and one of those was Mike Ramey, who was on the floor, weeping and crying out to God, surrounded by people who were praying with him. As I stood nearby, I heard someone say, 'God has called Mike to preach'. I thought to myself how wonderful it must be to have a calling, a sense of direction in life. As I gazed around the congregation and saw how the Holy Spirit was moving and working in people's lives, I began to praise God with all my heart. Completely occupied in praise and thoroughly engulfed in God's presence, I heard the voice of the Lord speak very clearly to me saying, 'I am calling you to preach'. It was the first time that I had ever heard the voice of God speaking to me (but it would not be the last).

I preached my first sermon at a home prayer meeting on Tuesday evening, November 27, 1973. My text was Gal. 6.16-26. I had no idea how to prepare a message or how to deliver it. The sermon was a disappointment both to me and to the audience, but I picked myself up and tried again two weeks later.

Lee College Years

> For the Lord satisfies the longing soul
> And fills the hungry soul with good things (Ps. 107.9).

In light of my call to the ministry, I decided to transfer to Lee College and major in biblical studies. I began in January of 1974 and graduated in May of 1977 with a BA in Biblical Education (with honors).

My years at Lee College made a significant impact upon my academic preparation, my spiritual formation, my ministerial development, and my personal life. In addition to OT and NT Survey and courses in history and theology, I also studied Acts, Romans and Galatians, 1 and 2 Corinthians, Prison Epistles, General Epistles, Daniel and Revelation, Wisdom Literature, Major Prophets, and Minor Prophets. Gifted and dedicated faculty members who influenced me include Robert O'Bannon, Sabord Woods, John Sims, Kyle Hudson, and Bill George. It was French Arrington, however, who best prepared me to become a Pentecostal Scholar. His courses were academically challenging and his lectures reflected serious engagement with critical scholarship. I enjoyed his New Testament Greek courses more than any in college. Learning Greek opened up for me a new world of possibilities in the study of the Bible.

My spiritual formation and ministerial development benefited from the college curriculum, but mostly they were furthered by my extra-curricular participation in 'Pioneers for Christ', a campus group founded by Lee College professor Charles Beach. Students in PFC held weekly prayer meetings, Wednesday evening worship, and services at the local nursing homes. PFC teams would also travel out of town on weekends, during breaks, and in the summer months to conduct revival meetings in Churches of God throughout the USA. We called those revival meetings 'Invasions'. My first sermon to a church congregation was delivered on an Invasion to the Florence, Alabama Church of God, March 8, 1974. I urged them to 'Wake Up!' (Rom. 13.11-12). I traveled with PFC to numbers of churches in Tennessee, Georgia, North Carolina, Louisiana, Ohio, New York, and Nebraska.

The Pioneers for Christ supplied me with a valuable 'internship' in ministry and gave me a community of faith in which to grow. I was encouraged by the spiritual example of students like Stan Rankin (who would become my brother-in-law), by Charlie Stott (my roommate), and by Milton Carter, who became one of my best friends. Milton led a PFC team of nine students to New York City in the summer of 1974, a summer which would prove to be major turning point in my life. I learned the value of daily communion with God, as Charlie and I arose early every morning for an hour of prayer. It was also during that summer that I began to practice fasting on a regular basis.

Along with daily Bible reading, the practices of prayer and fasting began to transform both my relationship with God and my approach to ministry. My passion for God intensified, and at times the Holy Spirit would move mightily when I preached. I was witnessing healings, miracles, and genuine revival. My hunger for God was intensified even further by my reading of John Wesley, George Whitefield, Charles Finney, Leonard Ravenhill, and E.M. Bounds.

My time at Lee College affected more than the academic, spiritual, and ministerial dimensions of my life. My personal life also took a 'right turn' during that time when I met and married my beautiful wife, Karen Luke. I quickly learned the depths of her love when, on our first Christmas together, she gave me the Bauer, Arndt, and Gingrich's *Greek-English Lexicon*. She outdid herself the next year by giving me Kittel's *Theological Dictionary of the New Testament*.

Karen's grandfather was a Church of God evangelist and pastor, and her parents attended the North Rocky Mount Church of God, making Karen a third generation Pentecostal. Her Pentecostal heritage has been a valuable component of our life together, and I have been deeply enriched by all the members of her family. In addition to her considerable gifts as musician, singer, teacher, and organizer, Karen is fully committed to the Pentecostal faith. When we began our pastoral ministry, she was probably more qualified to lead the church than I was.

Shepherding God's Flock

> The Lord lifts up the poor out of trouble's reach,
> And makes them families like a flock (Ps. 107.41).

I graduated from Lee College in 1977, and we moved immediately to Scottsbluff, Nebraska, to pastor a mission church. The area was predominately Lutheran and Roman Catholic, with the nearest Church of God 185 miles away in North Platte. We worked hard to get the church on its feet, paying all of the church bills ourselves. We went from there to Wichita, Kansas, where we followed a long-term pastor whose credentials had been revoked on account of adultery. The church was divided and our time there was difficult.

We enjoyed the adventure of ministering in Nebraska and Kansas, but by this time, our son Stephen had been born, and we were far away from the grandparents. We decided that we wanted to be closer to our families, so we moved east to a small church in Chatom, Alabama. I was learning that there was more to the ministry than what I had been taught in college. I realized that I could benefit from further preparation for pastoral ministry; therefore, we moved to Cleveland so that I could attend the Church of God School of Theology (now the Pentecostal Theological Seminary).

At the School of Theology, I studied with F.J. May and Robert Crick, whose courses offered me the opportunity to reflect upon my three years of pastoral experience. I already knew how to practice the Pentecostal faith, but Steve Land taught me how to understand Pentecostalism theologically and how to place the Pentecostal story with the larger Christian story. I appreciate Harold Hunter for introducing me to a wide array of contemporary issues in theology. Most important among those issues were the questions surrounding Spirit baptism both inside and outside of the Pentecostal tradition. He impressed me as a careful scholar who was not afraid to entertain hard questions. He insisted that the Scriptures can be trusted and that we should not be afraid to follow them wherever they may lead. I had two courses with Rickie Moore (Deuteronomy and Isaiah), who began teaching in my final year at the Seminary. Rickie's approach to the biblical text was based on the rhetorical/literary methods that were just beginning to gain traction in the academy. While studying with Rickie, I realized that my high school and college courses in literature and poetry might prove themselves valuable after all. I began to read books and articles on the interpretation of the Bible as literature. The Seminary was still in its infancy, but already there were signs that it would contribute significantly to a revisioning of Pentecostal theology and scholarship.

It was toward the end of my seminary studies that, for the first time, I began to entertain a future ministry of teaching. Knowing that a teaching career would require further education, I investigated a variety of ThM and PhD programs. Because I had so enjoyed my courses in Greek and Hebrew, my first choice of specialization was biblical languages. My second choice, however, was Old Testament, an area that was underrepresented in the Church of God. At that time I was unable to find a program that would be feasible. Karen was pregnant with our second son, Michael, and it seemed that the Lord was leading us to return to the pastorate and give attention to the children.

After graduation from the Seminary, I served for a short time as a pastor in Kentucky, where our second son, Michael, was born. We then moved to Arkansas. At the time, we did not understand why God placed us in Arkansas, but now we can see how the hand of God was working. During our time at McCrory, Arkansas, I adopted a regular routine of extended times for prayer and fasting. At the end of two years, the state overseer asked me if I would assume the pastorate at West Memphis. The church was in trouble and in danger of closing, so I told him that I was not at all interested. Nevertheless, I soon received a letter appointing me as pastor of the West Memphis Church of God. I called the overseer and registered my displeasure, but he would not reconsider the appointment. A few days later, I was contacted by people from the church who informed me of their own dissatisfaction with the overseer. It seems that they had requested Bud Jenkins as pastor, and if I came, they would not support me.

Under this cloud of uncertainty, we packed up and moved to West Memphis. As we were unloading our U-Haul, a man from the utility company came to shut off the church's gas because the bill was unpaid. I learned that many of the bills, including the mortgage payment, were two months behind. God helped us, and in four months we had all the bills caught up and seventy-five people in church. It was truly a miracle.

In view of the fact that I was remaining in pastoral ministry, I considered pursuing a DMin degree. As I was contemplating my options, I happened to be in Memphis for a hospital visit and passed by the Mid-America Baptist Theological Seminary, a reformed, fundamentalist institution. I stopped in and picked up a catalog, thinking that perhaps they would offer the DMin degree. If not, I might enroll in a course or two for my enrichment. To my amazement, I found that they offered a ThD in biblical languages, the very degree that I had desired to enter four years earlier.

I am convinced that, after I finished seminary, God was working without my knowledge to bring me to a place where I could enter a doctoral program. While I was complaining about the stubborn overseer, God was using him to bring me to West Memphis.

Mid-America required that I take twenty-six hours of upper level Greek and Hebrew courses as prerequisites to the ThD. I finished those courses in one year and then entered the doctoral program. The Greek and Hebrew courses at Mid-America were very helpful to me on three fronts. First, because we were not allowed to use the English text in class, my facility in reading the original languages improved dramatically. Second, the doctoral seminars included extensive exposure to recent innovative approaches to language study and textual analysis, including modern linguistics, semantics, structuralism, and discourse analysis. Third, I was able to study other Semitic languages besides Hebrew – Aramaic, Ugaritic, Akkadian, and Egyptian.

As far as I know, I was the only Pentecostal enrolled at Mid-America, and I wanted to be a positive representative for the Church of God School of Theology and for Pentecostalism. I avoided making my Pentecostal theology a distraction to the class or an annoyance to the teachers, but occasionally, someone would ask for my opinion on the subject of tongues, healing, or other related topics. On those occasions, I would respond briefly if the teacher gave me the opportunity. The teachers and the students were always kind and considerate, but their stance was clearly cessationist.

The ThD studies were requiring quite a bit of my time, and my wife had secured a good teaching position; therefore, I decided that I would resign my pastorate and attend school full-time. I called the new overseer, Wayne Taylor, to inform him of my decision. I had no intention of asking Bro. Taylor for his advice or for his help because by this time I had suffered a number of disappointments from state overseers. One overseer reneged on his promises and left me stranded. Another threatened me with retribution if I did not follow his orders – to be exact, he said, 'I will break your back'. At one church, I encountered a serious moral breach that could not be allowed to continue, so I visited my overseer to seek his guidance. His response was, 'What do you expect me to do about it? Next year, when my time is up, I'm out of here'.

To my surprise, Bro. Taylor did not accept my resignation, but instead he offered to find me a better situation within driving distance of Memphis. Subsequently, he appointed me as pastor of the Sharpe's Chapel Church of God in Wynne, Arkansas. God gave me a dream that confirmed to me the appropriateness of the new appointment, and we enjoyed three years of productive ministry while I attended doctoral seminars and began my dissertation at Mid-America. I also I taught a Monday evening Greek course for my fellow pastors, and I taught a course at the summer camp meeting on the subject of pastoral ministry.

The Open Door

> The Lord makes the storm a calm, so that the waves are still ...
> The Lord guides them to their desired harbor (Ps. 107.30).

By this time I had been elected to the State Council, and was also serving as chair of the State Ministerial Development Board. In that capacity I visited Cleveland in 1991, attending the MIP commissioning services as a representative from Arkansas. I happened to bump into Steve Land while I was in Cleveland, and after I had talked with him for a while, he asked me if I would consider moving to Cleveland and teaching part-time while I pastored. He knew of a local pastor who would be retiring soon and suggested that I might be able to assume his pastorate. I informed him that I had no desire to move at that time but that I would pray about it. Both of us understood that it would be nearly impossible for me, an out-of-state pastor, to receive an appointment in Cleveland. The next day, as I drove on Highway 64, along the Ocoee River, I began to pray about what had taken place. As I prayed, the Holy Spirit spoke to me saying, 'I have set before you an open door, and no man can shut it' (Rev. 3.8). I knew that I would be moving to Cleveland. Two months later we began our ten-year pastorate at the Prospect Church of God in Cleveland. While serving as pastor, I also taught part-time at the Seminary. I taught one course at the Seminary in 1992 (Biblical Hebrew), and I taught two courses at Lee College the same year (Old Testament Theology and Psalms). The next year, while Rickie Moore took a sabbatical leave, I taught a full load at the seminary and I taught Psalms again at Lee College. From 1993 forward, I taught only at the Seminary, where I was given a full load each year, along with student advising and committee work. I enjoyed both my preaching and my teaching ministries as they informed each other and grew simultaneously. Finally, after years of uncertain wandering, I felt like I had found my place in life.

Our move to Cleveland was naturally a stressful time for our family. However, as Stephen and Michael got adjusted to the new schools and new friends, they began to develop their impressive musical talents. In addition to his work on the piano, Stephen joined the school band and played the trombone. Michael also polished his skills on the keyboard, but he joined the show choir. Both of them performed vocal solos at school and at church. Stephen now leads music at his local church, and Michael is a performer at Dollywood theme park in Pigeon Forge, Tennessee.

Because of my busy schedule and because of insufficient supervision, I was finding it difficult to complete my dissertation for Mid-America. God knew that I needed to advance to a higher level of scholarship, and he knew how to push me to that higher level. Professor Willie Wessels, from the University of South Africa (UNISA), came to Cleveland to visit the Seminary, and he offered to accept me as a transfer student in the DTh program at UNISA. Professor Wessels had a strong background in historical critical methods, but he was also a Pentecostal pastor – a rare combination. I enrolled at UNISA and proceeded to work with Wessels as my supervisor in South Africa and with Rickie Moore as my supervisor in the USA.

As I pursued my thesis research, I began to sense that my time as a pastor was coming to a close, and that I should devote my full attention to teaching and scholarly pursuits. Knowing how easy it is for academics to lose touch with the realities of local church ministry, I tried to remain as long as possible with one foot in the pastorate and the other in academia. In 2005, however, I placed both feet firmly in the academy, but I retained the conviction that my pastoral experience should continue always to inform my scholarship.

In my first attempt to look at Judges from a Pentecostal perspective, I took the most obvious approach – I aimed to offer a fresh study of the passages where the Spirit of the Lord appears. After a good deal of work, however, I decided that the role of the Spirit in Judges was not prominent enough (or diverse enough) to justify a doctoral thesis. Therefore, I channeled that research into a journal article.[9] My second attempt centered on issues of purity and power that have surfaced in relation to the judges. The relationship between purity and power is a crucial one among Pentecostals, who value both purity and power and who find it difficult to account for the immoral behavior of the Spirit empowered judges. Again, I chose not to pursue this obviously 'Pentecostal' topic, and I wrote another journal article.[10] After many hours of reading Judges, meditating on its stories, and praying about the most prominent themes of the book, I was unable to discover anything that I deemed worthy of an entire thesis. My hope for writing a 'Pentecostal' interpretation of Judges was fading away. Then suddenly and surprisingly, my focus on Judges was redirected through a charismatic event, a Pentecostal experience, in which the Holy Spirit spoke to me, pointing me to the Shema: 'Hear O, Israel, the Lord is our God, the Lord is one. And you shall love the Lord your God with all your heart, with all your soul, and with all your strength' (Deut. 6.4-5). Through this charismatic experience I realized that I had been reading Judges but not hearing Judges, and I determined that the terminology of 'hearing' captured concisely my hermeneutical goal as a Pentecostal. Later, while I was discussing my approach with a colleague, he asked me if the term 'hearing' was used in the book of Judges. Upon investigation, I discovered in Judges the repetition of the phrase, 'You have not heard my voice' (Judg. 2.2; 2.17, 20; 6.10), and I realized that Israel's failure to hear the voice of Yahweh was fundamental to the narrative. I discovered further that Yahweh speaks three times directly to Israel and that these three speeches occur at crucial points in the narrative.

While studying Judges, I was affected most powerfully by the realization that God is passionate both in his anger and in his compassion. What I heard in the three speeches of God was the suffer-

---

[9] Lee Roy Martin, 'Power to Save!?: The Role of the Spirit of the Lord in the Book of Judges', *Journal of Pentecostal Theology* 16.2 (2008), pp. 21-50.

[10] Lee Roy Martin, 'Judging the Judges: Searching for Value in these Problematic Characters', *Verbum et Ecclesia* 29.1 (2008), pp. 110-29. While there is no shortage of material for developing a thesis around the topic of purity and power, I realized that further pursuit of the subject would carry me too far away from Judges itself and into theology and Christian ethics.

ing of God, his vulnerability, the risk that he accepts when he enters covenant, his desire that his people know him and relate to him. In Judges 10, Yahweh admits to feeling abused and manipulated. Yahweh is not a distant, detached God; rather Yahweh is a responsive, relational God. Pentecostal prayer, preaching, and worship all presuppose this kind of relational God. My years in the pastorate, ministering to wounded people, have taught me the value of God's relationality.

Expressing my 'hearing' of Judges through an academic medium presented me with a difficult challenge. For me, because of my many years in pastoral ministry, there is only a fine line between hearing the text and preaching a sermon. A theological interpretation of Scripture is clearly distinct from a sermon but not very far removed from it. The two are on a continuum that does not include clear lines of demarcation to indicate where one ends and the other begins. In the process of writing, I studied Judges with my church congregation and as I discussed my work at length with seminary colleagues.

The Seminary community as a whole provided a rich context for creative theological construction. I was able to engage in ongoing dialogue with faculty members like Ayo Adewuya, Kim Alexander, Ken Archer, Hollis Gause, Jackie Johns, Cheryl Bridges Johns, and Steve Land. I gained much through regular post-grad seminars organized by Chris Thomas that featured works in progress by people like Robby Waddell, Dale Coulter, and Bob Debelak. I benefited as well from colleagues in the Society of Pentecostal Studies who critiqued my work along the way as I presented parts of it at the annual meetings. My most helpful dialogue partner was Chris Thomas, who served as something of an unofficial supervisor of my thesis. We talked about my work almost daily. During the final stages of my thesis writing, I would go over a chapter informally with Chris, then I would submit it to Rickie, who would often require me to rewrite various parts two or three times. I would finally send the chapter to Willie Wessels, who would evaluate it on the basis of the South African requirements. One of my thesis examiners declared that it was the best thesis he had read. Another examiner, Walter Brueggemann, called my work 'impressive', 'compelling', and a 'fine work of which Mr Martin can be justifiably proud'. At the end of the process, I realized that I had been shaped into a Pentecostal scholar.

After finishing my thesis, I looked forward to a bit of rest, but new opportunities and responsibilities came to me fairly quickly. I was seated beside Melissa Archer in the Biblical Studies Interest Group Meeting of the Society for Pentecostal Studies when I checked my email and learned that all examiners had approved my thesis and that I would be graduating the next month. Robby Waddell, sitting nearby, spoke up and nominated me as Interest Group Leader. Thus began my five year tenure as leader of the largest interest group in SPS. Leading the Bible group requires a significant commitment of time and energy, but it is rewarding work that has allowed me to become acquainted with a large number of biblical scholars in the Pentecostal tradition. The SPS Bible group has become one of my most treasured group of friends and an important source of constructive dialogue and fruitful ideas. My years in SPS and my work with the Bible group led to my election as second vice-president of SPS (a position that leads automatically to president). SPS is a valuable fellowship for me, and it is even more valuable for those scholars who labor in non-Pentecostal settings and have no local community of Pentecostal scholars. If we are to forge ahead into ever deeper theological waters, we need places like SPS, where the collegial environment invites dialogue. We need a safe environment where budding scholars can spread their wings, and where all of us can take risks without the threat of being ostracized.

As soon as I finished my thesis and received my doctorate, a major adjustment became necessary when Rickie Moore left the Seminary to become Chair of the Department Theology at Lee University. I had lived under the false assumption that I would always teach beginning Hebrew at the Seminary (I had even authored a Hebrew Grammar for use in our course), but with Rickie's departure, I was needed elsewhere. Months earlier, the Lord had prepared me for the transition by mysteriously removing my 'burden' for teaching the beginning Hebrew course. We began utilizing adjunct and part-time faculty to teach beginning Hebrew, while I picked up the Bible courses that Rickie Moore had taught.

The semester after Rickie left the Seminary, we began offering a full slate of online courses, and I was asked to develop and teach

'Pentecostal Explorations of the Old Testament' online. The next year, I developed an online Bible course on the book of Judges, which I teach regularly.

While teaching at the Seminary, Rickie served as lead editor of the *Journal of Pentecostal Theology*, but his expanded responsibilities at Lee University caused him to resign as editor, and I was asked to step in and fill that role. Serving as Associate Editor of the JPT has added significantly to my work load, but also it has benefited me in important ways. I have become acquainted with many Pentecostal scholars from around the world, giving me a broader knowledge of the global Pentecostal/Charismatic movement. Moreover, I have been enriched by reading journal articles that are outside my field of specialization, articles that I would not have read were I not the editor.

Another life-changing event occurred on May 17, 2008, when I awoke suddenly because of a sharp, crushing pain in the center of my chest. I should have called an ambulance, but instead I took two aspirin and sat in a recliner until the pain subsided to a dull ache. I struggled through the morning and early afternoon, praying and believing God for healing. I recited to God all of the healing testimonies from Scripture, and I reminded him of the healings that I had witnessed and experienced. When one is faced with death, the doctrine of healing is not a point for theoretical debate, and the belief in God's present willingness to intervene on our behalf is not a dusty tradition. During that time of wrestling with God, I became convinced that God had kept me alive through the day and that I would 'not die, but live, and declare the works of the Lord' (Ps. 118.17). Nevertheless, with the pain continuing, I went to the hospital emergency room and underwent tests that showed a 99 per cent blockage in the left descending cardiac artery (but no heart damage). After four arterial grafts (bypasses) and five days of recovery, I returned home with a good prognosis.

I came home from my heart surgery with a desire to narrow my priorities and eliminate fruitless pursuits that can eat away at valuable time. As Red resolved near the end of the The Shawshank Redemption, 'Get busy living or get busy dying'.[11] Therefore, I now

---

[11] *The Shawshank Redemption* (directed by Frank Darabont; Los Angeles: Columbia Pictures, 1994).

focus my time and energy on two primary areas: (1) family and (2) ministry, which consists of teaching and scholarship.

Our family has grown over the years. Our daughter Kendra was born in 1995. Since that time, we have sponsored pajama parties; we have transported her to dance classes; we have attended recitals and ballet performances; we have chaperoned school field trips; and we have purchased formal gowns for school dances.

Not long after Kendra was born, our son Stephen married his wife Marilyn, and she has been a wonderful addition to the family. Stephen and Marilyn live in Miami, Florida and have two boys, Caleb and Joshua, whom we love dearly. A few years ago, Karen's father moved in with us. He is now eighty-six years of age and continues to be very active.

Because this narrative relates my journey in Pentecostal scholarship, I have omitted numerous important events from my personal life and pastoral experience. I would not want my reader to come away with the impression that those unstated moments are any less significant. My relationship with my wife, my children (and now grandchildren) has been and continues to be the most valuable part my life. I cannot imagine how I would have survived without Karen's steadfast love and companionship. Furthermore, my life would have been much diminished without the joy of watching Stephen, Michael, and Kendra grow into the amazing people that they have become.

My ministry, which started with preaching, continues to include regular preaching, both at my local church (Grace Community Church of God) and at other Church of God congregations. Most of my present ministry, however, consists of teaching, both at PTS, at other educational institutions, and in churches. In addition to teaching, I continue to be involved in research, writing, publishing, and editing. In the autumn of 2008, I joined with Chris Thomas and Steve Land in the founding of the Centre for Pentecostal Theology. Housed in its own facilities on the Campus of the Pentecostal Theological Seminary, the Centre is dedicated to facilitating the conception, birth, and maturation of constructive Pentecostal Theology across the theological disciplines. Chris and I also established CPT Press with modest hopes of publishing affordable constructive Pentecostal scholarship.

We live in opportune times for Pentecostal scholarship. Earlier generations of Pentecostals who sought post-graduate education were forced to leave their faith at the door of the university. Especially in the field of biblical studies, scholarship was dominated by modernist illusions of scientific objectivity. Today, however, the academy recognizes the legitimacy of ideological, sociological, contextual, and confessional readings of Scripture. Unfortunately, there are still a few people who argue against the viability of a Pentecostal hermeneutic. One such person remarked, 'I am an Old Testament scholar. I just happen to be Pentecostal'. In light of those kinds of statements, I have coined the phrase, 'Happenstance Hermeneutics'. As I have argued elsewhere, I contend that if we do not construct and adopt a Pentecostal hermeneutic, then we will adopt someone else's hermeneutic. We can choose either to adopt the current dominant models without considering the subsequent effect upon our tradition, or we can carefully and intentionally formulate contextual models of interpretation that integrate available contemporary methods with the ethos of our tradition. I propose that we follow the latter course and construct a Pentecostal hermeneutic that employs the hermeneutical methods that are more conducive to our ethos, theology and view of Scripture.[12]

My ministry of teaching and scholarship is motivated by a concern for the formation of present and future Pentecostal ministers and scholars (2 Tim. 2.2) who practice a Pentecostal faith that is genuine and vibrant. However, I would mention two caveats. First, global Pentecostalism is by no means monolithic, and we must appreciate the diversity within the movement. Second, Pentecostalism will continue to take on expressions different from those of the past. The preservation of an ancient, fictional, idealized version of Pentecostalism is not my desire. We cannot recover the past even if we wanted to do so. However, if the Pentecostal movement hopes to continue its growth and impact in the world, it must have ministers and scholars who understand and are committed to the distinctive heart of the tradition and who can hear what the Spirit is now saying to the Church. We must continue to practice the Full Gospel if we are to fulfill the role for which God raised us up.

---

[12] Lee Roy Martin, *The Unheard Voice of God: A Pentecostal Hearing of the Book of Judges* (JPTSup, 32; Blandford Forum, UK: Deo Publishing, 2008), p. 57.

Conclusion

> Oh, that people would praise the Lord for the Lord's goodness
> And for the Lord's wonderful works to all people (Ps. 107.15).

I am now closer to the end of my life than to the beginning. God has redeemed me from my wandering and drifting. I do not have answers to all my questions, but I think I have a better idea of what is important and what is peripheral. And I have hope. In 'The Shawshank Redemption', which I mentioned above, Red scoffed at the value of hope, but at the end of the movie he uttered these words of longing: 'I hope I can make it ... I hope to see my friend and shake his hand. I hope the Pacific is as blue as it has been in my dreams. I hope'.[13] I hope that I will continue to praise God for his goodness. I hope that I will not forget how he saved me, kept me, blessed me, changed me, guided me, loved me, and healed me. I hope that I can always teach others the 'wonderful works' of God. I hope that I will continue to grow and to listen to the Holy Spirit. I hope that, instead of just reiterating the past, I can participate with others in creative scholarship that propels us to a hopeful future.

I hope.

---

[13] Red, in *The Shawshank Redemption*.

9

THE SPIRIT, VOCATION, AND THE LIFE OF THE MIND: A PENTECOSTAL TESTIMONY

AMOS YONG[*]

I focus my autobiographical reflections on three periods of my life: my formative years growing up Pentecostal, my theological education, and my vocation as a Pentecostal scholar.[1] A generation or two ago, such a testimony would have been rare indeed. The following narrative shows that the possibilities actualized in my own life are due to my having been the blessed recipient of the gifts of many others, including other contributors to this volume. I would urge readers to consider these testimonies not as isolated accounts of private or individual lives, but as a more-or-less harmonious witness to the new thing that the Holy Spirit is working out of the modern Pentecostal movement at the beginning of its second century.

[*] Amos Yong (PhD, Boston University) is J. Rodman Williams Professor of Theology and Director of the PhD program in Renewal Studies at Regent University School of Divinity in Virginia Beach, VA, USA.

[1] In two other books I have provided autobiographical vignettes – preceding each major chapter in *Discerning the Spirit(s): A Pentecostal-Charismatic Contribution to Christian Theology of Religions* (JPTSup, 20; Sheffield, UK: Sheffield Academic Press, 2000), and *Theology and Down Syndrome: Reimagining Disability in Late Modernity* (Waco, TX: Baylor University Press, 2007) – although this essay is the first coherent account to date of at least the earlier parts of my life journey.

Pentecostal Formation

I was born in 1965 to Assemblies of God (AG) pastors Joseph and Irene Yong – themselves of the Chinese diaspora to Southeast Asia – in the small village of Taiping, West Malaysia. When I was four, my parents moved to a suburb of the capital city of Kuala Lumpur to pastor Glad Tidings AG in Petaling Jaya, which shared space with the then Bible Institute of Malaysia (now AG Bible College of Malaysia), founded and then still overseen by American AG missionaries. The congregation thrived under my father's leadership during the next six years. As a PK (pastor's kid), I responded to the salvation message many times. My most vivid memory occurred around the time I was six, at the end of a Sunday night service which showed the film, the Prodigal Son. I recalled crying at the altar and being deeply moved – I knew I had been 'born again'.

When I was ten, my parents moved our family (two younger brothers were with me in tow) around the world to pastor a small AG church in Stockton, California, one of a number of 'home-missions' congregations that were part of the 'Chinese section' of the Northern California-Nevada District of the AG. Rev. Lula Baird, under whose missionary efforts in Malaysia my mother converted to Christ, returned to Northern California to begin planting churches for first generation Chinese immigrants from Hong Kong and elsewhere, and she needed Cantonese-speaking ministers so she went back to her mission field to sponsor bilingual pastors like my parents. I thus became also a MK (missionary kid) – to the USA, no less! – an early example of what is now identified in missiology circles as the 'reverse missions' from the 'rest' back to the Euro-American West.[2]

The summer of my twelfth birthday (in 1977) brought me to our youth/church camp that set the trajectory for the rest of my life. Over the course of three nights, I experienced what Pentecostals call the baptism or infilling of the Holy Spirit. Responding to the invitation at the end of each evening's message to receive more of God, my friends and I encountered God in an undeniably palpable

---

[2] One of the earlier accounts of this phenomenon in Pentecostal circles was by Larry D. Pate, 'Pentecostal Missions from the Two-Thirds World', in Murray W. Dempster, Byron D. Klaus, and Douglas Petersen (eds.), *Called and Empowered: Global Mission in Pentecostal Perspective* (Peabody, MA: Hendrickson, 1991), pp. 242-58.

way, and we caught a glimpse of what the gospel writer said would happen when the Spirit is given and received: 'Out of the believer's heart shall flow rivers of living water' (Jn 7.37). We prayed, cried, worshipped, spoke in unknown tongues, and simply soaked in the presence of God. This sequence of experiences left a deep impression on my spirit. I know that I have never been the same. Even to this day my theological work is driven by a hunger to understand better this overwhelming experience, perhaps with the hope of being able to share it more effectively with others so that they also might experience something like this that might transform their lives once and for all.[3]

During my junior high and high school years, my good friend Steven Lo and I ran off with the annual Chinese section Bible quiz championship for at least three or four years in a row. We memorized large portions of the New Testament and didn't give other church teams much of a chance in the yearly summer camp competition. When I was in my junior year, I took up leadership of our small youth group as the PK to help out my father. It was during this time that I felt my first call to the ministry, although even then I had said, in light of the challenges I saw my parents facing after immigrating to pastor in a foreign country, that I did not want to have to labor with such struggle for what seemed like such minimal results (numerically, the church remained small, and that felt unsuccessful compared with the booming congregation they nurtured in Petaling Jaya). Of course, at that time, I knew only of ministry in its very traditional sense – that of being a pastor, or missionary, or evangelist – and so I received my call with a sense of ambivalence.

I went off to Bethany College (later University, now defunct) of the Assemblies of God in Scotts Valley, California, and studied for four years preparing for ministry, graduating in 1987 with a bachelor's degree in Ministerial Studies and with my ministerial 'license to preach' with the AG (which I have retained to this day). I took theology courses with Stan Steward (more an Arminian then) and Truett Bobo (then and forever a Calvinist, perhaps predestined to be such!),[4] who presented also contrasting styles, while we read

---

[3] This paragraph has been adapted from my, 'Faith at an Early Age: Formative Moments', *The Christian Century* 128.4 (22 February 2011), p. 22.

[4] I surmise that Bobo imbibed his Calvinism as a doctoral student at the predominantly Reformed evangelical Fuller Theological Seminary, where he wrote

Donald Bloesch and Millard Erickson.[5] I also took courses in exegesis on Hebrews and Revelation with Rick Howard, who modeled in the classroom the kind of expository teaching that I also learned from Norman Arnesen in his infamous course in biblical hermeneutics.[6] But my most formative learning was spiritual, of the heart: participating regularly in and leading for two semesters the early morning student intercessory prayer ministry and also serving as regular preacher for the school's student ministries team which went out to local churches almost every weekend. I have always enjoyed preaching – never turning down the opportunity whenever invited, and always being ready even on short notice (like the night before, in one instance) – and do not think there is as sacred a task as that of proclaiming the gospel under the unction of the Spirit (as it is said in Pentecostal circles). I also was inspired by the Sunday School classes taught by Steve Savelich at Christian Life Center in Santa Cruz, not too far from campus, even while I began to develop a respect for and look upon my professor, Dan Albrecht – himself at that time working through coursework for the PhD at the Graduate Theological Union in Berkeley – as an exemplar. Later on, when I was looking for seminaries to attend, I decided upon Western Evangelical Seminary (WES) in Portland, Oregon (now George Fox Seminary), since both Steve and Dan were alum; what was good enough for Steve and Dan was good enough for me!

Upon graduation from Bethany I married Alma Garcia – she was the team ministries leader during the spring term of 1985, when we started dating – and we began as youth pastors at a fairly decent size, predominantly Caucasian, AG church in Fairfield, California, under the leadership of Rev. Russell Umphenour. Our cross-

---

his doctoral dissertation on 'An Evangelical Theology of the Intermediate State' (1978).

[5] E.g. Millard J. Erickson, *Christian Theology*, 3 vols. (Grand Rapids: Baker Book House, 1983-1985), and Donald G. Bloesch, *Essentials of Evangelical Theology*, 2 vols. (San Francisco: Harper & Row, 1978-1979).

[6] I wrote my exegesis paper – 'Persevering through First Peter', specifically focused on Jesus' preaching the gospel to the dead in 1 Pet. 4.1-6 – for Arnesen in the fall of 1984; at over 100 pages it was my first sustained writing project, preparing me well for what has turned out to be a life of writing. Howard's teaching so deeply impressed me that I began reading biblical commentaries in my spare time, and I eventually dedicated one of my books to him (and two others): *The Spirit Poured Out on All Flesh: Pentecostalism and the Possibility of Global Theology* (Grand Rapids: Baker Academic, 2005).

cultural – Chinese American and Mexican American – relationship already presented us with a steep learning curve and now we had seventy 'kids' from the youth group to care for as well. I was called to the ministry and here we were. Needless to say we did not do well as youth pastors during our first year and decided that we should have taken the biblical advice: 'When a man is newly married, he shall not go out with the army or be charged with any related duty. He shall be free at home for one year, to be happy with the wife whom he has married' (Deut. 24.5).[7] We resigned after one year, internally ashamed that we did not do better or last longer. At one level, we had failed; but at another level, maybe this was God's way of getting our attention? If we had been more successful according to conventional standards, perhaps I would never have attended seminary and maybe even never taken a theological turn toward academia.

Pentecostal Theological Education

Our second year of marriage was spent learning to be with one another, in Moses Lake, Washington, my wife's home town. Then, I got a job transfer and we moved to Vancouver, Washington, right across the river from Portland and WES, where I intended to enroll. After all, since I had not done too well in the ministry position for which I thought I was well prepared coming out of college, what else could I do but go back to school? I was a good student and this was my fall-back response. And I certainly had no excuse since I had a full time position working for the State of Washington's Support Enforcement Agency (collecting child support from absent parents) and one of the benefits of this position was full tuition reimbursement, regardless of the field of study!

There is space to mention only three of the many highlights during my time at WES. The first was W. Stanley Johnson's lectures on contemporary theology (since Descartes)[8] in the spring term of 1991. I remember sitting in amazement as I followed the unfolding

---

[7] Unless otherwise noted, all quotations of Scripture are from the New Revised Standard Version.

[8] Our main text was James C. Livingston's *Modern Christian Thought from the Enlightenment to Vatican II* (New York: Macmillan, 1971), which remains one of the most highlighted and marked up books in my personal library.

of the modern theological conversation, mesmerized by Stan's grasp of the issues (Stan's PhD from St. Louis University was on H. Richard Niebuhr's theology of sin and grace). That was my own theological *Aufklärung*, and it was during that class that I fell in love with theology, and began to wonder about a vocation as a theologian and professor. Was it possible that I could have received a call to ministry but live out that call as a scholar and an academic? The possibilities were intriguing, but I still wasn't sure what was happening to me or where I was headed.

That same spring semester I took the 'History of the Holiness Movement' with historian Susie Stanley. Susie recognized my potential as a student from a Pentecostal background and gave me two pieces of advice: join the Society for Pentecostal Studies (which I did shortly thereafter), and start publishing by writing book reviews (which I finally took up in 1996, and have not stopped since). That term, I wrote a paper for her, 'The Transition from Holiness to Pentecostal Terminology: A Study of the Life and Thought of Charles Fox Parham', working primarily off James Goff's recent (at that time) biography of one of the alleged founders of the modern Pentecostal movement.[9] Research for this paper introduced some intellectual dissonance for this lifelong Assemblies of God kid who was used to the thesis that the modern Pentecostal outpouring of the Spirit came not through historical factors or agents but providentially, 'suddenly from heaven', as it were.[10] This, along with a paper I wrote for Stan in the introductory theology course in the fall of 1990 titled '*Glossolalia*, the Evidence of Spirit Baptism, and the Witness of the Book of Acts', led to a kind of crisis of faith: was I going to be able to hold on to the distinctive doctrine of my Pentecostal faith, that of speaking in tongues as the evidence of Spirit baptism, taught as derived from an inductive study of the book of Acts and restored to the church with the modern Pentecostal revival; or was that doctrine also subject to historical development and really a novel introduction by Parham at his Bible school in Topeka, Kansas, at the turn of the twentieth century?

---

9 James R. Goff, Jr., *Fields White unto Harvest: Charles F. Parham and the Missionary Origins of Pentecostalism* (Fayetteville, AR: University of Arkansas Press, 1987).

10 E.g. Carl Brumback, *Suddenly ... from Heaven: A History of the Assemblies of God* (Springfield, MO: Gospel Publishing House, 1961).

I almost gave up my ministerial credentials with the AG (which requires that its ministers reaffirm the denominational stance annually), in part because I still wasn't sure that ministry involved a calling to theological academia, and in part because I didn't know how to reconcile my Pentecostal theological and doctrinal self-understanding with what I was learning in seminary. Amidst my theological crisis, I remembered that Dan Albrecht had pursued his PhD with the Graduate Theological Union – and I knew enough about the theological landscape by this time to know that it was much more radical and liberal than the WES curriculum or environment – and yet he had somehow been able to reconcile his learning and his faith. So I had at least a couple of extended phone conversations with my mentor, and he led me to see that I did not need to make any rash decisions. After all, now historically astute – I was then in the midst of my masters degree in Christian History and Thought – I knew that doctrinal developments did not occur overnight, so Dan reminded me there was no need to go into panic mode so quickly and that I could live with the tensions for awhile. Further, if in fact I felt that this doctrine was not defensible, then it needed to be revised, and aspiring theologians like me could not lead that conversation if we gave up on the denomination at this point. Dan's was the best advice anyone has ever given to me.[11] I remained in the AG and have not looked back since.[12]

During my last year at WES (1992), I took courses on Wesley with Irv Brendlinger, a historical theologian, who then asked me if I thought I might pursue PhD studies on Wesley.[13] At that time, I told him no, Wesley just wasn't interesting enough, although those

---

[11] My *Spirit Poured Out on All Flesh* was also dedicated to Dan, alongside Rick Howard and Frank Macchia, who we will meet in a moment.

[12] A few years later, during PhD studies, I wrote and published 'Tongues of Fire in the Pentecostal Imagination: The Truth of Glossolalia in Light of R.C. Neville's Theory of Religious Symbolism', *Journal of Pentecostal Theology* 12 (April 1998), pp. 39-65, which presents my own coming to peace with the initial evidence doctrine. I am currently writing a systematic and dogmatic theology oriented around the World Assembly of God Fellowship's Statement of Fundamental Truths wherein I make some proposals for how to understand further this specific doctrine; see note 27.

[13] I wrote two papers for Irv: '"Enthusiasm" and the Charismology of John Wesley' and 'Reassessing the Quadrilateral: Wesley's Epistemological Method in Philosophy, the Sciences, and Religion'. I sent them off to the *Wesleyan Theological Journal* for publication consideration; as I never heard back from them, I wonder if they ever got to their intended destination.

familiar with my work in the last ten years will know that I now align myself as a Pentecostal theologian more in the Wesleyan tradition than with any other set of theological sensibilities.[14] During the fall of 1992 I successfully defended my MA thesis, 'The Doctrine of the Two Natures of Christ: A Historical and Critical Analysis' before Irv, Susie, and Stan (who advised the thesis).[15] My years at WES were profoundly transformative intellectually. I am grateful not only for Stan, Susie, and Irv but to all my teachers – Joseph Coleson in Hebrew Bible, Donald Hohensee in missiology and in theology of holiness, Richard Taylor in the doctrine of the atonement, among others – for welcoming this Pentecostal enthusiast but yet gently introducing me to the breadth and depth of the ecumenical and Christian tradition as a whole and to the Wesleyan stream more particularly.

My time at WES convinced me I needed to pursue the PhD in theology, but I felt that I was just coming into my second naïveté and needed to ramp up some more before diving into doctoral studies. Since I was still working for the State of Washington and tuition reimbursement was still available, I enrolled in a second MA in History at Portland State University (PSU). The highlights of my studies were baptism in the history of philosophy, in particular Kant and the development of the process philosophy of Whitehead and Hartshorne with professor John Hammond;[16] a course on the history of Buddhist traditions with professor Linda Walton; and lectures in the intellectual history in the West under professors Craig Wollner and Michael Reardon. Besides papers hovering around the above mentioned topics, I also wrote on Augustine's rhetoric, Arminianism in eighteenth and nineteenth–century Ameri-

---

[14] Besides sections on Wesley and Wesleyan theology in my books, see also my essays, 'The "Baptist Vision" of James William McClendon, Jr.: A Wesleyan-Pentecostal Response', *Wesleyan Theological Journal* 37.2 (Fall 2002), pp. 32-57, and 'Wesley and Fletcher – Dayton and Wood: Appreciating Wesleyan-Holiness Tongues, Essaying Pentecostal-Charismatic Interpretations', in Christian T. Collins Winn (ed.), *From the Margins: A Celebration of the Theological Work of Donald W. Dayton* (Eugene, OR: Pickwick Press, 2007), pp. 179-90.

[15] I have dedicated *The Bible, Disability, and the Church: A New Vision of the People of God* (Grand Rapids: Eerdmans, 2011), to these three of my WES teachers.

[16] I eventually revised and presented a paper on Whitehead at a conference and it was published as part of the conference proceeding: 'Personal Selfhood(?) and Human Experience in Whitehead's Philosophy of Organism', *Paideia Project: Proceedings of the 20th World Congress of Philosophy* (1998), http://www.bu.edu/wcp/MainPPer.htm.

ca, John Henry Newman, St. Louis Hegelianism, idealism in twenti-eth–century philosophy of religion, Reinhold Niebuhr, Paul Tillich, and Fidel Castro and the Cuban Revolution.

In the spring of 1995, I defended my thesis, 'From Pietism to Pluralism: Boston Personalism and the Liberal Era in American Methodist Theology, 1875-1953', under Craig, but with solid input from Rufus Burrow, Jr. (now Indiana Professor of Christian Thought and Professor of Theological Social Ethics at Christian Theological Seminary in Indianapolis), who was then and remains the foremost expert on the Boston personalist tradition. Rufus was under no obligation to help out this student who approached him out of the blue (I was referred to Rufus by dean emeritus of Boston University's School of Theology Walter G. Muelder when I con-tacted him expressing my interest in learning more about Boston Personalism), but his kindness, patience, respectful reception of me, and willingness to take me under his wing and go the extra mile showed me what it meant to open our hearts as scholars in the ser-vice of Christ's reign. The result was a thesis that would have been nowhere as good without his input (which is not to say it is per-fect!). Although a historical study, my thesis topic also bridged my growing interests in philosophy developed at PSU while yet broad-ening my theological horizons; in part, it led me to do my PhD at Boston University.[17] My time at PSU also initiated me into thinking philosophically about theological matters and impressed upon me the importance of engaging with the theological task in a pluralistic world of many faiths.

While I did not do much at PSU directly related to Pentecostal studies, I attended my first Society for Pentecostal Studies (SPS) meeting when it convened at Wheaton College in early November 1994. It was at that meeting that I met Frank Macchia, who at that time had just published his Basel University doctoral thesis on the Blumhardts in relationship to a Pentecostal theology of social en-gagement.[18] I recall standing in a hallway as a starry-eyed student

---

[17] Elsewhere I tell more of the story of my theological development begin-ning with my PhD studies: Yong, 'Between the Local and the Global: Autobio-graphical Reflections on the Emergence of the Global Theological Mind', in Dar-ren C. Marks (ed.), *Shaping a Global Theological Mind* (Aldershot, UK: Ashgate, 2008), pp. 187-94.

[18] Frank D. Macchia, *Spirituality and Social Liberation: The Message of the Blum-hardts in the Light of Wuerttemberg Pietism* (Metuchen, NJ: Scarecrow Press, 1993).

listening to a conversation he was having with Roman Catholic theologian Ralph Del Colle, who had also been deeply formed by the charismatic renewal in the Catholic Church, about Frank's theology of *glossolalia*, barely grasping the significance that here Pentecostal theology was being done with the help of and in dialogue with the work of Karl Rahner and a Catholic sacramental philosophy![19] Here the seeds were sown about the possibility of doing constructive Pentecostal theology, but one that was out of the Pentecostal ghetto, with possible implications for contributing to and even advancing broader theological conversations. More importantly, Frank retained his AG ordination, even after studying for his MDiv at Union Theological Seminary in New York City and then also at Basel under Jan Lochmann, a student of Karl Barth! It was possible to be Pentecostal, be called to ministry, and to fulfill that calling as a theologian, academic, and scholar, after all! There was no necessary conflict between my speaking in tongues and in theological German! I struck up relationships with both Frank and Ralph then, and have been privileged to have had them as mentors, later as colleagues, and now as friends and collaborators.[20] In any case, this meeting solidified my commitment not just as a Christian theologian, but as a specifically Pentecostal one. I was beginning to discern now the possibility of being Spirit-filled while yet cultivating rather than rejecting or neglecting the life of the mind.

---

[19] Frank's ground-breaking articles then were 'Tongues as a Sign: Toward a Sacramental Understanding of Pentecostal Experience', *PNEUMA: The Journal of the Society for Pentecostal Studies* 15.1 (1993), pp. 61-76, and 'Sighs too Deep for Words: Toward a Theology of Glossolalia', *Journal of Pentecostal Theology* 1 (1992), pp. 47-73; he has since published two major volumes expanding on this early work toward distinctively Pentecostal and yet robustly ecumenical theology of the Spirit and of Spirit-baptism: *Baptized in the Spirit: A Global Pentecostal Theology* (Grand Rapids: Zondervan, 2006), and *Justified in the Spirit: Creation, Redemption, and the Triune God* (Grand Rapids: Eerdmans, 2010).

[20] In 1994, Ralph had just published his dissertation, *Christ and the Spirit: Spirit-Christology in Trinitarian Perspective* (New York: Oxford University Press, 1994); later, he, Frank, and myself engaged in an extensive email conversation with Dale T. Irvin, following a session at the SPS on my just published doctoral dissertation, which was then published as, 'Christ and Spirit: Dogma, Discernment and Dialogical Theology in a Religiously Plural World', *Journal of Pentecostal Theology* 12.1 (2003), pp. 15-83.

Pentecostal Scholarship and Vocation

As already indicated, I have retained my minister's credentials with the AG since 1987. Over the last twenty-five years, however, we have ministered in a variety of churches and denominations. While in Vancouver (completing my masters degrees at WES and PSU), we helped to found, with Pastor Toby Johnson, and establish Turning Point Christian Center (1990-1996). Then in Massachusetts while working on my PhD, we were graciously invited to serve as part-time associate pastors by Rev. Dr Dennis Cheek for a small congregation in Mansfield (1996-1998).[21] From 1999-2005 while teaching at Bethel University in St. Paul, Minnesota, which belonged to the Baptist General Conference (BGC), a broadly evangelical group of churches rooted in the Swedish Pietist immigration to the upper Midwest region of the USA in the nineteenth century, we attended and ministered regularly at Olivet Baptist Church (a BGC congregation) while also serving regularly and providing pulpit supply to BGC churches throughout Minnesota and even into Wisconsin and Iowa. Since moving to Chesapeake/Virginia Beach (to teach at Regent University) in 2005, we have been a part of the Great Bridge Presbyterian Church (GBPC);[22] and, more recently we have been attending the Hillsong-connected Wave Church and the independent charismatic New Life Providence Church. As a megachurch, Wave Church's strengths are its capacity to reach the younger generation, emphases on conversion without ignoring the social dimension of the gospel, and vital and inspirational congregational worship. New Life is more neopentecostal but also intentionally trans-ethnic, which is a blessing for myself and my wife.

---

[21] What is noteworthy is that Dennis himself was a bi-vocational pastor who volunteered his time to the church so he was not paid, but himself had a PhD (at that time in science education, since then adding a second PhD in theology) and recognized that a young PhD student like me with a family needed all the support, financial and otherwise, available, and so created a salary for us to help us get by! I have more recently dedicated the following volume to Dennis, in recognition of his mentorship, friendship, and never-failing encouragement of my work: Yong (ed.), *The Spirit Renews the Face of the Earth: Pentecostal Forays in Science and Theology of Creation* (Eugene, OR: Pickwick Publications, 2009).

[22] I wrote my *Who is the Holy Spirit? A Walk with the Apostles* (Brewster, MA: Paraclete Press, 2011), from out of a year-long Sunday school class I taught at GBPC in 2008 on Luke–Acts.

During the time when I was completing my PhD (1996-1998), I understood my calling then to work consciously not just as a Christian theologian but as a Pentecostal theologian. Trained and mentored by systematic philosopher Robert Cummings Neville,[23] I envisioned myself as a systematician as well, albeit one thoroughly Pentecostal in confession, approach, and orientation. Needless to say, Pentecostal theology was still in its gestating stages at that time,[24] and there was a deep inferiority complex among the handful of us Pentecostals who were emerging on the theological scene – this was the case at least for me! Hence I needed to shed my reputation as a 'tongues-speaker' and 'prove' myself as a theologian, and as a systematician to boot! I thus rejected labeling anything I was doing as 'confessional', 'apologetic', or 'missional' – these all sounded the death-knell for aspiring systematicians in the guild. I needed to show I could soar with those who I felt were the most erudite speculative thinkers, adeptly cover the same ground as the historical theologians, and develop a general conceptual framework that exhibited the same kind of sophistication as the great systematicians had in the last century. My Pentecostal sensibilities were fully attuned to the renaissance in the doctrine of the Holy Spirit (pneumatology) and in trinitarian theology during this time, so I began to conceive of what others were calling a Theology of the Third Article in service of a robustly trinitarian theology;[25] this would thus be

---

[23] I will always remain indebted to my *doktorvater*, whose charity and grace I have long desired to imitate, whose sageliness I aspire to develop, and whose scope, brilliance, and vision is simply inspiring; I dedicated to him my second book: *Spirit-Word-Community: Theological Hermeneutics in Trinitarian Perspective* (New Critical Thinking in Religion, Theology and Biblical Studies Series; Burlington: Ashgate Publishing, 2002; reprint: Eugene, OR: Wipf & Stock Publishers, 2006).

[24] Led by Donald W. Dayton, *The Theological Roots of Pentecostalism* (Peabody, MA: Hendrickson Publishers, 1987), and Steven J. Land, *Pentecostal Spirituality: A Passion for the Kingdom* (JPTSup, 1; Sheffield: Sheffield Academic Press, 1993). Dayton was a Wesleyan Holiness historical theologian; only Land was confessionally Pentecostal, now president of the Pentecostal Theological Seminary of the Church of God, Cleveland, Tennessee.

[25] E.g. D. Lyle Dabney's 'Otherwise Engaged in the Spirit: A First Theology for the Twenty-first Century', in Miroslav Volf, Carmen Krieg and Thomas Kucharz (eds.), *The Future of Theology: Essays in Honor of Jürgen Moltmann* (Grand Rapids: Eerdmans, 1996), pp. 154-63; cf. Clark H. Pinnock, *Flame of Love: A Theology of the Holy Spirit* (Downers Grove: InterVarsity Press, 1996). Here I should mention that Pinnock was a Baptist theologian touched by the charismatic renewal and he has also encouraged me over the years, until his untimely death in 2010, to develop as a Pentecostal theologian. Dabney's story, conversely, is a little differ-

a trinitarian theological system precisely because it was pneumato-
logically inflected and informed through and through. I even wrote
a whole book on theological method and hermeneutics to flesh out
the possibilities of such a systematically organized theological intui-
tion.[26]

In hindsight, almost fifteen years out of my PhD, I can now see
that I have been doing all along what I had feared to acknowledge
at one time: straining to articulate a 'confessional', 'apologetic', or
'missional' theology. I am a confessional theologian insofar as I
have never identified myself as anything less than Pentecostal. True,
Pentecostalism is less a denomination or a confession; truth be told,
it has been called a mood, a spirituality, a sensibility, or a movement, arguably not any one thing but a plurality of 'Pentecostalisms'. Yet in reality it is and has always also been constituted by a
range of confessions – among which is the AG's 'Statement of
Fundamental Truths'. In that sense, I have embraced my Pentecostal identity and attempted to theologize from out of that specific
location. I anticipate going forward that I will be playing a greater
role as a theologian of the church, especially in its Pentecostal expressions. Perhaps, God willing, what my undergraduate teacher
Dan Albrecht mentioned before will yet come to pass: that I may
be able to play some small role in the theological renewal of the
church, especially of the denomination and 'fellowship' (as the AG
likes to understand itself) of my youth and of my life.[27]

But I have also been an apologist. At one time I disdained that
label because I associated it with the defensive-mindedness of conservative evangelical and even fundamentalistic theological dis-

---

ent. He grew up Pentecostal but when he told one of the denominational leaders
that he felt led to pursue a doctorate in theology, he was told that that was not
needed for the movement. Dabney went to Germany to study under Jürgen
Moltmann and came back to the USA after that and joined the Methodist
Church. He has remained in conversation with Pentecostal theologians over the
last decade, but who knows how many other Pentecostals the movement lost in a
similar fashion?

[26] See note 23.

[27] I have begun to conceive of a one-volume mini-systematic pneumatological, and trinitarian theology that is also dogmatically rooted in – in terms of being
organized by – the World Assembly of God Fellowship's Statement of Fundamental Truths, tentatively titled *The Renewal of Christian Theology: Systematic and
Dogmatic Reconsiderations for a Global Christianity* (Waco, TX: Baylor University
Press, forthcoming).

courses that operated from out of a foundationalist worldview.[28] And because much of my Pentecostal tradition had aligned itself with a fundamentalistic outlook,[29] I was especially sensitive to the charge of being guilty by association. So from a post-Enlightenment, post-modern, and post-conservative – not to mention post-liberal – framework, I explicitly eschewed apologetics altogether. However, if apologetics is nothing less than 'Always [being] ready to make your defense to anyone who demands from you an account of the hope that is in you' (1 Pet. 3.15), then I need to now fess up that I've been doing apologetics for a long time, interpreting my Pentecostal experience for the wider post-denominational and ecumenical conversation. Further, my work, I now see, has been motivated by the felt need of translating Pentecostal tongues into a set of discourses palatable to, acceptable within, and understandable by the wider theological and post-secular academy. Last but not least, I have been working diligently attempting to provide a rational articulation of what my Pentecostal faith means in a post-Christian world.[30]

I can now also see that I have been an evangelist and a missionary. In the theological guild, of course, missiology and evangelism for a long time had been relegated to the realm of practical theology, or at best they were done as part of the professionalized training for the ministers of the church (in Doctor of Ministry programs rather than in PhD programs). I was neither a practical theologian nor a missiologist, so I thought; instead I was a systematician, a philosophical theologian, a constructive theologian, etc. But I was wrong on two counts. First, I now realize that there is a hermeneutical circle between theology and practice, between reflection and praxis, between the life of the mind and the life of the hands, hearts, and spirit. The dualism between systematics and practics is itself a misguided severance bequeathed by the modernist mentality.

---

[28] I was cured of modernist foundationalism during the course of my doctoral studies, most clearly articulating the reasons why in a seminar paper I wrote under Neville, eventually published as, 'The Demise of Foundationalism and the Retention of Truth: What Evangelicals Can Learn from C.S. Peirce', *Christian Scholar's Review* 29.3 (Spring 2000), pp. 563-88.

[29] The anti-intellectualism of which is well documented by Rick Nañez, *Full Gospel, Fractured Minds: A Call to Use God's Gift of the Intellect* (Grand Rapids: Zondervan, 2005).

[30] My books on theology and science, on theology and disability, and on political theology can all be classified as apologetic in these senses.

Rather, all theology flows out of the life of the church, and actually reflects on the lived realities of the Christian life. My books in the last ten years all arise from out of the questions of how to live faithfully and Pentecostally in a post-secular, post-modern, and post-Christian world. In all of these senses, they are efforts to think authentically in a time in which there is little stability for Christian self-understanding in general, much less Pentecostal self-identity in particular.

But more precisely — and here I happily confess my previous ignorance about what I was actually doing — I had defined missiology in a very narrow sense related to the classical model of 'Christianizing the other'. And in a postcolonial academic environment, then, I did not want to be associated with those who proclaimed a gospel but yet presented it in American or Western dress. Yet a missionary is only merely one who is sent or comes with the message of the gospel of salvation in Christ, in the power of the Spirit. My work in theology of religion, interreligious dialogue, and theology of pluralism[31] may not be explicitly oriented toward achieving the conversion of people of other faiths — in an academic environment honest encounter with others requires a measure of risk and vulnerability on the part of the missionary[32] — but I have surely been engaged in bearing witness to the work of Christ in the Spirit as a Pentecostal in these scholarly forums. In other words, I have been attempting to testify 'about God's deeds of power' (Acts 2.11) as a Pentecostal believer and theologian in a world of many faiths. In that sense, I may not be a traditional evangelist or missiologist, but I can no longer deny there is a very real, even if subtle, evangelical and missiological aspect to my work.

Of course, the danger of all of these efforts is that translation attempts inevitably lose something of the original — and some would say that they compromise the primordial faith stance or risk syncretism with the target audience. I cannot guarantee that I have been successful in all that I have endeavored, and my reviewers have

---

[31] Three full books so far on this set of topics, two more coming on the Buddhist-Christian dialogue, and many published book chapters and journal articles.

[32] See my, 'Francis X. Clooney's "Dual Religious Belonging" and the Comparative Theological Enterprise: Engaging Hindu Traditions', *Dharma Deepika: A South Asian Journal of Missiological Research* 16.1 (2012), pp. 6-26.

surely been right in many of their criticisms.[33] But I would also say that those who remain too worried about reforming the old risk becoming irrelevant, and that the eschatological nature of the Christian faith calls us to embrace the forward-looking dimension of life in the Spirit with boldness.[34] Thus have I also accepted my task, albeit always accompanied with fear and trepidation, of being a culture theologian or theologian of culture, one who attempts to make sense of the community of faith within a contemporary context, whatever that is, and of being a mediating theologian or theologian of mediation, one who attempts to arbitrate between diverse worlds, in my case between Pentecostalism, whatever that is, and 'the world', whatever that is. This is a perilous undertaking and not for the faint of heart since the pitfalls are innumerable. All I can say is that my colleagues and friends, particularly in the Society for Pentecostal Studies, have been encouraging, helpful in giving me feedback whenever I have asked for it (which has been often), and gracious in being patient with my musings even when they have been half-baked or not fully coherent.[35] They have been the ones who I have relied upon to navigate the issues, and many have provided the needed admonishment at crucial moments. And the prayers of my wife are invaluable, as is the fellowship of the saints amidst the body of Christ – the fellowship of the Spirit – in the various

---

[33] A few of my critics, especially those on the internet, have been quite strident, very worried that I might be misleading to the unwary; I admit that some of my formulations have been open to some of the criticisms that I have received. But I would also say that these particular critics also have not displayed the charity with which we should approach all who we think are headed in the wrong direction. Inevitably, as fallible creatures, we get some things wrong and can always do better. I have to walk a fine line between a conservatism that holds in high regard the responsibilities that pertain to being a teacher of the faith (Jas 3.1-5) and an openness that is required to fuel the kind of exploratory work so desperately needed for the confessional, apologetic, missional, and scholarly tasks of our time.

[34] I emphasize this eschatological orientation to Pentecostal spirituality and theology in my short rejoinder article, 'Performing Global Pentecostal Theology: A Response to Wolfgang Vondey', *PNEUMA: The Journal of the Society for Pentecostal Studies* 28.2 (2006), pp. 313-21.

[35] I have edited or in the process of editing over fifteen books, almost all of them related to Pentecostal studies, with many of these involving members of the SPS, not to mention having served as book review editor for the Society's journal since 2000 and as co-editor since 2010; in short, my work is unthinkable apart from this network of like-minded global scholars and sojourners. I owe whatever is worth emulating about the life of the mind to these, my exemplars, colleagues, and friends.

churches and congregations within which we have been blessed and nurtured.

Conclusions, for Now

I am still on the way, trying to understand who I am as a Pentecostal Christian in a complicated world. At one level, things are fairly simple, as we need only the faith of a child to experience the salvific touch of the Spirit of Jesus. At another level, even a charismatic theologian of the level of St. Paul, in the middle of reflecting on life in the Spirit and within the charismatic congregation (1 Corinthians 12-14), admitted that 'For now we see in a mirror, dimly, but then we will see face to face' (1 Cor. 13.12a). I have come to live in this tension-filled space, resting only in the fact that there is no rest except that in the Spirit, whose 'wind blows where it chooses, and you hear the sound of it, but you do not know where it comes from or where it goes' (Jn 3.8a).

And I have also come to realize that unless we Pentecostals develop and model the possibility of a Spirit-filled life of the mind, our children will not be inspired to seek earnestly after the life of the Spirit. Ours is a calling to love God not only with all our heart, our soul, and our strength, but also with our mind (Lk. 10.27) – these cannot finally be partitioned because we are created holistically, not compartmentalistically. As I indicated at the beginning of this chapter, I have been blessed with mentors who have come alongside me and helped me to find my own identity and vocation as a Pentecostal minister and scholar. One person who has not yet appeared in the preceding pages but deserves mention at this juncture is Cecil M. Robeck, Jr., known by his friends as Mel. When I was beginning to do work on a Pentecostal theology of interreligious dialogue, I knew that Mel had for years blazed an ecumenical trail in the footsteps of David DuPlessis. Whenever I would write Mel, I always received back many pages – single-spaced and in small print – of wisdom, encouragement, and guidance. Mel modeled the Spirit-filled life in at-that-time forbidden territory.[36] I have received

---

[36] When I edited Veli-Matti Kärkkäinen's *Toward a Pneumatological Theology: Pentecostal and Ecumenical Perspectives on Ecclesiology, Soteriology and Theology of Mission* (Lanham, MD: University Press of America, 2002), we agreed to dedicate that volume jointly to Mel and to Catholic ecumenical theologian, Kilian McDonnell

inspiration from his exemplary life to do what I can to encourage others who may feel a divine call of the Spirit into the world of academia and scholarship. Mentors are available, more so today than ever before, who have cultivated the life of the mind precisely in response to a Spirit-filled vocation. Find them at the Society for Pentecostal Studies, or other like networks (e.g. the European Pentecostal Theological Association, the Canadian Pentecostal Research Network, and the European Research Network on Global Pentecostalism [GloPent], among other scholarly venues). Perhaps the next generation of theologians and scholars whom the Spirit calls will face fewer obstacles, just as I was able to follow in the footsteps of those who paved the way before me.

The possibilities for Pentecostal theological reflection remain endless as we are only in its first generation of undertaking. Take practically any topic and a Pentecostal theology of that topic remains to be written. Among the most important issues to be taken up today include Pentecostalism as a global renewal movement in relationship to the political, economic, social, and environmental forces of globalization, the relationship between theology and science (especially the applied, medical, and technological sciences and the ethical issues raised by exponential advances in these arenas), and social justice issues related to the plight of women, people with disabilities, and war. It seems to me that there are plenty of biblical and distinctively Pentecostal theological resources to be brought to bear on thinking afresh about these issues. Substantive theological work in all of these domains will be of aid to the global renewal movement as we seek to live faithfully in anticipation of the coming reign of God and bear witness to the living Christ in the power of the Spirit. May the Lord of the Harvest call, anoint, empower, and send forth many more to this vocational task of making sense of the work of the Spirit in the beautiful, complex, and yet fallen world that we inhabit.[37]

(Kärkkäinen's mentor for his habilitation thesis). I am now privileged to be co-editing with Mel *The Cambridge Companion to Pentecostalism* (Cambridge University Press), which is scheduled for publication in 2014.

[37]Thanks to Steven Fettke and Robby Waddell for the invitation to contribute to this important volume, and for urging development of important themes in response to an initial draft, and to my graduate assistant Timothy Lim for helping proofread and format this paper according to the preferred publisher style.

10

'I HAVE COME TO GIVE YOU LIFE AND MORE ABUNDANTLY' (JOHN 10.10)

KENNETH J. ARCHER[*]

'In Jesus name we pray. Amen!' Wow. This is great and so different. I still had not grown accustomed to prayer being offered prior to the beginning of a class. I was in my first few weeks of college at Central Bible College in Springfield, Missouri. I was 20 years old and had been saved just over one year.

How I became a committed Christian, went to college and eventually became Professor of Pentecostal Theology at Southeastern University in Lakeland, Florida, is a testimony of grace-filled deliverance and hope-filled determination. My academic journey is interwoven into my salvific journey. I am extremely grateful to the Lord for the abundant life he has provided. It is my heartfelt prayer that my testimony of God's grace will be a blessing to you and a source of encouragement in your journey with the living God.

---

[*] Kenneth J. Archer (PhD, University of St. Andrews) is Professor of Pentecostal Theology and Christian Studies and Director of the Master of Arts in Theological Studies at Southeastern University in Lakeland, FL, USA.

Pre-conversion[1]

I have a memory that stands out to me from my teen years. On one particular morning, as I reached to retrieve the cereal box from the cupboard, I noticed my mom's small notebook sitting on top of her Bible on the counter. Normally I would not have looked twice; after all, her Bible was always in the house, either in the kitchen or in the living room. It was the notebook itself that distracted me. As my eyes glanced down, I saw a list of names. I sat the cereal box down on the counter and picked up the notebook. I was tired and, truth be known, trying to shake off the lingering effects of another night of partying. I began to read the page. On it she was praying for the salvation of her family, and my name was on the list!

Even though that event took place some 30 years ago, I vividly remember it. God was trying to get my attention. I had drifted away from the Lord and from my mother's early religious influence upon my life. I had not become agnostic or an atheist. I believed in God. I accepted the Christian understanding of the triune God and the basic tenants of the Christian faith, but my life had become a constant pursuit of 'worldly' pleasures. I had relationally drifted away from God. Promiscuity and the abuse of drugs and alcohol had become very serious issues, and my life was on the verge of destruction. Toward the end of my teenage years, I was riddled with loneliness, filled with emotional pain, and spiritually dead. I was, to quote a line from a 1980's hard rock band, 'on the highway to Hell'. How had I arrived at such a place?

I am the oldest of five children. I was raised in a loving, hardworking blue collar family in northern Ohio. My father worked at

---

[1] I understand my salvific journey from a Pentecostal synergistic perspective. All grace is redemptive, especially from an eschatological perspective, but not necessarily regenerative. My understanding is more Wesleyan, moving from prevenient to converting to sanctifying and on into perfecting grace. Prevenient grace is the grace that comes before conversion. God always initiates and yet we are called to respond positively to the Spirit, thus salvation is a gift of grace (Eph. 2.1-10). I use 'Wesleyan' to signal the importance of experiential synergistic soteriology. As Randy L. Maddox in his *Responsible Grace: John Wesley's Practical Theology* (Nashville, TN: Abingdon Press, 1994), has demonstrated, a Wesleyan understanding of Christianity calls for a 'responsible grace'. 'Without God's grace we *cannot* be saved; while without our grace-empowered, but uncoerced participation, God's grace *will not* save' (p. 19). Pentecostal theology will breach any previously existing Christian tradition because Pentecostal theology is its own theological tradition.

an engine plant for the Ford Motor Company and my mother was a stay-at-home mom who devoted all of her energies to my dad and her children. My parents attended our school functions, but we were never encouraged to get involved in extra-curricular activities such as sports or clubs. We took yearly vacations together during the summers, but we did not socialize with other families. I spent most of my time hanging out with my cousins who lived a few miles away. I was raised in the Roman Catholic tradition and was baptized as an infant. My parents, especially my mother, made sure the family attended mass fairly regularly, especially on Christmas Eve and Easter Sunday. When my siblings and I were young, we also attended catechism where we received instruction in the Catholic faith. I took my first communion in second grade and was confirmed in eighth grade. Both events were significant for me.

As I prepared myself for first confession, my mom explained that the priest represented God, and he would hear my confession and extend God's forgiveness. She made it clear, however, that it is God the Father who forgives us. She reminded me that it is Jesus who saves us. She asked me if I had a personal relationship with Jesus. After her explanation and in response to her question, I invited Jesus into my life. She was raised and confirmed as an 'evangelical' Episcopalian. She married into the Catholic tradition.[2] Her pietism was evident in how she presented Catholicism to me.

During the eighth grade, I again attended catechism regularly because I was preparing for confirmation. This was an important event since I would reaffirm the water baptismal vows my parents and the Church took in my stead and embrace the Catholic faith as an adult. I was motivated to this by one promise that my parents made to me. After I confirmed my faith, I could choose whether I wanted to attend mass or not. If I chose not to go to church, my parents would respect my wishes. I was responsible for my relationship with God. By this time I had no interest in attending church. I was confirmed, not because of religious desire but because I wanted to keep the family tradition. After confirmation, I stopped attending Mass. This was only made easier because my father had become disenchanted with the Catholic Church and quit attending except for an occasional Christmas Eve service. In time, my mom became

---

[2] Their marriage took place in 1963 which was prior to the implementation of the changes made at Vatican II.

part of a Charismatic prayer group and eventually began attending a Pentecostal church.

The summer of seventh grade marked a major transition in my life. I began smoking cigarettes and using alcohol. Through these vices I was able to make new friends who were experimenting with the same things. I was identified in school as a 'freak' which meant I was not into sports and used drugs and alcohol. By the time I turned 16, I was smoking daily, drinking and using marijuana regularly. I was committed to partying as a lifestyle.

In spite of being high most days during school hours, I did fairly well with my grades in high school. Math and shop classes were where I excelled. English grammar, spelling, reading, and composition were extremely difficult for me. Even in grade school I had difficulty with spelling. I had a hard time passing spelling tests even when I cheated! Throughout all my school years, I had a difficult time with language.[3] Nevertheless, by the tenth grade I had a B average in school.

During my junior and senior years, I attended a county vocational school.[4] The goal was that after graduation I would be able to find a job. There were a number of reasons why I made this choice. One significant reason was that my family did not encourage me to attend college.[5] We were encouraged to be hard workers and were expected to find a job in which we would be able to support our future family. Since college was not encouraged, it made sense to learn a skill which would give me an advantage at finding a higher paying job as a skilled employee in the blue collar work force. I chose the Tool and Die program because it was more demanding than other programs offered at the school. Math was an important prerequisite and a subject that I enjoyed and in which I excelled. While at the vocational school, I focused on learning the trade even while continuing to party.

---

[3] While attending college, I would be diagnosed with a mild form of dyslexia.

[4] The vocational School was for students who most likely would not succeed in college or had no desire to go to college. In addition to the course work related to a vocation, students would take one English course and one American history course. My program, Tool and Die, required advanced math courses as well as drafting and design.

[5] I was one of the first persons on my father's side of the family to earn a four year college degree.

After I graduated from High School, a series of events transpired which had a snowball effect in my life. First, the job market crashed and I could not find a job in Tool and Die; instead, I found a job working as a laborer for a concrete company. I also went through a painful breakup with my fiancé. Then, my uncle Harold, whom I respected, died suddenly of heart complications at the age of 48.[6] I felt like my life was spinning out of control. In December, after leaving a Christmas party, I ran into someone on the road and was arrested for driving under the influence. The charges would be reduced to reckless operation but I had to attend drug/alcohol awareness classes which brought me to the realization that my lifestyle was more destructive and out of control than I had even realized.

The Turning Point: Converting Grace[7]

The point of surrendering my life fully to God came through the direct witness of my cousin, Dan Archer, and his wife, Lisa. Prior to his conversion, Dan had been one of my drinking buddies.[8] Dan invited me to attend his church, New Life Assembly of God, located in Wellington, Ohio. I was nineteen and my life had hit bottom, so I agreed to go with them to church.[9] After all, what did I have to lose? I went to church but I was not ready to give up my lifestyle.

Two weeks later, I attended a high school graduation party. I had made up my mind that I was not going to use alcohol, but as the party went on, my resolve gave out and I drank a lot. I do not remember much of that night. Because I was too wasted to drive home, someone volunteered to drive me and my friend back home.

---

[6] Harold was my dad's older brother.

[7] Converting grace involves the experience of justification and initial sanctification.

[8] Dan and I became close because I worked for his father, Harold, at his trucking company from the time I was 14 until I graduated from high school. I worked with Dan a few days a week.

[9] I was curious about the Pentecostal church because of some of the testimonies I had heard, such as healings, tongues, and even exorcisms. The supernatural had always fascinated me. Pentecostal churches in the USA that have marginalized opportunities for the gifts to operate during worship services because they have embraced seeker sensitive models of church growth have diminished the Full Gospel. Such pastors and churches may have lost much more than what they think they have gained.

On the way home something strange happened to me. I became so overwhelmed with a strong sense of hopelessness and despair that I decided to jump out of the car window. I had never before had suicidal thoughts, but suddenly I was pushing myself through the opened window. My friend grabbed for my legs as the car slowed down, but by the time the car came to a complete stop I had already rolled into the ditch. My knees were bleeding, but I had no broken bones. My friend jumped out of the car and ran after me. The next thing I remember was when they dropped me off at my house. I began crawling on the ground, heading for a small stream that ran next to our house. I was trying to end my life. My friend intervened again and walked me up to the porch. For reasons unknown to me at the time, I could not seem to get into my house. When I tried, I was tossed over the porch rail onto the ground. Something was keeping me from getting into the house. My friend knocked on the door and woke my parents from sleep. My dad came to the door and brought me into the house. I was using strong profanity, something I had never done before around my parents. My mom rolled me up in a blanket because they were afraid that I would hurt myself or someone else. She later told me that she sat up all night praying and interceding in tongues for me. I believe that there was a spiritual battle being waged for my very life that night. I woke up the next morning sick and tired. I hardly remember anything except that I wanted to end my life. My Dad called me that morning from work. He told me he loved me and then gave me an ultimatum: If I continued in such a lifestyle I would have to leave home. I knew he was serious. I decided to attend the Sunday evening service with my cousin Dan.

I do not remember the sermon, but the pastor gave an invitation to accept Jesus as Lord and Savior. I unenthusiastically surrendered to the Lord. I knew that my lifestyle had to change; sex, drugs and rock and roll had to go. From my perspective I was a failure. I did not walk to the front of the church; instead, I stood at my seat and prayed to God to forgive me of my sins and to deliver me from the evil trying to destroy me. As I surrendered, I experienced the grace of forgiveness, deliverance, and the hospitable embrace of the community.[10] On a muggy night in June of 1983, I became part of the family of God.[11]

The Journey Begins: New Life Assembly of God (June 1983 to August 1984).

The Pentecostal congregation in Wellington encouraged me to press forward in the faith. I knew that Jesus had forgiven me of my past sins and accepted me. I was encouraged to read my Bible, attend all church services and, of course, honor God with my tithe. Besides attending the services on Sundays, I attended the youth service on Wednesday nights. The youth pastor spent additional time with me after services to pray and counsel me. I started making new friends and participating in various church social activities. I was being 'socialized' into the Christian community.

I was very aware that my former lifestyle had to change. At the closing of the sermons, I responded to the altar calls further experiencing God's sanctifying grace. I did receive immediate deliverance from the demonic presence, yet certain vices would take some time

---

[10] Many people in the community were genuinely concerned about me as a person. They took me in as one of their own and they knew me by name.

[11] During my time of study at Ashland Theological Seminary, I would come to appreciate better my Roman Catholic upbringing. No doubt it provided me with a Christian worldview and opportunities for prevenient grace to work in my life. I had memorized the Apostle's Creed and the Lord's Prayer. I was indoctrinated into core Christian beliefs and partook of communion. The Catholic Church did affirm miracles. Yet in my darkest hours of desperation it was not the Catholic Church that drew me to the crucified Christ, but instead it would be the testimony of hope proclaimed boldly by the Pentecostals that caused me to look to the crucified and risen Lord. I consider that particular day in June of 1983 to be my real conversion in the sense of an adult surrender to follow Jesus by turning away from my rebellious lifestyle. It was the Pentecostal 'Full gospel' message that brought real hope to my desperate situation and a radical change to my life. This understanding of adult conversion would be in keeping with a more Anabaptist-pietistic perspective involving a conscious commitment to follow Jesus which is bound up in a real effort of responsibility to a local community and discipleship. On this see my essay co-authored with Andrew Hamilton, 'Anabaptism-Pietism and Pentecostalism: Scandalous Partners in Protest', *Scottish Journal of Theology* 63.2 (2010), pp. 185-202. I do not deny that as a child I had a 'personal relationship' with Jesus and my new commitment may be more in keeping with the parable of the prodigal son (Luke 15). I was really lost but now I was found!

to break.[12] Church folk, both young and old, would pray with me, and I was encouraged to pray for others. It was this community that nurtured me into the Pentecostal Christian way of life. Sunday services included times of praying for the sick and struggling. People were invited to the front for prayer where they were anointed with oil and had hands laid on them (Jas 5.17). At the altar one could hear people praying in tongues. During services the gifts of tongues and interpretation (1 Corinthians 12-14) were operational. I was excited to be a part of a church that believed in the present power of God to change lives.[13] At this church, the doxological themes of the Full Gospel, Jesus as Savior, Sanctifier, Spirit Baptizer, Healer and King who is coming again, were preached. Testimonies were also encouraged. The first testimony I offered was a testimony of provision. I was grateful for the car that God enabled me to purchase. I learned that God was concerned about everything; He was *Jehovah Jireh*, my provider.

Approximately one month after my conversion, I was (re)baptized by immersion in water at a church picnic. Prior to being water baptized, I was also asking God to baptize me with the Holy Spirit. I wanted to come up out of the water speaking in tongues. As I went under the water and came back out I sensed God's Spirit in a special way. I had died with Christ and I had been raised with him into a new life. I desired to be a faithful follower of Jesus, for I was a new creation to bring praise and glory to God. After I came out of the lake, a woman in her early forties met me. She had a large bath towel, and as she wrapped it around me she hugged me and said, 'Welcome to the family of God!' Her warm embrace further mediated God's redemptive grace. I knew the living God loved me not just because the Bible said so but more importantly because this particular Pentecostal community showed me so. Her actions exemplified a Pentecostal community who passionately loved Jesus

---

[12] Sanctification is a series of crises in which one experiences grace that sets us free to love God more fully and yet it is also a process in growing in grace of God as we are transformed into the image of Christ.

[13] My first pastor was Norm Beetler, later to become my father-in-law. He preached expository sermons with excitement. Nancy, his wife, often prayed for me, especially after I started dating their only child, Melissa. Her prayers echoed and quoted promises of Scripture and the seriousness of spiritual battles with the kingdom of darkness.

and compassionately reached out to the sick, sinful, and struggling in society.

After a month of seeking God for the gift of Spirit baptism, I received my personal Pentecost in August of 1983. Jesus baptized me in the Holy Spirit. The biblical sign of tongues accompanied my Spirit baptismal experience. I was at the altar praying.[14] People were gathered around me praying and finally after some time I lost myself in worship and mumbled a few syllables.[15] I began praying in tongues as part of my personal devotions and during times of intercessory prayer at the church. A couple of weeks later I felt the Spirit come upon me and I spoke out in tongues during a worship service. I remember falling down on my knees and asking God to provide the interpretation to the message. Someone did, and I was greatly relieved!

I began sensing a call to full time pastoral ministry. I was not sure what all this meant for me. Initially my father was not too excited about my going into ministry. Yet he came with my mother (and other family members) to hear my first public sermon. My pastor invited me to share my testimony and preach on a Sunday evening. I went to the pulpit and cried my way through my testimony. I made sure that I apologized to my parents for the way I had lived my life. I did the best I could to make restitution to my parents. I asked them to forgive me. (Later I would apologize to each of my siblings for not being there for them). I shared how my lifestyle had contributed to a deep spiritual emptiness but Jesus had changed my life. Through my testimonial exhortation, I gave God glory for delivering me from Satan and sin. At the end of my testimony, I invited people to come and pray. The altars were filled with youth and many adults came forward to pray for their lost children. As a congregation, we cried out to God to bring healing and salvation to our families!

---

[14] For a further description of my Spirit Baptism experience and how I understand it sacramentally see my 'Nourishment for our Journey: The Pentecostal *Via Salutis* and Sacramental Ordinances', *Journal for Pentecostal Theology* 13 (2004), pp. 79-96, and chapter four in my *The Gospel Revisited: Towards a Pentecostal Theology of Worship and Witness* (Eugene, OR: Pickwick publications, 2011), Chapter 4.

[15] For the first week following, I questioned my experience and wondered if it was just me. However, as time went on and as I continued praying in and with the Spirit, I came to accept the experience as authentic.

Over the next year various individuals in the community confirmed the call of God on my life. The pastor said I needed to go to a bible college to prepare for fulltime pastoral ministry. I did think that maybe Southeastern College would be a nice place to go because it was close to the beach; however, I decided that Central Bible College would be a better choice since my girlfriend, the pastor's daughter, was going to be attending Evangel College after her high school graduation. The next fall, I packed my car and headed to Springfield, Missouri, to attend Central Bible College. My formal academic adventure had begun. Yet the academic journey was interwoven into my relationship with God in such a way that I cannot separate it from my salvific journey. As Christians our vocational callings should be an important aspect of our relationship with God.

Bible College: The Beginning of My Formal Theological Education

In August of 1984, I began attending Central Bible College. Over the next three years the faculty grounded me in the Bible, Arminian-Pentecostal theology, pastoral leadership, and Assemblies of God doctrine and polity. The four cardinal doctrines of the AG – Salvation, Healing, Spirit Baptism and the imminent return of Jesus Christ – were especially emphasized. These experiences were understood to be promises available to Christians because they were wrought in the atoning work of Jesus Christ. The themes were explicitly addressed in certain doctrinal courses, yet the emphasis overall was more implicit. The themes of the Full Gospel were articulated throughout the various chapels and ministry experiences which further developed and refined my 'embedded theology'.[16] The college provided an atmosphere for further Pentecostal spiritual formation. It was here that I first became indoctrinated into clas-

---

[16] For a helpful discussion of embedded and deliberative theology see Howard W. Stone and James O. Duke, *How To Think Theologically* (Minneapolis, MN: Fortress Press, 1996), pp. 13-21. I adapted their definition of embedded theology. They define it as an implicit theological understanding of Christian faith disseminated by the Christian community's various ministry practices and assimilated by its members that is expressed in their daily lives. The Pentecostal community contributed primarily to my embedded theology, but it would also include my more limited and detached involvement with the Roman Catholic community.

sical Pentecostalism from a more fundamentalist perspective. And towards the end, I began to be introduced to evangelical critical biblical scholarship and modern yet conservative philosophical reasoning.[17]

I will always be grateful for the school and its faculty because they were willing to accept me as a student on academic probation. I was accepted into college because of my pastor's recommendation letter. Even though I had earned a B average in High School, I did not score well on the entrance or the ACT exams. The faculty helped me to develop further basic skills in reading and writing. During the first semester I took remedial grammar. I also decided that it would be beneficial to improve my reading skills, so I spent a great deal of time in the library.

My favorite subject was theology. My first theological paper (on God's omniscience, of all things!) was only two pages long and took me almost 20 hours to write! The textbook for the course was written from a more Reformed perspective; however, I argued for an Arminian view of God's foreknowledge.[18] After earning my PhD, I would publish a series of essays affirming an openness view of the future. I argued that it was consistent with Scripture and the Pentecostal experience of intercessory prayer.[19] The point is that most of my early theological writings were academic critical reflections on my embedded Pentecostal spirituality.

During my third year of college, Melissa and I were married. I decided to take additional classes so that I could finish my degree in three years instead of four. I pushed hard that year because I wanted to get into the harvest field; Jesus could return at any time! I graduated in August of 1987 with a major in Bible and a minor in biblical Greek. Through God's grace, hard work, and the attentive help and encouragement of friends and the faculty, I completed my degree. The Lord had truly helped me to develop my intellectual

---

[17] The course on Introduction to Philosophy used Norman L. Geisler and Paul Feinberg, *Introduction to Philosophy: A Christian Perspective* (Grand Rapids, MI: Baker Book House, 1980) as the textbook.

[18] The textbook was Henry Clarence Thiessen, *Lectures In Systematic Theology* (Grand Rapids, MI: Eerdmans, rev. edn, 1979). The Arminian view of omniscience affirmed that God simply knew the future without determining or causing the specific events to transpire. The focus of the discussion centered upon personal salvation.

[19] See my *The Gospel Revisited*, Chapter 5.

abilities and experience academic growth. I was encouraged by a few teachers to go on and do graduate work.

Interestingly, my introduction to the history and theology of Pentecostalism left out some of the more critical details of the movement. During my time at CBC, the argument was that Pentecostals were Evangelicals who added on the doctrine of the Baptism in the Holy Spirit with the initial evidence of speaking in unlearned tongues. Concerning the 'distinctive' doctrine of Spirit Baptism, it was understood to be a biblical doctrine that had been recovered by Charles Fox Parham at his Bible Institute in Topeka, Kansas. Parham was the originator of the doctrine.[20] A significant part of my PhD thesis would challenge the argument that Pentecostals were Evangelicals who spoke in tongues. I have argued that Pentecostals share some theological concerns with Evangelicals but Pentecostalism should be appreciated as a distinct theological tradition.[21]

First Pastorate and Continuation of Academic Theological Education

After graduation Melissa and I served as Youth pastors at the same Pentecostal church where I had given my life to Christ. Nine months later, I became the senior pastor of that church after the pastor resigned to pursue full-time missions work. At the time I was one of the youngest senior pastors in the state of Ohio. As the pastor, I began engaging in various responsibilities. I continued to study both academic works as well as more popular level publications. I began a quest into the various interpretive arguments that whetted my appetite for further theological studies. More importantly, I felt that God was calling me to continue my education in a formal academic setting. I shared this with the leadership of the

---

[20] As well as I can remember, the professors did not focus on the Azusa Street revival nor did they discuss the controversial details of Parham's life, such as his maintaining the Jim Crow laws, his racial attitudes, and other interesting theological doctrines he held to such as the annihilation of the wicked. (I would discover Parham's theological and racial views during my PhD research). It was Parham's contribution to the development of the doctrine of Spirit baptism with speaking in other tongues that was highlighted.

[21] See my 'A Pentecostal Way of Doing Theology: Method and Manner', *International Journal of Systematic Theology* 9.3 (July 2007), pp. 301-14.

church. I desired to further my education so that I could teach theology to future ministers.

Our church was about 40 miles from Ashland Theological Seminary. Ashland Seminary had a good reputation among AG ministers in Northern Ohio. My former youth pastor was a graduate. I decided to attend Ashland in order to further my theological training. I enrolled in the 144 quarter-hour MDiv program. I attended the fall quarter and did very well, but I knew that if I was ever going to finish the degree I would have to attend full-time. Due to time demands and lack of support from church leadership, I did not enroll in the winter or spring quarters. As the following fall rolled around, I again approached the church leadership about the possibility of attending Seminary on a full-time basis. I explained to them that the Holy Spirit was calling me to pursue further studies. The leadership of the community which nurtured me into the Pentecostal faith saw no value in my attending Seminary on a full-time basis. One board member expressed the sentiment of the rest. He explained to me that I already had more education than most of the members of the congregation. I had a college education; they had High School diplomas. In addition, to further my education would take away from church responsibilities. The church was not *paying* me to attend Seminary. If I really felt called of God to pursue a graduate degree, I would need to resign from my pastorate. This was a painful time for Melissa and me. We decided to resign and seek a church that would allow me to be their pastor and attend the Seminary full-time. We resigned without having another pastorate in place. I enrolled for fall courses at the Seminary. God opened the door for us to begin pastoring a small Assemblies of God home missions church in Twinsburg, Ohio.

MDiv: Ashland Theological Seminary

During my time at Ashland, I encountered a broader and more diverse evangelical pietistic faculty who were much more open to academic critical scholarship (both Modern and Postmodern) than what I had encountered at Central Bible College. While I was at Ashland Seminary, my critical thinking skills were further awakened and developed. Here, I began to assess my Pentecostal and Christian faith critically. I became much more aware of the influences of

Modernity upon Christian belief and practice. An evangelical perspective of the exegetical historical critical methodology was affirmed with an ongoing critique of the liberal presupposition beliefs that gave rise to the method. A few biblical scholars were more affirming of literary and liberation readings of Scripture as well as some emerging postmodern methodologies.

During my last year I took upper level courses which introduced me to various theoretical concepts that pushed me to rethink further my Pentecostal and even Christian faith. I had entered the 'wilderness' of academic criticism. I found it both liberating and troubling. I had not abandoned Pentecostal faith and practice; however, I was in the process of revisioning aspects of my Pentecostal theological understanding. Through times of struggle, surprise, and even embarrassment, I came to see that Pentecostalism had both strengths and weaknesses. Although I was informed by a professor that sometimes we intellectually outgrow our more anti-intellectual traditions, my desire was to integrate the emotional and intellectual dimensions of a human being. Pentecostals are passionate about the Lord and God's reign. We cannot or should not reduce academic theology to just the cognitive aspect of a human being. Indeed, I saw my theological studies as an important part of my vocational calling; hence I understood 'study' as an aspect of worship.

Ashland Theological Seminary offered one course on Pentecostalism. The course would contribute to my future PhD studies. The critical history and early theology of Pentecostalism would come into focus through a course titled 'The History of Methodism and the Roots of Pentecostalism'. The textbooks for the course included Vinson Synan's *The Holiness-Pentecostal Movement in the United States*[22] and Donald Dayton's *The Theological Roots of Pentecostalism*.[23] The course gave me an opportunity to reflect critically upon the prehistory and early theology of Pentecostalism. I did a research paper on the Azusa Street Revival. The attempt at racial reconciliation, the volume of miraculous healings, and the transformation experienced by individuals who had received Spirit Baptism were of particular interest to me. William Seymour, the African American

---

[22] Donald W. Dayton, *The Theological Roots of Pentecostalism* (Peabody, MA: Hendrickson Publishers, 1987).

[23] Vinson Synan, *The Holiness-Pentecostal Movement in the United Sates* (Grand Rapids, MI: Eerdmans, 1971).

leader of the Azusa Street Revival, became my new hero. The early literature I read reinforced Dayton's theological analyses of early Pentecostalism. The theological DNA that produced the Pentecostal movement fused particular 19th century themes into a new gestalt identified as the Full gospel of Jesus Christ.

When I read Dayton's monograph, I had already been a senior pastor for over five years. The proclamation of the Full Gospel of Jesus Christ as the Savior, Healer, Spirit Baptizer, and Soon Coming King was the focus of most, if not all, my ministry. We included in our weekly Sunday worship services a time to lay hands on the sick and anoint them with oil as we believed God for their healing. I practiced the 'shot gun' approach to altar calls: I began with a call to salvation, then included calls for consecration and recommitments (sanctification), followed by opportunities for those to experience healing and deliverance. We all knew that Jesus was coming; the signs were everywhere. Therefore, it was important to be baptized in the Holy Spirit. Hence, calls for being baptized in the Holy Spirit were also included at times in the invitation. This approach, albeit an approach that was consistent with more of the radical revivalist tradition, may not have been the normative ministry practices of most Pentecostal preachers at that time; however, I venture to suggest that themes of the Full Gospel were heard regularly through sermons and testimonies in many Pentecostal and even charismatic churches.

The Full gospel served as the very heart of my Pentecostal spirituality – a dynamic pietistic Christocentric soteriology. Dayton's book impacted me because it brought into critical focus my embedded spirituality. As a result of reading Dayton's book, I began to think about the possibilities of writing a Pentecostal systematic theology based upon the Full Gospel. Towards the end of my Seminary studies, I was convinced that Pentecostalism had more to offer the larger Christian theological traditions than what most evangelicals thought. I knew that I wanted to offer a constructive contribution to the small but growing academic field of Pentecostal theology.[24]

---

[24] For a more thorough discussion on the importance of the Fivefold Gospel see my 'The Fivefold Gospel and the Mission of the Church: Ecclesiastical Implications and Opportunities' in John Christopher Thomas (ed.), *Toward a Pentecostal Ecclesiology: The Church and the Fivefold Gospel* (Cleveland, TN: CPT Press, 2010). I

I graduated from Ashland Theological Seminary with a Master of Divinity degree with an interdisciplinary major in Theology, Church History, and Philosophy. My critical thinking skills were strengthened, which enabled me to graduate with High Honors (3.93 GPA). I was encouraged by several faculty members to pursue a PhD. I had decided that I wanted to attend a University rather than a Seminary for my PhD studies. My rationale was straightforward. I had attended a Pentecostal Bible College which gave me a working theological language and indoctrinated me into a 1970s Assemblies of God Pentecostal system of beliefs and practices. By now I realized that many of the professors I had at CBC were immersed in modernistic philosophical categories which were used by academic conservative evangelicals. The epistemological categories were tweaked from a Pentecostal perspective, but they were not yet thoroughly reworked or abandoned. Postmodernity had not yet made an impact upon the faculty. Ashland Seminary favored pietistic and Anabaptist theological perspectives. The faculty was from diverse Protestant theological traditions, including the Reformed, which added to the breath, beauty and diversity of the Christian faith. I believed I was ready to venture into a liberal and secular University environment. I wanted to attend a University that was considered academically astute by the broader circles of academia and by the public. I wanted to prove to myself and to others that a Pentecostal from a non-academic upbringing could earn a degree from what might be considered a top-tiered or ivy league University. In addition, a degree from such a University would definitely be an advantage when it came to landing a teaching post either in a Christian or secular University.

During my last quarter at Ashland Seminary, I contacted Professor Richard Bauckham who taught at the University of St Andrews in Scotland. He was suggested by one of the faculty members at Ashland as a possible supervisor for PhD research. I had become aware of Bauckham through his work on Jürgen Moltmann which I read for a course in contemporary theology. He was recognized as both a theologian and leading biblical scholar. I also knew he was a committed Christian and open to the charismatic movement. His

---

am still in the process of writing a fully developed Pentecostal narrative theology grounded in the Fivefold Gospel. For a provisional attempt see my *The Gospel Revisited: Towards a Pentecostal Theology of Worship and Witness.*

scholarship, his commitment to Christian community, and his openness to 'charismatic movements' were extremely important attributes that I was looking for in a supervisor. Furthermore, the University of St Andrews only required a one-year residency; thus it was a financially viable option. I would be able to return to the States and finish my research on a part-time basis while I continued to pastor.

I wrote to Professor Bauckham and explained to him my desire to engage in Hermeneutics and Pentecostalism.[25] He was interested in my topic and extended an invitation for me to become one of his research students. Along with the invitation to study was the opportunity to work as a Teaching Assistant which helped to reduce my tuition for that year.

PhD: A Seven Year Process

After graduating from Ashland Theological Seminary and resigning our pastorate, Melissa and I, with our two young sons Trent (age 4) and Tyler (age 3) moved to St Andrews, Scotland. I enthusiastically began my research on Pentecostalism and hermeneutics. My year of postgraduate research at St Andrews brought many opportunities to engage in critical dialogue on various subjects.

I began to reflect critically on Pentecostalism and Christian faith. I also knew that I needed to put some distance between me and the subject of my studies. This was difficult because of my commitment to the Pentecostal tradition. Yet, this time was extremely beneficial for me. I read deeply and widely, and found myself surprised and amazed. I discovered a growing genre of critical academic work on Pentecostalism. I had read some of the academic historiography on Pentecostalism, but now I had become aware of biblical and theological contributions. Journals such as *Pneuma* and the *Journal of Pen-*

---

[25] My doctoral research focused on Pentecostal hermeneutics. The Pentecostal community, as a distinct narrative tradition, is an essential and necessary component of a Pentecostal hermeneutic. I argued that the Full Gospel was the very heart of the 'central narrative convictions' of the Pentecostal story which shaped its community's identity. See the published version of my PhD thesis, Kenneth J. Archer, *A Pentecostal Hermeneutic for the Twenty-First Century: Spirit, Scripture and Community* (JPTSup, 28; London and New York: T&T Clark, 2004), and the paperback edition, *A Pentecostal Hermeneutic: Spirit, Scripture, and Community* (Cleveland, TN: CPT Press, 2009).

tecostal Theology and its supplement series became significant resources for me as I pursued my studies. In the second semester of my studies, I presented a paper on Pentecostalism and hermeneutics to the post-graduate seminar. The paper enabled me to move from a research student to a PhD candidate.[26]

I must say that I experienced some difficult times in my theological critical reassessment of Christianity. I had read various works that rejected Christianity. I had discussions with those of other religious faith traditions. I even came to understand why some would reject Christianity. Also, as a pastor I had counseled individuals who experienced painful events that led them to question seriously their faith in God. Even though difficult, it is not uncommon for Christians to reexamine their faith, and this becomes especially true for those who enter into formal academic education. I remember times when I would walk around the cathedral ruins in St Andrews arguing with God! I reaffirmed my Christian faith commitment to God. To this day, I am convinced that cognitive rationalistic arguments alone cannot *prove* or *disprove* the existence of God. The heart of Christianity is first and foremost relational spirituality.

After one school term we returned to the States. I took Professor Bauckham's advice and found someone to read through my research, especially the early Pentecostal historiography and theological sections. I was blessed to have Dr Bill Faupel work through the drafts of my chapters. His insight into the tradition was extremely beneficial to my research.

The next six years were filled with research and writing. I also began teaching as an adjunct instructor at Ashland Theological Seminary. Additionally, we began pastoring a non-denominational community church in Mohicanville, Ohio. During my time of researching and writing my PhD thesis, I regularly presented papers at the Society for Pentecostal Studies (SPS). I also attended the Society for Biblical Literature (SBL) and the American Academy of Religion (AAR) annual conferences. SPS was especially helpful because here I met other scholars who were committed to the Pentecostal tradi-

---

[26] I revised the paper and submitted it for publication. It was my first publication. See my 'Pentecostal Hermeneutics: Retrospect and Prospect', *Journal of Pentecostal Theology* 8 (April 1996), pp. 63-81. To my surprise selections of this essay would be included in David F. Ford and Mike Higton (eds.), *The Modern Theologians Reader* (UK: Willy-Blackwell, 2012), pp. 360-65. There are only two entries under Pentecostal and Charismatic Theology.

tion and serious academic scholarship. I found myself among those who were more open to Postmodernism. These scholars were not committed to modern or even postmodern epistemological systems. They were forging new paths into critical scholarship which offered critical assessment and helpful revisioning to the Pentecostal tradition. As a result of such engagement, I crossed the desert of skeptical (Modern and/or Postmodern) criticism. I had journeyed through the wilderness of the first naïveté and entered into the 'second naïveté'.[27]

The second naïveté is a post-critical stance in which I recognize that commitment to community is not an option but a reality, and my participation in a Christian community shapes my view of reality. I am not suggesting that one cannot understand other peoples' views, but I am saying that one's participation in a community nevertheless makes life meaningful. I am unashamedly and unabashedly committed to the Pentecostal traditions, and more importantly, I am committed to Jesus Christ and his Church. I embraced the Pentecostal traditions without trying to make excuses for the challenges and problems within them.

Ten Years at the Church of God Theological Seminary: Further Development and Refinement in My Academic Vocation

After submitting my PhD and successfully defending it, I was contacted by Dr John Christopher Thomas from Church of God Theological Seminary in Cleveland, Tennessee.[28] The Seminary was searching for a theologian, and Chris encouraged me to apply for the position. I felt honored that they were interested in me and my work. I was hired in July, 2001 and thus began the fulfillment of my calling to full-time theological education. I respected the theological view of this community. They really were pioneers in attempting to forge a distinct Pentecostal hermeneutic and Spirituality, grounded

---

[27] Paul Ricoeur, *The Symbolism of Evil* (New York, NY: Harper and Row Publishers, 1967), p. 351.

[28] The first time I met Chris was during my final quarter at ATS. We sat and talked for about an hour. I explained to him my concern to work on a Pentecostal hermeneutic. He was delighted and encouraged me. I would get better acquainted with him and COGTS faculty through my involvement at the SPS. He would be an important dialogue partner in my future work at COGTS.

in the first ten years of the Pentecostal movement and the experiential dimensions associated with the Fivefold Gospel.[29]

We moved to Athens, TN, a small town north of Cleveland. We immediately started attending Woodward Avenue Church of God. Melissa and I believe that becoming part of this particular church community was as important as landing the job at the Church of God Seminary.[30] The community was diverse ethnically (even though the majority were Anglo), socially, and economically. The community had a strong revivalist flavor and more 'raw' demonstrative manifestations of spirituality. Tongues and interpretation as well as prophetic prayer, praying for the sick, and altar calls were regular aspects of the experientially charged worship services. Even though there was not an official emphasis upon holistic mission, individuals in the community were active in various forms of ministry outreach and service. I appreciate the fact that the Pentecostal Full Gospel generates hope and healing for a broken world. The Lord continued to confront and transform us in this community. I am sure my time at Woodward seeps through my academic work.

My time at COGTS continued to contribute to the development of my theological understanding. I was privileged to teach there for ten years. Those ten years were very fruitful for me academically and professionally. I gleaned a great deal from the faculty members and their publications. Steve Land lifted up the importance of the Fivefold Gospel in his first monograph, and Chris Thomas made a significant connection between the Fivefold Gospel and ecclesiastical signs associated with it. I continue to develop that initial paradigm in productive and creative ways.[31] Rickie Moore and Chris Thomas' work in hermeneutics has also been influential in my own

---

[29] Not all the faculty would affirm the Fivefold gospel as the essential identity marker of Pentecostal theology, yet all recognized the significance of it and the essential importance of the first ten years of the Pentecostal movement. No doubt, Steven Jack Land's *Pentecostal Spirituality: A Passion for the Kingdom,* which is considered a seminal contribution, served as a Pentecostal manifesto for the COGTS community.

[30] We were active members. From 2002 until leaving to teach at Southeastern, Melissa and I served as the college and career pastors. One of the highlights of our time at Woodward was praying for our sons to receive Spirit Baptism. They both experienced the Baptism in the Holy Spirit and spoke in tongues as the Spirit gave them utterances. My sons were and still are active in the music ministry at Woodward.

[31] For example see my 'Nourishment for our Journey: The Pentecostal *Via Salutis* and Sacramental Ordinances'.

endeavors. Cheryl Bridges Johns' work in formation and ecumenism played an important role in my understanding of the necessity of praxis and a hospitable yet sectarian identity. The majority of my academic publications emerged during these 10 years. Prior to resigning to respond to God's call to come to Southeastern University in Lakeland, Florida, I published my second monograph, *The Gospel Revisited: Towards a Pentecostal Theology of Worship and Witness*. The book reflects my theological development and is my attempt at laying out the beginning of a constructive Pentecostal narrative theology. I dedicated the book to the faculty and staff at Church of God Theological Seminary, now known as Pentecostal Theological Seminary.

Today I consider myself a post-critical Pentecostal with a postmodern accent. I affirm Scripture as the Spirit-inspired penultimate witness of God's revelation to humanity.[32] For me the Bible is a self-authenticating metanarrative which offers readers an opportunity to enter into a verbally construed world. Through the Spirit, Scripture creates a world so that one can encounter the mediated transforming presence of the living God. It does so through open-ended conversation with its readers shaped by their communities and personal stories. The Full Gospel is the formational story of Jesus Christ which shapes Pentecostal spirituality and theology. We find our true identity only in a redemptive relationship with the almighty God. Hence we testify that Jesus is our Liberator, Savior, Deliverer, Healer, Spirit Baptizer, Sanctifier, and King who is returning so very soon. Such worshipful confessions are born out of our redemptive relationship with God and serve as reminders of God's gracious redemptive activity.

I have been blessed to make a small yet significant contribution to the academic development of a constructive Pentecostal hermeneutic and theology. The journey has not been easy. But as I said, my academic journey is interwoven into my journey with the Living God. The journey has been filled with surprise and disappointment, grief and joy. I am grateful for God's redemptive grace and holistic

---

[32] By penultimate, I mean second only to Jesus Christ the Living Word. See my, 'A Theology of the Word ... and that's the Point!' in S.J. Land, R.D. Moore, J.C. Thomas (eds.), *Passover, Pentecost and Parousia: Studies in Celebration of the Life and Ministry of R. Hollis Gause* (JPTSup, 36; Blandford Forum: Deo, 2010), pp. 125-44.

salvation. I desire all the glory to go to my Lord and Savior Jesus Christ.

Implicit and Explicit Themes: A Brief Reflection on my Testimony

I would like to offer a few concluding remarks. First, the Lord has brought me a long way, both spiritually and academically. Who would have thought that God would call a construction laborer (which I consider respectable work) into pastoral ministry that would eventually lead him to becoming a Professor of Theology? I give all the glory to the living God! Second, significant persons walked beside me on the journey. Academic mentors who can pray with and for you are indispensable faithful guides. They did not keep me from entering into the wilderness nor encourage me to avoid it; rather, they led me through the wilderness. They were able do so because they had been through it themselves. Third, Pentecostal communities, both academic and local churches, played an important role in keeping me anchored in the faith tradition. I am Pentecostal not so much because I pray and speak in tongues but because I am part of a Pentecostal community. Fourth, the journey has been costly financially. Academic pursuit is expensive! Without hesitation, I can say that God has *always* showed himself to be faithful. Fifth, there were times where I questioned my faith. I had and still have times of the 'dark night of the soul'. I believe everyone has such experiences, but it seems that academic study encourages it. I feel that this is not a sign of weakness nor is it something we can avoid; rather, it is an essential part of the journey. Sixth, I am grateful for my spouse Melissa. I cannot express how significant she has been to me as a source of strength, encouragement and spiritual insight. Finally, life is a storied reality. The triune God shares life with us, and through the biblical story we find our story. I pray that the Lord will continue to lead you into the journey of a lifetime, a redemptive expedition filled with mystery and surprise. I pray that the Spirit will sustain you as the Spirit 'drives you' into the wilderness and empower you to overcome. May God lead you to the mountain so that you too can see the promised land, and this I pray in Jesus' name. Amen!

Epilogue

Whence Pentecostal Scholarship? The Coming of Age of the Pentecostal Critical Tradition and a Forecast for Its Future

Robby Waddell[*]

The Origins of Pentecostal Scholarship

Determining the precise beginning of the Pentecostal movement is an impossible task. Throughout the nineteenth century and continuing into the first decade of the twentieth century numerous revivals exhibiting a renewed emphasis on the gifts of the Spirit sprung up around the world. Although historiographers of the movement continue to uncover more information about its origins, the Azusa Street Revival in Los Angeles remains arguably the most influential of these early events.[1] The majority of the initial adherents of the movement, at least in the USA, joined newly formed denominations such as the Church of God in Christ, the Interna-

---

[*] Robby Waddell (PhD, University of Sheffield) is Professor of New Testament and Early Christian Literature and Director of the Center for Faith and Higher Learning at Southeastern University in Lakeland, FL, USA.

[1] For an introduction to the various international expressions of early Pentecostalism, especially those outside North America and independent of the Azusa Street Mission, see Allan H. Anderson, *Spreading Fires: the Missionary Nature of Early Pentecostalism* (Maryknoll: Orbis Books, 2007). The leading work on the Azusa Street Revival is Cecil M. Robeck, Jr., *The Azusa Street Mission and Revival: The Birth of the Global Pentecostal Movement* (Nashville: Thomas Nelson Publishers, 2006).

tional Pentecostal Holiness Church, the Church of God (Cleveland, TN), the Assemblies of God, and the International Church of the Foursquare Gospel. These groups shared characteristics including exuberant worship services and a combination of doctrines none of which were completely new in church history, though this particular mix of beliefs and practices – such as Spirit baptism with the accompanying glossolalia, divine healing through the laying on of hands, exorcisms, sanctification (discursively defined), and a strong belief in the imminent return of Jesus Christ – distinguished the new movement as an identifiable expression of Christianity.[2]

Throughout the twentieth century the movement would continue to expand exponentially through evangelism and by means of other related renewal movements within the Catholic Church and many of the mainline Protestant denominations. Given the growth rate of Pentecostal indigenous churches in Asia, Africa, and South America many religious experts are predicting that Pentecostalism – broadly conceived – will represent the face of Christianity in this century.[3] As a sociological and religious phenomenon the impact of Pentecostalism on global Christianity is undeniable, and yet for the purpose of this chapter the question remains: 'What contribution does Pentecostalism have to make to the critical tradition of religious studies?' or 'What does Athens have to do with Azusa Street?'

The first generation of Pentecostals produced books, pamphlets, and newspapers, though this work was written at a popular level. Owing in part to the anti-intellectualism which plagued much of the movement, the question as to whether or not Pentecostals had anything to contribute to the critical tradition of Christian theology was hardly considered in the first half the twentieth century. As Pentecostal denominations gained more cultural acceptance and joined evangelical organizations such as the National Association of Evangelicals, it appeared as though – theologically at least – Pentecostals

---

[2] Historical and theological assessments of early Pentecostalism may be found in D. William Faupel, *The Everlasting Gospel: The Significance of Eschatology in the Development of Pentecostal Thought* (JPTSup, 10; Sheffield: Sheffield Academic Press, 1996) and Donald Dayton, *Theological Roots of Pentecostalism* (Grand Rapids: Zondervan, 1987).

[3] See Harvey G. Cox, *Fire from Heaven: The Rise of Pentecostal Spirituality and the Reshaping of Religion in the Twenty-first Century* (Reading: Addison-Wesley, 1995), and Philip Jenkins, *The Next Christendom: The Coming of Global Christianity* (New York: Oxford University Press, 2007).

may be nothing more than a version of conservative evangelicalism with some added zest related to worship style and the doctrine of Spirit baptism. Pentecostals had a distinct identity that was rooted in a particular worldview and spirituality but did they truly have a unique theological contribution?[4] The answer to this question appears to be a resounding yes!

The Coming of Age of Pentecostal Scholarship

In the inaugural issue of the *Journal of Pentecostal Theology* the editors outlined what they saw as three distinct phases in the history of critical-constructive Pentecostal scholarship. According to their historical sketch the first generation included the earliest Pentecostal scholars who completed post-graduate work despite 'an environment which did not encourage nor even perceive the viability of interaction between Pentecostal faith and critical theological scholarship'.[5] Although the editorial did not name specific examples from this generation, it would include among many others the work of scholars like Vinson Synan, whose testimony is included in this volume.[6] A second generation of scholarship emerged when for the first time Pentecostals were afforded the opportunity to bring 'their Pentecostalism to bear upon their graduate research',[7] though most of this work was restricted to descriptive historical study or social scientific analysis of the movement. Included in this generation

---

[4] The question about a distinctively Pentecostal theological contribution has for the most part been answered, though it continues to receive some attention. Helpful discussions of this topic include Terry L. Cross, 'The Rich Feast of Theology: Can Pentecostals bring the Main Course or only the Relish?' *Journal of Pentecostal Theology* 16 (April 2000), pp. 27–47; *idem*, 'A Proposal to Break the Ice: What can Pentecostal Theology offer Evangelical Theology?' *Journal of Pentecostal Theology* 10.2 (April 2002), pp. 44–73; and Dale M. Coulter, 'What Meaneth This? Pentecostals and Theological Inquiry', *Journal of Pentecostal Theology* 10.1 (October 2001), pp. 38–64.

[5] Steven J. Land, Rickie D. Moore, and John Christopher Thomas, 'Editorial', *Journal of Pentecostal Theology* 1 (1992), p. 3.

[6] Any attempt to list scholars who would fit into this generation would inevitably be limited and fall far short of naming all those who deserve mention, nevertheless, a complete list would include the work of scholars such as Stanley Horton, French Arrington, Gordon Fee, Robert Cooley, Russell Spittler, William Menzies, Leonard Lovet, and Del Tarr.

[7] Land, Moore, and Thomas, 'Editorial', p. 3.

would be scholars such as Edith Blumhofer and William Faupel as well as John Christopher Thomas' early work on footwashing. With the rise of the third generation, Pentecostal scholars were given the opportunity to integrate the distinctives of Pentecostal faith with their critical theological research. A well-documented hallmark of this generation is the debate that arose in biblical studies around whether the metaphor of Spirit baptism represented initiation into the Christian community (e.g. James D.G. Dunn and Max Turner) or a subsequent experience of empowerment for vocation (e.g. Roger Stronstad and Robert Menzies).[8] The *Journal of Pentecostal Theology* along with its monograph series was established as a venue for this expanding phase of the critical tradition of Pentecostalism.

In the 1998 presidential address of the Society for Pentecostal Studies, John Christopher Thomas suggested that perhaps the rise of a fourth generation of Pentecostal scholarship was being experienced. This generation, according to Thomas, benefits from the increasing number of Pentecostals within academia and the attention that accompanies any group with such extensive demographics, but more importantly this generation will have the 'opportunity to read, assess, and critique academic works by Pentecostal scholars, an opportunity largely impossible just a few short years ago'.[9] I find this description of the critical tradition of Pentecostalism helpful. In fact, I would categorize my own work as part of this fourth generation identified by Thomas. Be that as it may, the sheer volume of Pentecostal scholarship has reached such a pace of proliferation that identifying what generation a particular piece derives from may have reached its limits as a useful metaphor. In the following pages, I offer a brief sketch of the current state of Pentecostal scholarship – not attempting to be comprehensive but hoping to provide a general sense of the current state of Pentecostal scholarship. In the spirit of this book, my hope is also to invite young people from within the spiritual tradition of Pentecostalism to engage in a creative and critical construction of Pentecostal theology for the twenty-first century.

---

[8] For a discussion of this scholarship see Martin William Mittelstadt, *Reading Luke-Acts in the Pentecostal Tradition* (Cleveland, TN: CPT Press, 2010).

[9] John Christopher Thomas, 'Pentecostal Theology in the Twenty-First Century', *Pneuma* 20 (1998), p. 5.

Academic Journals

The number of journals dedicated to Pentecostal studies is on the rise. The longtime established standards of Pentecostal scholarship include *Pneuma: The Journal of the Society for Pentecostal Studies*, which is under the joint editorial leadership of Amos Yong and Dale Coulter, and the *Journal of Pentecostal Theology* led by editors John Christopher Thomas and Lee Roy Martin. In the inaugural issue of *JPT* – now two decades ago! – Walter Hollenweger, the godfather of Pentecostal historiography, wrote that the criticism of Pentecostalism as being anti-intellectual can no longer be applied without qualification owing to the critical mass of scholarship that had coalesced by the early 1990s.[10] Other established journals in the tradition are *JEPTA* (the *Journal of the European Pentecostal Theological Association*) edited by William Kay and the *Asian Journal of Pentecostal Studies* published by the Asia Pacific Theological Seminary in Baguio City, Philippines. In the last decade other journals have been established including *PentecoStudies: An Interdisciplinary Journal for Research on the Pentecostal and Charismatic Movements* edited by Mark J. Cartledge, and *Pax Pneuma: The Journal of Pentecostals and Charismatics for Peace and Justice* edited by Paul Alexander. Another notable new journal is *The Journal of Biblical and Pneumatological Research*. *JBPR* is not explicitly dedicated to the Pentecostal tradition, though it deserves to be mentioned in this list because its focus is of importance to Pentecostal theologians and biblical scholars. Paul Elbert, the editor of *JBPR*, is a Pentecostal as are the majority of its editorial board members. In addition to the journals in print, there are a couple of peer-reviewed web journals – the *Canadian Journal of Pentecostal-Charismatic Christianity* edited by Peter Althouse and Michael Wilkinson and *Australasian Pentecostal Studies* edited by Shane Clifton, which is now in its second decade. Also available online is the annually published *Cyberjournal for Pentecostal-Charismatic Research* edited by Harold Hunter. The opportunity for articles to be published about Pentecostalism has never been greater. It should be noted that these journals are not the exclusive arenas of Pentecostal scholars but include significant dialogues with scholars from other

---

[10] Walter J. Hollenweger, 'The Critical Tradition of Pentecostalism', *Journal of Pentecostal Theology* 1 (1992), pp. 7–17.

traditions, notable examples including Harvey Cox, Walter Brueggemann, and Jürgen Moltmann.

Book Series

The number of quality monograph series dedicated to Pentecostalism is also on the rise. The *Journal of Pentecostal Theology* Supplement Series, edited by John Christopher Thomas, has almost forty volumes. The series was originally published by Sheffield Academic Press and then had a short stint at Continuum before finding a more permanent home at Deo Publishing. This series contains a number of significant pieces including the seminal and often cited monograph by Steven Land, *Pentecostal Spirituality: A Passion for the Kingdom.* More than any other series the JPTSS has made room for volumes on biblical studies and hermeneutics.

John Christopher Thomas is also the editor of the *Pentecostal Commentary Series*, published by Deo Publishing. Volumes in this series are written primarily for Bible students, pastors, and lay persons; and therefore, the technical arguments are located in the footnotes and kept intentionally to a minimum. The authors of the commentaries, however, are experts in the field of biblical studies and are conversant with the swell of secondary literature. Intentionally attempting to represent the ethos of the Pentecostal movement, the format of the commentary is unique and deserves mention. The volume begins with an introduction containing a series of questions 'designed to lift up corporate and individual issues that are illuminated in the biblical book under examination' (p. ix). The questions invite the readers to contextualize the message of the ancient text in a reasonably useful manner. Following the initial set of questions the introduction proper includes normal introductory matters of literary genre, authorship, date, place of composition, audience, and theological emphases. A brief but helpful section on the role of the Holy Spirit in the book is included in the introduction. The heart of the book is the commentary proper, which like all commentaries contains a running exposition of the text including discussions on various interpretative options. Throughout the commentary reflections are periodically included, summarizing the main ideas in each major section followed by a series of questions directly inviting the readers to reflect on key dimensions of the text. Following the reflections, the readers are presented with specific ways to respond. This format makes the volumes in this series very applicable for a pastor preparing a sermon or for a small group Bible study in a local church.

The global effects of Pentecostalism have inspired two relatively new series. The first is edited by Andrew Davies and William Kay, *Global Pentecostal and Charismatic Studies*, published by Brill. The series focuses on 'different themes within the Pentecostal-Charismatic movements from with a combination of historical, social scientific, and theological approaches'.[11] Secondly, The Center for the Study of World Christian Revitalization Movements at Asbury Theological Seminary publishes a series titled *Revitalization: Explorations in World Christian Movements*. This project contains subseries on Early Church Studies, Medieval and Reformation Studies, Pietist and Wesleyan Studies, Intercultural Studies, and Pentecostal and Charismatic Studies. The series on Pentecostal and Charismatic Studies is edited by D. William Faupel.

Paul Alexander is editing a new series of books with Wipf and Stock Publishers under the title *Pentecostals, Peacemaking, and Social Justice*. In the series preface, Alexander, who is known for his outspoken commitment to peace and justice, explains that 'peace and justice issues are not separate concerns but different ways of talking about and seeking *shalom* – God's salvation, justice, and peace'. Alexander defines the peacemaking aspect of the series as a focus on 'peacemaking, peacebuilding, conflict transformation, nonviolence, forgiveness and other peacemaking-related themes and issues within Pentecostal-Charismatic traditions and from Pentecostal-Charismatic perspectives'. The justice aspect of the series is defined as a focus on issues of 'gender, race, ethnicity, sexuality, economics, class, globalization, trade, poverty, health, consumerism, development, and other social issues'. This series represents a new phase in Pentecostal critical scholarship that contributes to contemporary thinking and practice of just-peacemaking as it attempts to recover and expand upon a widespread commitment to a peaceful witness within early Pentecostalism.

James K.A. Smith and Amos Yong are editing a series for William B. Eerdmans Publishing Company titled *Pentecostal Manifestos*.

---

[11] http://www.brill.nl/publications/global-pentecostal-and-charismatic-studie s#EDIBOA_0

The expressed purpose of the series is to 'provide a forum for exhibiting the next generation of Pentecostal scholarship'. Acknowledging the valuable work over the last fifty years that has focused on the articulation of a distinct Pentecostal theology and vision, this series looks to build on this foundation and move Pentecostal scholarship forward by 'engaging in theological and cultural analysis of a variety of issues from a Pentecostal perspective'. In particular the volumes in *Pentecostal Manifestos* intentionally seek to focus 'on important issues that are concerns not only for Pentecostals and charismatics but also for the whole church'. Less encumbered by the anti-intellectualism of the early days of the tradition, the editors of this series expect the volumes to be able to engage 'the conversations of the wider theological academy'. The initial volumes in the series, in my opinion, have lived up to the ambitious goals of the editors, making this series especially promising.[12]

Research Centers and PhD Programs

Owing partially to the numerical growth of the movement and partially to the expanding critical tradition of Pentecostalism, a number of research centers and PhD programs have been developed around the world over last few decades. A leading consortium of Pentecostal research is the European Research Network on Global Pentecostalism.[13] Known simply as GloPent, this network – founded in 2004 – is the collaborative effort of the Centre for Pentecostal and Charismatic Studies at the Graduate Institute for Theology and Religion at the University of Birmingham, the Hollenweger Center at the Vrije Universiteit Amsterdam, the Department of History of Religion and Missions Studies at the faculty of Theology, Heidelberg University, and the Institute for Pentecostal Studies at the University of Uppsala, who joined the steering group of the network in 2010.

---

12 The initial volumes in this series include Frank D. Macchia, *Justified in the Spirit: Creation, Redemption, and the Triune God* (Grand Rapids: Eerdmans, 2010); James K.A. Smith, *Thinking in Tongues: Pentecostal Contributions to Christian Philosophy* (Grand Rapids: Eerdmans, 2010); and Wolfgang Vondey, *Beyond Pentecostalism: The Crisis of Global Christianity and the Renewal of the Theological Agenda* (Grand Rapids: Eerdmans, 2010).

13 The following information on GloPent comes from the network's website http://www.glopent.net.

The objectives of the network are: (1) to link researchers on global Pentecostal and Charismatic Christianity, aiming especially to make available to the European academic community the research from African, Asian, and Latin American scholars; (2) to promote study exchange by providing short-term classes and workshops for post-graduate students working on their dissertations; (3) to facilitating the discussion and practice of various methodologies and theoretical frameworks currently being used to study global Pentecostalism; (4) to pursue common research projects that are both international and interdisciplinary with the hope of securing funding; and (5) to stimulate academic publications at highest standards of academic excellence. The publication efforts of GloPent include the journal *PentecoStudies* (mentioned above) and an edited collection of workshop papers.

In addition to its publications and workshops, a most valuable contribution of GloPent is its website which serves as a clearing-house for academic resources. It is a veritable treasure trove including bibliographies on a variety of topics, collections of papers, doctoral research projects, and lists of websites and research institutions. GloPent also has created a search engine comprising several thousand sites that is tailored in order to query a collection of websites highly relevant to the study of Pentecostal and Charismatic movements. Students interested in pursuing doctoral programs focusing on Pentecostal and Charismatic Christianity should certainly consider studying at one the four institutions represented by Glo-Pent – the University of Birmingham (with Allan Anderson, Mark Cartledge, and Andrew Davies), the Vrije Universiteit Amsterdam (with André Droogers), Heidelberg University (with Michael Bergunder), or University of Uppsala (with Jan-Åke Alvarsson).

In October 2001, William Kay founded the Centre for Pentecostal and Charismatic Studies at the University of Wales, Bangor. The Centre formed a partnership with Mattersey Hall, an Assembly of God Bible college. Kay directed the Centre until his departure to become Professor of Theology at Glyndŵr University in Wrexham, Wales. Under Kay's leadership, numerous students completed post-graduate degrees in areas of Pentecostal/Charismatic history, theology, and missions. The Centre also received funding the British Academy in 2002 for a project titled, 'Pentecostal and Charismatic Christianity in the UK: Texts and Contemporary Trends'. This project sought 'to provide as full a description as possible of the Pentecostal and charismatic movement's institutional and geographical influence within the UK and to provide internationally key and core Pentecostal and charismatic texts to make them readily available to teachers within the fields of theology and cultural studies'.[14] The Centre is now under the leadership of John Christopher Thomas. In June 2010, the Centre hosted a conference on Pentecostal ecclesiology – the first conference of its kind. The papers presented at the conference were collected and published in a monograph, *Toward a Pentecostal Ecclesiology: The Church and the Fivefold Gospel.*[15]

Located on the campus of the Pentecostal Theological Seminary in Cleveland, TN, the Centre for Pentecostal Theology is 'a residential library dedicated to facilitating the conception, birth, and maturation of constructive Pentecostal Theology across the theological disciplines'.[16] In addition to housing the library the goals of the centre include (1) providing a research environment for both established scholars and those completing post graduate level degrees on Pentecostal themes, topics, and methodologies; (2) coordinating the publication of the *Journal of Pentecostal Theology*, the *Journal of Pentecostal Theology* Supplement Series, the *Pentecostal Commentary Series*, and other manuscripts at both the scholarly and popular levels, published under the imprints of the center – CPT Press and Cherohala Press, respectively; (3) assisting 'prospective research students in identifying and gaining admission to appropriate courses of research at various institutions around the world and, in some instances, arranging for direct supervision';[17] and (4) promoting 'significant dialogue on a number of issues and themes crucial to the tradition by sponsoring conferences and consultations designed to allow specific scholars opportunity for focused interaction and to make the results available to a wider audience in published form'.[18] John Christopher Thomas, who co-founded the centre with Lee Roy Martin, is the Clarence J. Abbott Professor of Biblical Studies at the Pentecostal Theological Seminary and the Director of the

---

[14] http://www.bangor.ac.uk/trs/centres/pcs/projects.php
[15] John Christopher Thomas (ed.), *Toward a Pentecostal Ecclesiology: The Church and the Fivefold Gospel* (Cleveland, TN: CPT Press, 2010).
[16] The following information on the Centre for Pentecostal Theology comes from the center's website at http://www.pentecostaltheology.org.
[17] http://www.pentecostaltheology.org
[18] http://www.pentecostaltheology.org

Centre for Pentecostal and Charismatic Studies at Bangor University, Wales. Many of the students who conduct their research at the centre are pursuing their degrees at Bangor under Thomas' supervision.

Regent University and the Assemblies of God Theological Seminary (AGTS) are currently the only two American-style PhD programs available from a Pentecostal-Charismatic perspective. The School of Divinity at Regent offers the PhD in renewal studies with concentrations in biblical studies, history of global Christianity, and Christian theology. Directed by Amos Yong, this ecumenical program offers both breadth and depth and is supported by a very impressive faculty. AGTS offers both the PhD in Intercultural Studies and the PhD in bible and theology.

Research Grants

In recent years Pentecostal and Charismatic Christianity has been the subject of a variety of studies funded by multimillion dollar grants. At times this money has been awarded directly to institutions that identify with the spiritual tradition and other times the studies have been facilitated by large research universities. In 2003 the Lilly Endowment awarded grants of two million dollars to a number of colleges and universities in the USA to explore the topic of vocation and calling from within particular Christian traditions. Lee University, which is affiliated with the Church of God (Cleveland, TN), and Evangel University, which is affiliated with the Assemblies of God, received this grant. Five years later, both of these schools received a renewal grant of half a million dollars. The Lilly Endowment also funded through its Sustaining Pastoral Excellence Program a multimillion dollar grant to the Pentecostal Theological Seminary which funded a program for pastoral covenant groups, conducted under the leadership of the seminary's Center for Pentecostal Leadership and Care.

More recently the John Templeton Foundation has funded a couple of multimillion dollar grants supporting the study of Pentecostalism from a social scientific perspective. The Flame of Love Project is seeking to establish a 'new field of interdisciplinary scientific study and transform social science by taking God seriously as a perceived actor in human events'. The co-directors of the project include the University of Akron's Margaret Poloma, John Green, and Matthew Lee and the president of the Institute for Research on Unlimited Love, Stephen Post. Included in the core research group for this project are Pentecostals Arlene Sanchez-Walsh of Azusa Pacific University and Amos Yong of Regent University. Principal investigators of the funded sub-projects include a number of Pentecostals researchers, namely Kimberly Ervin Alexander and Mark J. Cartledge's project, 'Learning to Love and Loving to Serve: A Study of the Socialization of Godly Love and Its Influence on Vocation', Paul Alexander's (and Robert Welsh's) 'Risking Death for the Love of God: A Theological and Psychological Study of Pentecostal Engaged in High Risk Social Action', and Peter Althouse and Michael Wilkinson's 'Charismatic Renewal as Mission: Godly Love and the Toronto Airport Christian Fellowship's Soaking Centers'.

The Templeton Foundation has also funded the Pentecostal and Charismatic Research Initiative (PCRI), a project housed at the University of Southern California's Center for Religion and Civic Culture. Intending to provide a scholarly framework to investigate Pentecostalism and the various renewal movements that have emerged in Roman Catholicism and mainline Protestantism, the PCRI has provided funding for research in four specific geographic regions: Africa, Asia, Latin America and the former Soviet Union. One of the individually funded projects is being conducted by Pentecostal scholar William Kay. His project is titled, 'Asian Pentecostal-style Church Growth: an international comparative project'.

Finally, there is one more exciting development that warrants mentioning, the establishment of The Foundation for Pentecostal Scholarship. Although this group is currently operating at a much smaller scale than the granting organizations mentioned above, it is nonetheless a significant advancement in the tradition to have an organization that is dedicated to the advancement of Pentecostal studies. Robert Graves, the president of the foundation, and those working with him deserve to be commended for their work in the promotion the tradition's critical tradition. Established scholars who are working within the tradition and graduate and post-graduate students interested in Pentecostal theology should keep the foundation on their radar as a potential place for travel and/or subvention funds.

Scholarly Societies

The Society for Pentecostal Studies (SPS) is an international community of scholars working within the Pentecostal and Charismatic traditions. Established in 1970, the 'purpose of the society is to stimulate, encourage, recognize, and publicize the work of Pentecostal and charismatic scholars; to study the implications of Pentecostal theology in relation to other academic disciplines'.[19] Student membership in the society, which includes a subscription to *Pneuma*, is available at a reduced rate, and graduate students who are members are also eligible to present their research at the annual meetings. SPS has joint meetings every five years with the Wesleyan Theological Society, and it also has relationships with both the Society of Biblical Literature and the American Academy of Religion. SPS is listed as a 'Program Affiliate' with SBL, and SPS members James K.A. Smith and Amos Yong were founding co-chairs of the Pentecostal–Charismatic Movements Consultation at AAR.

Other Pentecostal academic societies exist that focus their mission on particular geographical areas. Since its initial meeting in 1981 at the Catholic University of Louvain, Belgium, the European Pentecostal Charismatic Research Association has fostered dialogue in various fields and disciplines relevant to Pentecostal/Charismatic history, theology, and church life. The European Pentecostal Theological Association, founded in 1979, is another fellowship of scholars actively engaged in Pentecostal education and ministerial training in Europe. The European Pentecostal Theological Association, founded in 1979, is a fellowship of scholars actively engaged in Pentecostal education and ministerial training in Europe. Two groups focus their attention on Asia: the Asian Pentecostal Society, a platform for Asian Pentecostal scholars to share their understanding of historical, biblical, and spiritual developments of Asian Pentecostalism and the Asia Pacific Theological Association, which was established for the Assemblies of God Bible schools in the Asia Pacific region. Global Pentecostalisms in the Americas (also known as GloPent-Americas), founded by Arlene Sanchez Walsh and Anthea Butler, focuses on Pentecostalism in the Americas and gives special attention to issues of gender, race, sexuality, and embodiment. Last but certainly not least is the Canadian Pentecostal Re-

---

[19] http://www.sps-usa.org

search Network (CPRN), a resource for the study of Pentecostalism in Canada and throughout the world. Led by Michael Wilkinson and conducted largely via a Facebook group, CPRN is quickly becoming a premier place for quality academic dialogue.

A Bright Forecast for the Future of Pentecostal Scholarship

It is not uncommon for the development of Pentecostalism in the twentieth century to be categorized chronologically and ecclesiastically. The early years when new Pentecostal denominations were being formed is defined as classical Pentecostalism, which is contrasted with the Charismatic renewal that took place in the second half of the century among the Catholics and mainline denominations. A third group – primarily consisting of evangelicals and dubbed the Third Wave – shares the emphases on healing, exorcisms, and prophetic speech with the first two movements, but avoided such self-designations as 'charismatic' and 'Spirit-filled' in order to accommodate those in their congregations who do not participate in the charismatic style of worship. If indigenous Pentecostal groups around the globe are added to this list then a fairly accurate sketch of the first century of the modern Pentecostal movement comes into view. Although these labels have been helpful in distinguishing certain aspects of the development of Pentecostalism, I question whether or not the future of Pentecostalism is best defined along these chronological, ecclesial, and geographical boundaries. The growth and diversity of the movement requires a different tack at categorization.

Donald Miller and Tetsunao Yamamori have identified orientations within the tradition that cut across the different types of Pentecostalism previously discussed; examples include (1) legalistic and otherworldly churches, (2) prosperity churches, and (3) progressive churches.[20] It is this third category that piques my interest because it best represents, in my opinion, the next generation of Pentecostals. Young Pentecostals are interested in making the world a better place and so their academic interests are drawn toward highly prac-

---

[20] Donald E. Miller and Tetsunao Yamamori, *Global Pentecostalism: The New Face of Christian Social Engagement* (Berkeley: University of California Press, 2007).

tical ways of putting their faith to work. They want to open medical clinics, minister to orphans, feed the hungry, house the homeless, and educate the uneducated. The future of Pentecostal studies is going to be fueled by interdisciplinary efforts that seek to leverage skills and knowledge in community development, micro-enterprises, advocacy for the poor, and equal rights for all people. The work that has been done in social justice and public policy is only the beginning of what is to come. The works of theological ethicists such as Murray Dempster and Paul Alexander and the social scientific study of Pentecostalism such as the empirical theology of Mark Cartledge and the work done by the Flame of Love Project are all going to have a very long shelf life if my understanding and prediction is accurate.[21] Another aspect of social justice that will see further development is a Pentecostal theology of disability. This otherwise neglected issue has recently received theological and practical treatment by Amos Yong and Steven Fettke.[22] This research must find its way into the curriculum of our Pentecostal colleges, universities, and seminaries and in turn inspire the next generation to be better than previous ones.

The next generation of Pentecostal scholars is already postdenominational, which means the movement is poised for further development in ecumenical studies and dialogue. Largely owing to global migration of people groups, the next generation of rank and file Pentecostals will be more versed in interfaith dialogue simply based on living in closer proximity to people of various faiths. Thus, the works of Pentecostal ecumenists such as Cecil M. Roebeck, Jr., Tony Richie, and especially the pneumatological theology of religions of Amos Yong will become foundational for future Pentecostals living in global village.

Although some initial work has been completed on a Pentecostal perspective of faith and science, this field of study remains wide open.[23] The integration of faith and science has long been the work of the John Templeton Foundation and the Biologos Foundation,

---

[21] Mark J. Cartledge, *Practical Theology: Charismatic and Empirical Perspectives* (Carlisle: Paternoster Press, 2003).

[22] Amos Yong, *Theology and Down Syndrome: Reimagining Disability in Late Modernity* (Waco: Baylor University Press, 2007); and Steven M. Fettke, *God's Empowered People: A Pentecostal Theology of the Laity* (Eugene: Wipf & Stock, 2011).

[23] See James K.A. Smith, and Amos Yong (eds.), *Science and the Spirit: A Pentecostal Engagement with the Sciences* (Bloomington: Indiana University Press, 2010).

but now that Pentecostals are getting involved with these funding agencies a more robust Pentecostal theology of creation is inevitable, one that does not require such an adversarial polemic against evolution.[24] A more developed theology of creation opens the door to ecological hermeneutics, an area of study that has only recently been found on the radar of Pentecostal biblical scholars.[25]

A number of areas that have already seen significant contributions remain, nevertheless, fruitful topics of study including biblical hermeneutics, theologies of race and gender. Although Pentecostal hermeneutics has been a topic of numerous theoretical studies, the practice of the proposed strategies has only been applied to a handful of texts. Future generations should be able to contribute to the further development of Pentecostal hermeneutics and offer readings of texts that reflect the theories. The monograph length studies that will be the standard for future work in this area include the work of Kenneth Archer, Amos Yong, and a new book edited by Kevin Spawn and Archie Wright.[26] Works on ethnic expressions of Pentecostalism have been the topic of research for years, for example see the early work of Villafañe or Solivàn.[27] However, the area of study is still a rich feast for future scholars who have interest in the field. Recent works on black Pentecostalism have also been very informative, though this is certainly a ripe field for additional research.[28] Gender studies, sexuality, and embodiment are areas that have received relatively little attention in Pentecostal circles, which is not too surprising given the mostly conservative ethos of the

---

[24] A substantial contribution has already been made by Amos Yong, *The Spirit of Creation: Modern Science and Divine Action in the Pentecostal-Charismatic Imagination* (Grand Rapids: Eerdmans, 2011).

[25] Jeffrey S. Lamp, *The Greening of Hebrews? Ecological Readings in the Letter to the Hebrews* (Eugene: Pickwick, 2012).

[26] Kenneth J. Archer, *A Pentecostal Hermeneutic for the Twenty-first Century: Spirit, Scripture and Community* (JPTSup, 28; New York: Continuum, 2004); Amos Yong, *Spirit-Word-Community: Theological Hermeneutics in Trinitarian Perspective* (Eugene: Wipf & Stock, 2006); and Kevin L. Spawn and Archie T. Wright (eds.), *Spirit and Scripture: Exploring a Pneumatic Hermeneutic* (New York: T & T Clark International 2012).

[27] Eldin Villafañe, *The Liberating Spirit: Toward an Hispanic American Pentecostal Social Ethic* (Lanham: University Press of America, 1992), and Samuel Solivàn, *The Spirit, Pathos and Liberation: Toward an Hispanic Pentecostal Theology* (JPTSup, 14; Sheffield: Sheffield Academic Press, 1998).

[28] See Amos Yong and Estrelda Alexander, *Afro-Pentecostalism: Black Pentecostal and Charismatic Christianity in History and Culture* (New York: New York University Press, 2012).

movement. However, if my expectation is correct then future Pentecostal scholars and ministers will be addressing these issues in fresh and creative ways.

It may come as a surprise that my final prediction for future development in Pentecostal studies is in the area of church history and theological distinctives. Volumes of valuable material have already been produced on these topics both by Pentecostals and by other interested scholars. Nevertheless, much history remains to be uncovered. The Azusa-centric narrative needs to be interrogated in light of stories of other independent revivals around the world. More works need to be completed on the theological roots of the Pentecostal movement, works that are geographically broader and historically earlier.[29] Dale Coulter's work on medieval theology vis-à-vis Pentecostal theology is a prime example of what is needed in this area. In regards to other theological distinctives, future scholars have much on which to draw, for example Frank Macchia on justification and Spirit baptism, Kimberly Alexander and John Christopher Thomas on healing and exorcism, and Steven Land on spirituality.[30] These impressive works notwithstanding, the future will hopefully see even more work in these key doctrines.

In closing, my hope is that the testimonies in this book will inspire future generations of Pentecostals to respond to the divine call of scholarship and engage in the wide and wonderful dialogues of critical scholarship. Pentecostalism has much more to offer to Christian theology and I expect that the future of Pentecostal studies is even brighter than its past.

---

[29]Dale M. Coulter, 'Continuing the Critical Tradition of Pentecostalism', *Pneuma: The Journal of The Society for Pentecostal Studies* 32.2 (July 2010), pp. 177-79.

[30] Frank D. Macchia, *Justified in the Spirit: Creation, Redemption, and the Triune God* (Grand Rapids: Eerdmans, 2010); Kimberly Ervin Alexander, *Pentecostal Healing: Models in Theology and Practice* (JPTSup, 29; Dorset: Deo Publishing, 2006); John Christopher Thomas, *The Devil, Disease, and Deliverance: Origins of Illness in the New Testament Thought* (JPTSup, 13; Sheffield: Sheffield Academic Press, 1998); and Steven J. Land, *Pentecostal Spirituality: A Passion for the Kingdom* (JPTSup, 1; Sheffield: Sheffield Academic Press, 1993).

Index of Biblical References

Index of Names

Made in the USA
Charleston, SC
28 August 2014